Don't forget to check out the excellent <u>free</u> online resources to help you learn more about human exceptionality!

Visit the Companion Website that accompanies the text to find many features and activities to help you in your studies:

- Web links to interesting sites to help expand your knowledge on each chapter.
- Text-related activities, such as Debate Forum and Case Study analysis, allow you to integrate technology into your studies.
- Practice tests to assess your understanding of key concepts in each chapter.
- Text correlations to national and state professional standards and the Praxis II exams to help you prepare for teacher certification
- Vocabulary flash cards to test your knowledge of key terms in each chapter
- An interactive Timeline that highlights the people and events that have shaped special education through history that expands on the discussion in chapter 1.
- 30 articles from the *New York Times* archive to give color to the discussions in the text.

www.ablongman.com/hardman8e

Study Guide

for

Hardman, Drew, and Egan

Human Exceptionality
School, Community, and Family

Eighth Edition

prepared by

Christine K. Ormsbee
University of Oklahoma

Joyce A. Brandes
University of Oklahoma

PEARSON

Boston   New York   San Francisco
Mexico City   Montreal   Toronto   London   Madrid   Munich   Paris
Hong Kong   Singapore   Tokyo   Cape Town   Sydney

ISBN   0-205-43532-7

Printed in the United States of America

10 9 8 7 6 5 4 3 2 1   09 08 07 06 05 04

Table of Contents

This guide corresponds with the chapters of the text it accompanies, *Human Exceptionality: School, Community, and Family*. It is designed to provide readers with the opportunity to connect new information presented in the text with information they already hold, to put those perceptions in context with the local and state special education system, and to identify additional resources and contexts, which readers can access to expand on their perspectives.

Each chapter is organized into three sections that support active learning. These sections include Preview, Guided Review, and Best Practices. Finally, an answer key is provided so that immediate feedback if available to check for accuracy and understanding of key special education concepts.

The Preview section provides a brief overview of the corresponding text chapter, asks the reader to identify what they already know, make connections to newly acquired information, and delineate how that new information relates with their previously held perceptions. It also provides specific questions that help focus the reader on the primary concepts of the chapter.

Guided Review offers the reader various activities that practice the key concepts and vocabulary of the field to support mastery. Using selected response items, puzzles, and a practice test, the reader is given multiple opportunities to review the key concepts and vocabulary of the corresponding chapter. Special education, while seemingly common knowledge, is a distinct discipline that often surprises people with its comprehensive nature. This section provides the reader with the structure for accommodating the specificity and detail of the field.

The Best Practices section helps the reader apply newly acquired concepts in artificial situations AND identify situations that demonstrate special education principles locally. This section includes resources that provide even more information and opportunities for professional growth for the reader.

We hope that these elements, in combination, provide the optimal learning and practice environment for readers to learn about individuals with special needs and become comfortable with the concepts and practices of special education and disability-related law.

Note: All puzzles were created with Puzzlemaker at DiscoverySchool.com

Understanding Exceptionality

In Chapter One the author introduces you to the language and history of differences: how those differences are named, how people with differences have suffered and triumphed, and how society has dealt with the differences of its people. An historical perspective regarding services for those with differences is presented, including various issues that influenced passage of federal laws ensuring the educational rights of all children and the basic human rights of people.

Weaving together the many disciplines that make up special education is also a focus of this chapter. Addressing how the fields of medicine, psychology, and sociology have impacted individuals with differences at home, at school, in the community, and at work, readers are shown how expansive the needs are of individuals with differences and how society has responded to address those needs.

Concept Reflection

A. What did I understand about exceptionalities before this class?	B. How did reading the chapter enhance or change what I already knew? (Relate this to Column A.)	C. What new information did I learn? (This may or may not be associated with your responses in A or B.)
1.	1.	1.
2.	2.	2.
3.	3.	3.
4.	4.	4.
5.	5.	5.

Keep the following questions in mind as you read this chapter.

1.1   Why do we label people?

A.

B.

C.

D.

1.2   Identify three approaches to describing human differences.

A.

B.

C.

1.3   Describe the services for people with disabilities through most of the 20th century.

A.

B.

C.

D.

E.

1.4   What is the purpose of the Americans with Disabilities Act?

A.

B.

1.5	**What services and supports must be available to ensure that an individual with a disability is able to live and learn successfully in a community setting?**

A.

B.

1.6	**How did the work of 19th century physicians and philosophers contribute to our understanding of people with disabilities?**

A.

B.

1.7	**Distinguish between abnormal behavior and social deviance.**

A.

B.

Guided Review

Read – Matching Vocabulary

Following are a number of the key terms and concepts used in this chapter. Try to complete this matching exercise before you read the chapter. Match each term with the phrase that you think most closely describes or defines it.

A. Pathology
B. Neurotic
C. Disability
D. Trephining

E. Handicap
F. Geneticist
G. Deviant
H. Labeling

1.8 _____ The process society creates to identify people who vary significantly from the norm.

1.9 _____ Drilling holes in a person's skull to permit evil spirits to leave.

1.10 _____ An inability to establish interpersonal relationships.

1.11 _____ This results from a loss of physical functions (e.g., loss of sight, hearing, or mobility).

1.12 _____ Limitation imposed on the individual by the demands in the environment and the individual's ability to adapt to those demands.

1.13 _____ Alterations in an organism that are caused by disease.

1.14 _____ A person who specializes in the study of heredity.

1.15 _____ Behavior characterized by combinations of anxieties, compulsions, obsessions, and phobias.

Reflect – Matching Vocabulary

This exercise is intended to provide practice in recalling what you have just read. Try not to refer back to the chapter as you match the following items with their descriptions below. As you work through this exercise, consider how this new information relates to other knowledge, concepts, and/or principles you learned before taking this course.

A. Conformity   E. Disability
B. Section 504   F. Psychotic
C. Itard   G. Culture
D. Normalcy   H. Reasonable accommodations

_____

1.16 _____ Labels communicate whether a person meets the expectations of the _____.

1.17 _____ People doing what they are "supposed" to do.

1.18 _____ A person (1) having a physical or mental impairment that substantially limits him or her in some major life activity, and (2) having experienced discrimination resulting from this impairment.

1.19 _____ Levels of maladjustment range from slightly deviant/eccentric to neurotic disorders to _____ disorders.

1.20 _____ Provision within the Vocational Rehabilitation Act of 1973 that prohibits discrimination against persons with disabilities in federally assisted programs and activities.

1.21 _____ These "level the playing field" for individuals with disabilities.

1.22 _____ Doctor who believed that the environment contributed to the learning potential of any human being.

1.23 _____ In the medical model, _____ is defined as the absence of a biological problem.

Supply a word/phrase in each sentence in order to make sense out of the statement of a concept, definition, or principle that is otherwise incomplete or lacks closure. Several answers, other than those listed in the key, may be acceptable for an item. Focus on whether or not your answer is equivalent to the answer supplied and be prepared to explain why you completed the statement(s) as you did.

1.24 When applied as an educational label, *handicapped* has a _____ focus and a _____ meaning.

1.25 When a person's intellectual, physical, or behavioral performance differs substantially from the norm, either higher or lower, that individual is regarded as _____ .

1.26 Labels can promote stereotyping, exclusion, and _____ .

1.27 Self-imposed labels reflect how we perceive _____.

1.28 Three approaches to describing human differences include developmental, individual, and _____.

1.29 The Civil Rights Act of 1964 did not mention people with _____.

1.30 Normalcy and _____ are the two dimensions of the medical model.

1.31 The science of human and animal behavior is known as _____.

Review – True/False

Please indicate whether the statements are true (T) or false (F) by circling the corresponding letter. You should be able to briefly describe the rationale for your answer.

T	F	1.32	Mentally retarded and gifted can both be considered *exceptional*.
T	F	1.33	Labels are based on facts.
T	F	1.34	Labels help professionals communicate more effectively with each other.
T	F	1.35	A cultural view defines "normal" according to societal values.
T	F	1.36	One of the risks of using labels is that the individual can be defined by his/her label as opposed to being a human being.
T	F	1.37	Though encouraged, compulsory sterilization was never legalized.
T	F	1.38	By the mid-1950s, the vast majority of people with disabilities were living in institutions.
T	F	1.39	ADA is intended to affirm the right of Americans with disabilities to participate in the life of their communities.
T	F	1.40	Homosexuality is not considered an impairment by ADA.
T	F	1.41	It is against the law to provide services for individuals with disabilities only in institutions when they could be served in a community-based setting.
T	F	1.42	Individuals with disabilities who work are less satisfied with their money and life.
T	F	1.43	Deviance must be defined within the context of the culture.

T	F	1.44	Jean-Marc Itard demonstrated through his work with Victor the Wild Boy that individuals with severe disabilities can learn new skills.
T	F	1.45	Due to the division of church and state, the ADA did not provide a mandate for individuals with disabilities regarding religious activities.
T	F	1.46	*Abnormal* is a term used by educators in labeling a person with a disability.
T	F	1.47	Self-labeling reflects how we perceive ourselves.

Chapter Review – Practice Test

In the following activity, select the most appropriate of the four answers provided for each item. Try to do this without looking at your text in order to get an idea of your comprehension level.

1.48 Students who do not meet the educational expectations of society may be
    A. labeled according to the extent of their deviation.
    B. labeled by the type of deviation they exhibit.
    C. provided specialized services.
    D. All of the above.

1.49 The term *exceptional* describes individuals who
    A. are limited because of environmental demands.
    B. have higher than average general ability.
    C. are sufficiently higher or lower than the norm to require specialized services.
    D. have a general malfunction of mental processing.

1.50 Typical development can be described statistically, by observing in large numbers of individuals those characteristics that occur most frequently at a specific age. This is a
    A. developmental approach.
    B. conforming approach.
    C. cultural view.
    D. self-labeling.

1.51 Thousands of people were committed to mental hospitals throughout the U.S., while thousands of persons with mental retardation lived in colonies, hospitals, or training schools during the early _____.
    A. 1800s
    B. 1900s
    C. 1950s
    D. 1990s

1.52 The civil rights of people with disabilities was recognized with the passage of the
    A. Americans with Disabilities Act.
    B. P.L. 99-457.
    C. P.S. 94-142.
    D. Individuals with Disabilities Education Act.

1.53 The major provision(s) of ADA include
    A. telecommunications.
    B. public accommodations.
    C. transportation.
    D. All of the above.

1.54 Successful inclusion requires the individual's ability to adapt to societal expectations,
    A. along with learning how to use generic community services.
    B. as well as willingness of society to adapt to and accommodate individuals with differences.
    C. to the degree defined by that society.
    D. without additional support being provided by the community.

1.55 A profession dedicated to assisting individuals in developing worthwhile leisure activities is known as
    A. therapeutic recreation.
    B. occupational therapy.
    C. play therapy.
    D. physical therapy.

1.56 _____ is essential to the creation of healthy lifestyles for individuals with disabilities.
    A. Work
    B. Physical activity
    C. Music and the arts
    D. Paid employment

1.57 Only _____ of people with disabilities (ages 18 to 64) work full- or part-time, compared to _____ of people who are not disabled.
    A. 20%, 25%
    B. 26%, 34%
    C. 32%, 81%
    D. 38%, 89%

1.58 The classic controversy over the role of heredity and environment is known as
    A. Itard's theory.
    B. Locke's opinion.
    C. the medical intervention model.
    D. nature versus nurture.

1.59 The approach that views abnormal more as a result of an individual's interaction with the environment than as a disease is referred to as the
    A. psychological approach.
    B. ecological approach.
    C. environmental approach.
    D. conditioning approach.

1.60 Deviance is defined as a violation of
   A.   the law.
   B.   family rules.
   C.   educational guideline.
   D.   social norms.

1.61 Doctors and philosophers contributed to our understanding of individuals with disabilities during the 19th century by emphasizing
   A.   humane treatment and their ability to learn new skills.
   B.   the importance of assessment and the need to be with people without disabilities.
   C.   that most were unable to learn new skills but needed to be treated fairly.
   D.   the advantages of group homes and medication.

1.62 _____ is a comprehensive label for persons who need special services in school.
   A.   *Retarded*
   B.   *Slow*
   C.   *Exceptional*
   D.   *Handicapped*

1.63 During most of the 20th century, people viewed individuals with disabilities as
   A.   a product of the environment.
   B.   social problems.
   C.   a result of poor parenting.
   D.   better off in public school classrooms.

Cryptogram

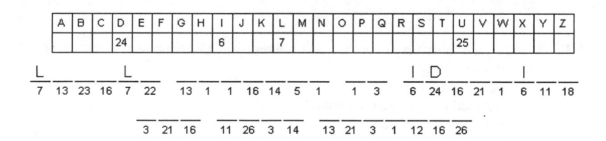

Double Puzzle

Unscramble each of the clue words. Copy the letters in the numbered cells to other cells with the same number.

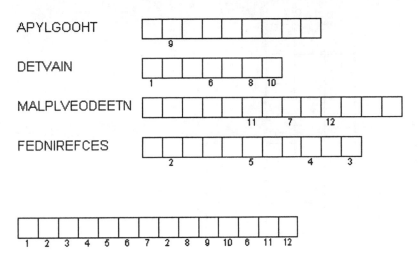

APYLGOOHT

(9)

DETVAIN

(1) (6) (8) (10)

MALPLVEODEETN

(11) (7) (12)

FEDNIREFCES

(2) (5) (4) (3)

1 2 3 4 5 6 7 2 8 9 10 6 11 12

Scramble

Unscramble the tiles to reveal a message.

I V I L	E D T	R I G	E O P L	R E C O	E W I

A D A	I S A B	G N I Z	O F P	I L I T	H E C

T H D	H T S	I E S .

Across

1. Violation of social norms
7. Results from a loss of function
8. Person who specializes in study of heredity

Down

2. Behavior characterized by combinations of anxieties, compulsions, obsessions, and phobias
3. Comprehensive label for people who need special services
4. Believed nature contributed to learning process
5. Science of human behavior
6. Recognition of civil rights of individuals with disabilities

Dionna is a junior in high school who has been on the school's honor roll every semester and is completing a college preparatory curriculum. She is a popular student with her peers and her teachers and is a favorite math tutor among the underclass students. Dionna's academic skills are above many in her class, her ability to think abstractly is unmatched, and her motivation to learn is very high.

In classes, it is easy to find Dionna because she is usually sitting in the front of the classroom in her wheelchair. Dionna has cerebral palsy, which interferes with her mobility and communication. She uses a voice-controlled laptop computer to participate in instructional activities because her writing is slow, laborious, and illegible.

Dionna spends all of her school time in the general classroom with her same-age peers and participates fully in the curriculum and class instruction. However, many of her teachers and peers will tell you that when they first met Dionna they expected someone entirely different. Now, as Dionna is preparing for college, the counselors are concerned about her success on a university campus and those unique issues that might be problematic for her.

1. What law would address Dionna's rights to a barrier-free educational environment? What kinds of barriers might Dionna face in a school setting?_____
_____
_____
_____

2. How could the school address those barriers? _____
_____
_____
_____

3. What kinds of problems might Dionna face in a university setting that other students without physical differences would not? _____
_____
_____
_____

4. How could the university address those barriers?_____
_____
_____
_____

1. Interview a school superintendent or principal who has been in education since before 1975. Ask them to describe what special education was like before P.L. 94-142 and what it is like today in terms of: integration with same-age peers, curriculum expectations, assessment, and parental expectations.

_____

_____

_____

2. Visit a local children's shelter and spend time reading to a small group of children. As you are reading and interacting with them, observe their social/emotional and communication skills. Then, repeat this experience with a similar group of children who come from homes with involved, active parents. Compare the developmental skills of these two groups of children. How were these children alike and different in terms of language skills, interpersonal competence, and peer relationships? How was your behavior/experience with the two groups?

_____

_____

_____

Resources

Books
Savage Inequalities: Children in America's Schools by Jonathan Kozol. Available through HarperCollins Publishers.
You Will Dream New Dreams: Inspiring Personal Storries by Parents of Children with Disabilities by Parents of Children with Disabilities by Stanley D. Klein. Available through Kensington Publishing Corporation.
Helping the Child Who Doesn't Fit In by Stephen Nowicki and Marshall P. Duke. Available from Peachtree Publishers.

Videos
My Country
Unfinished Business by Irene M. Ward and Associates – 1996, 32 min.
As I Am by James Brodie, www.fanlight.com
Kiss My Wheels by Thunder Road Productions, www.fanlight.com

Websites
Council for Exceptional Children: www.cec.sped.org
American Psychological Association: www.apa.org
Office of Special Education and Rehabilitation Services:
www.ed.gov/about/offices/list/osers/osep/index.html
Curry School of Education, University of Virginia:
http://curry.edschool.virginia.edu/go/cise/ose/information
The Disability Rag: www.ragged-edge-mag.com
National Information Center for Children and Youth with Disabilities (NICHCY):
www.nichcy.org/

This chapter starts by addressing the history of special education. This discussion includes the stance of education as a privilege and not a right for students with disabilities and the expanding role of the federal government in the 1960s. Eligibility requirements are briefly discussed. Criteria specific to individual disabilities are briefly discussed since they are defined and described in greater depth in subsequent chapters of this text. The five major provisions of IDEA are presented from an historical and current perspective. These provisions include FAPE, assessments, parental rights, IEPs, and the least restrictive environment.

The final segment addresses the purpose of the IEP as well as its development, components, and implementation. Current trends in the education of students with disabilities includes a discussion of effective special education practice, access to the general curriculum and greater accountability for student learning, ensuring reasonable accommodations in assessment and instruction, and establishing safe schools.

Concept Reflection

A. What did I know about educational services for individuals with or without disabilities before reading this chapter?	B. How did reading the chapter enhance or change what I already knew? (Relate this to Column A.)	C. What new information did I learn? (This may or may not be associated with your responses in A or B.)
1.	1.	1.
2.	2.	2.
3.	3.	3.
4.	4.	4.
5.	5.	5.

Keep the following questions in mind as you read this chapter.

2.1 What educational services were available for students with disabilities during most of the 20th century?
A.
B.
C.
2.2 Identify the principal issues in the right-to-education cases that led to eventual passage of the national mandate to educate students with disabilities.
A.
B.
C.
2.3 Identify six major provisions of the Individuals with Disabilities Education Act.
A.
B.
C.
D.
E.
F.
2.4 Identify the four phases of the special education referral, planning, and placement process.
A.
B.
C.
D.

2.5 Identify three characteristics of effective special education that enhance learning opportunities for students with disabilities.
A.
B.
C.

2.6 Identify four principles for school accountability as required in No Child Left Behind. Under IDEA, what must a student's IEP include relative to accessing the general curriculum?
A.
B.
C.
D.

2.7. Distinguish between students with disabilities eligible for services under Section 504/ADA and those eligible under IDEA.
A.
B.

2.8 Distinguish between the principles of zero tolerance and zero exclusion in America's schools.
A.
B.

Read – Matching Vocabulary

Following are a number of the key terms and concepts used in this chapter. Try to complete this matching exercise before you read the chapter. Match each term with the phrase that you think most closely describes or defines it.

A. 504/ADA Plan
B. IEP
C. LRE
D. Public Law 99-457

E. IDEA – Public Law 101-476
F. IFSP
G. Public Law 94-142
H. FAPE

_____

2.9 _____ Legislation that extended the rights and protections of Public Law 94-142 to preschool-age children (ages three through five). The law also established an optional state program for infants and toddlers with disabilities.

2.10 _____ A written plan that provides for reasonable accommodations or modifications in assessment and instruction as a means to "create a fair and level playing field" for students who qualify as disabled under Section 504 of the Vocational Rehabilitation Act and the American with Disabilities Act.

2.11 _____ The new name for the Education for All Handicapped Children Act (Public Law 94-142) as per the 1990 amendments to the law.

2.12 _____ Federal law made available a free and appropriate public education to all eligible students regardless of the extent or type of handicap (disability).

2.13 _____ Provision in IDEA requiring that students with disabilities receive an educational program based on multidisciplinary assessment and designed to meet individual needs.

2.14 _____ Provision within IDEA that requires every eligible student with a disability be included in public education at no cost.

2.15 _____ Students with disabilities are to be educated with their peers without disabilities to the maximum extent appropriate.

2.16 _____ A plan of services for infants and toddlers and their families.

Reflect – Matching Vocabulary

This exercise is intended to provide practice in recalling what you have just read. Try not to refer back to the chapter as you match the following items with their descriptions below. As you work through this exercise, consider how this new information relates to other knowledge, concepts, and/or principles you learned before taking this course.

A. Adaptive fit
B. Functional life skills
C. Individualization
D. Prereferral interventions

E. Related services
F. Self-determination
G. Zero tolerance
H. Zero-exclusion

_____

2.17 _____ A principle which advocates that no person with a disability can be rejected for a service regardless of the nature, type, or extent of their disabling condition.

2.18 _____ Those services necessary to ensure that students with disabilities benefit from their educational experience.

2.19 _____ Practical skills that facilitate a person's participation and involvement in family, school, and community life.

2.20 _____ Compatibility between demands of a task or setting and a person's need and abilities.

2.21 _____ The ability of a person to consider options and make appropriate choices regarding residential life, work, and leisure time.

2.22 _____ The consequences for a student's misbehavior are predetermined and any individual reasons or circumstances are not to be considered.

2.23 _____ Instructional adaptations or accommodations designed to provide additional support to children who are at risk for educational failure prior to referring them for special education services.

2.24 _____ A student-centered approach to instructional decision making.

Recite – Fill in the Blank

Supply a word/phrase in each sentence in order to make sense out of the statement of a concept, definition, or principle that is otherwise incomplete or lacks closure. Several answers, other than those listed in the key, may be acceptable for an item. Focus on whether or not your answer is equivalent to the answer supplied and be prepared to explain why you completed the statement(s) as you did.

2.25 The goal of education is _____ _____ of everyone.

2.26 At one time "special education" always meant "_____" education.

2.27 Education was reaffirmed as a _____ and not a _____ by the U.S. Supreme Court in the landmark case of *Brown v. Topeka, Kansas, Board of Education* (1954).

2.28 IDEA reflects "_____ _____" language and national use of the term _____.

2.29 The ten disability conditions recognized by the federal government as qualifying for special services include mental retardation, specific learning disabilities, serious emotional disturbances/behavior disorders, speech or language impairments, vision loss/blindness, hearing loss/deafness, orthopedic impairments, other health impairments, deaf-blindness, multiple disabilities, traumatic brain injury and _____.

2.30 IDEA has _____ major provisions.

2.31 The value upon which IDEA is based is that "every student can _____."

2.32 No student can be excluded from a public education based on a _____.

2.33 Assessment of students must be conducted in their _____ language.

2.34 Characteristics of special education that enhance learning opportunities for students of all ages and across multiple settings include intensive instruction, explicit teaching of academic, adaptive, and/or functional life skills, and _____.

2.35   The teaching of explicit skills to students with disabilities includes instruction in core academic areas, adaptive skills, and _____ life skills.

2.36   At one time, students who were blind, deaf, or labeled emotionally disturbed or mentally retarded were _____ from public schools.

Review – True/False

Please indicate whether the statements are true (T) or false (F) by circling the corresponding letter. You should be able to briefly describe the rationale for your answer.

T   F   2.37   In the 1960s the federal government provided financial support to university programs for the preparation of special education teachers.

T   F   2.38   The right to education for children with disabilities came to the public forum because of the civil rights movement of the 1950s and 1960s.

T   F   2.39   PL 99-457 extended all the rights of protections of school-age children to preschoolers ages three through five.

T   F   2.40   Individualized Family Service Plans address the needs of students six to twenty-one

T   F   2.41   The Individuals with Disabilities Education Act (IDEA) reflected "people first" language and national use of the term *disabilities*.

T   F   2.42   ADHD is one of the qualifying conditions for provision of special education services.

T   F   2.43   The Supreme Court established that a state must provide an ideal education for students with disabilities.

T   F   2.44   Parents must give written consent for an initial evaluation but not for an initial placement in special education.

T   F   2.45   General and special educators must acquire a core of knowledge and skills that facilitates their ability to teach all students.

T   F   2.46   In the 1970s educators became aware of the need for students with special needs to be educated in an environment that would promote "normal" social interaction.

T   F   2.47   The functional life skills approach is based on the premise that if these special skills are not taught through formal instruction, they will not be learned.

T   F   2.48   Children with disabilities remain the most at risk of being left behind.

In the following activity, select the most appropriate of the four answers provided for each item. Try to do this without looking at your text in order to get an idea of your comprehension level.

2.49 In the 1970s, the likelihood of exclusion was greater for children with disabilities living in
    A. rural communities.
    B. urban school districts.
    C. suburban communities.
    D. middle-income neighborhoods.

2.50 A 504 plan provides for reasonable accommodations or modification as a means to
    A. create a "fair and level playing field."
    B. create meaningful goals and objectives on IEPs.
    C. create easier access to support for teachers.
    D. create meaningful opportunities in leisure activities.

2.51 One of the events of the 1950s that had a significant impact on the evolution of educational programs for students with disabilities included:
    A. behavioral and medical professionals became interested in services for individuals with disabilities.
    B. lawmakers began to push for better legal considerations.
    C. parents sued school districts for better IEPs and related services.
    D. families pushed the government to improve the conditions of the institutions in which individuals with disabilities were living.

2.52 The Pennsylvania Association for Retarded Citizens v. Commonwealth of Pennsylvania,1971 suit resulted in
    A. students being labeled mentally retarded.
    B. provision of a free and appropriate public education for all children with mental retardation of ages 6 to 21.
    C. provision of alternative educational services being made available.
    D. provision of speech-language therapy in all public schools.

2.53 Public Law 94-142 (1975) made provisions for
    A. nondiscriminatory and multidisciplinary assessments.
    B. procedural safeguards to protect the rights of students and their parents.
    C. an education in the least restrictive environment.
    D. All of the above.

2.54 A recent survey by Johnson, Duffett, Farkas, and Wilson (2002) found that a vast majority of parents were convinced that when their child needed special education they
    A. had to fight an uphill battle.
    B. needed to pay for assessments.
    C. would have to provide medical documentation.
    D. hire a lawyer.

2.55 Related services can include
    A. transportation.
    B. physical and occupational therapy.
    C. counseling.
    D. All of the above.

2.56 The purpose of the IEP is
    A. provide an opportunity for parents and professionals to develop and deliver specially designed instruction to meet student needs.
    B. create a legal document that binds the school system and the parents to a specific guideline for the child's education.
    C. generate assessment guidelines that everyone understands and agrees to implement when determining a child's success.
    D. All of the above.

2.57 Intensive instruction involves
    A. instructional cues and prompts.
    B. feedback.
    C. matching students' ability and skill.
    D. All of the above.

2.58 An IEP team must include at least
    A. special education teacher, general education teacher, and a local education agency representative.
    B. special education teacher, student's parents, and a general education teacher.
    C. special education teacher, student's parents, general education teacher, and a local education agency representative.
    D. special education teacher, student's parents, and a speech therapist.

2.59 An IEP must include a statement of the child's present level of educational performance, measurable annual goals, special/related services and supplementary aids, and:
    A. modifications, physical education programs objectives.
    B. modifications, a statement of how the student's progress toward the annual goals will be measured.
    C. modifications, number of students in general education classrooms.
    D. names of bus drivers and classroom assistants.

2.60 Special education means specially designed instruction provided at no cost to parents. Services can be provided in
    A. hospitals.
    B. home.
    C. physical education facilities.
    D. All of the above.

2.61 In order for a student to receive specialized services available under IDEA, two criteria must be met. One of these includes having one of the disability conditions identified in federal law or a corresponding condition defined in a state's special education rules and regulations. The other is
- A. demonstration of a financial need by the family.
- B. provision of documentation that members of the family want the services provided for the student.
- C. a demonstrated need by the student for specialized instruction and related services.
- D. All of the above.

2.62 Which of the following does not address school accountability under No Child Left Behind (NCLB)?
- A. Emphasis on challenging academic standards that specify the knowledge and skill levels
- B. Recommended books provided to all students with IEPs
- C. Focus on students achievement as the primary measure of school success
- D. Reliance on achievement testing to spur the reforms and to monitor their impact

2.63 Assessment of a student must include
- A. a team of school professionals.
- B. several pieces of information.
- C. validated instruments.
- D. All of the above.

2.64 The intent of the parental safeguards is
- A. to assist the school system in evaluations.
- B. to involve parents in decisions regarding their children.
- C. to protect the student and family.
- D. B. and C.

2.65 "Least restrictive environment" means
- A. full inclusion with non-disabled peers in general education classrooms.
- B. education with non-disabled peers to the maximum extent possible.
- C. partial inclusion with non-disabled peers in general education classrooms.
- D. full inclusion of non-disabled peers in special education classrooms.

2.66 The special education referral, planning, and placement process, as mandated in IDEA, is intended to ensure that all eligible students with disabilities have
- A. the opportunity to receive a free and appropriate public education.
- B. assessments conducted and paid for the by the state agencies.
- C. the option to select the school in which they will receive services.
- D. extra assistance provided as they progress through school.

2.67 The sequential phases in the referral, planning, and placement process include
   A. initiating the referral and assessing student's eligibility.
   B. developing the IEP and determining the least restrictive environment (LRE).
   C. Both of the above.
   D. None of the above.

2.68 The hallmark of special education is
   A. individualization.
   B. classroom assistants.
   C. parental involvement.
   D. special education classrooms.

Cryptogram

Unscramble each of the clue words. Take the letters that appear in circles and unscramble them for the final message.

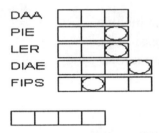

DAA

PIE

LER

DIAE

FIPS

Scramble

Unscramble the tiles to reveal a message.

EDUC	OF	N IS	IPAT	EVER	FOR
YONE	ION	THE	L PA	ATIO	FUL
GOAL	RTIC	.			

22

Unscramble each of the clue words. Copy the letters in the numbered cells to other cells with the same number.

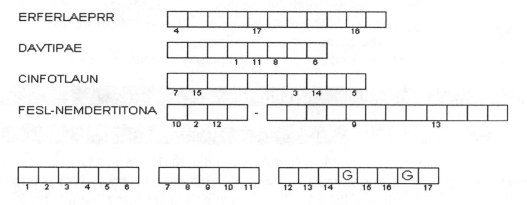

ERFERLAEPRR

DAVTIPAE

CINFOTLAUN

FESL-NEMDERTITONA

Across

3. Student-centered approach to instructional decision making
4. A plan for infants/toddlers and their families
7. Education is a _____, not a privilege
8. Every student can _____
10. IDEA reflects national use of this term
12. No student can be excluded from a public education based on _____
13. New name for Education for All Handicapped Children Act

Down

1. Practical skills
2. Educational plan written specifically for a particular child with disabilities
5. Public education made available to everyone at no cost
6. Assessment of students must be conducted in their _____ language
7. Services necessary to ensure that students with disabilities benefit from their education
9. Educated with peers to the greatest extent possible
11. Compatibility between demands of a task and a person's need/abilities

Best Practices

Case Study

Oscar, a 3rd grade student who has an identified attention deficit disorder (ADD), has been struggling to keep up in the general curriculum since the first day of school. He has difficulty staying on task and spends much of his school time drawing violent scenes on notebook paper. He has completed only about 50% of in-class assignments and only 25% of homework. His unit tests are always barely passing.

In addition to general academic difficulties, Oscar is difficult to handle: he is often noncompliant, emotional, even belligerent when addressed about his academic performance or behavior, and can be aggressive with his peers. The 3rd grade teacher states that he spends at least 50% of his time managing Oscar and trying to get him to complete the assigned work. It is now the end of the first semester and the teacher is tired and frustrated and thinks Oscar doesn't belong in the 3rd grade classroom.

Oscar's parents are insistent that Oscar be taught the 3rd grade curriculum in the general education classroom and believe that the teacher simply isn't trying to teach Oscar "the way he learns." Oscar's IEP has the 3rd grade classroom identified as the least restrictive environment and calls for some consultant support for the teacher. This has been documented as infrequent, informal contacts between the 3rd grade teacher and the resource room teacher.

1. What principles of special education address Oscar's educational placement in the general education classroom?

   _____

   _____

2. What kind of information might be helpful to a multi-disciplinary team in determining the appropriate educational placement for Oscar? How might this information be obtained?

   _____

   _____

3. Based on the limited information above, is Oscar experiencing success in his current educational placement? Why or why not? What needs to happen next?

   _____

   _____

1. Contact a local organization that serves families with disabilities. Interview a staff member of the organization to determine the following:
    A. What are the key pieces of special education law?
    B. How has IDEA improved educational opportunities for children with disabilities?
    C. What is the most common concern of parents of children with disabilities today?

2. Contact your State's department of special education department. Ask about the due process procedures for your state: How does due process work? Who can file for a due process hearing? For what reasons can a person request a due process hearing? How many due process hearings are requested each year? How many due process hearings are actually held for a decision? Is the due process procedure effective for safeguarding children with disabilities rights to an appropriate education?

3. Arrange to attend a due process hearing. Who initiated the hearing? What are the legal issues in conflict? Based on the evidence offered by both parties, what would your decision be and why?

Resources

Books

A Mind at a Time: America's Top Learning Expert Shows How Every Child Can Succeed by Mel Levine. Available through Simon & Schuster.
Disability Rights Movement by Deborah Kent. Available from Scholastic Library Publishing.
No Pity; People with Disabilities Forging a New Civil Rights Movement by Joseph P. Shapiro. Available through Random House.
Joey Pigza Swallowed the Key by Jack Gantos. Available from HarperCollins Children's Books.
Critical Issues in Special Education: Access, Diversity, and Accountability by Audrey McCray Sorrells, Paul T. Sindelar, and Herbert J. Rieth. Available through Allyn & Bacon.

Videos

Without Pity. www.films.com
A Mind of Your Own by Gail Sweeney, www.fanlight.com
One of Us: Four Stories of Inclusion by Ron Gould, www.fanlight.com

Websites

Disability Rights Commission: www.drc-gb.org
The Council for Disability Rights: www.disabilityrights.org
Online Resource for Americans with Disabilities: www.disabilityinfo.org

3

Inclusion and Collaboration in the Early Childhood and Elementary School Years

Preview

Chapter Three describes education and other services for young children with disabilities, from infancy through the transition into the early years of elementary school. A brief historical review of early intervention, a discussion of the rationale for such services, and a description of service delivery options are provided. The chapter also describes the early elementary school years, including the roles and responsibilities of the classroom teacher in meeting the needs of all students in the classroom.

Throughout the chapter collaboration is emphasized, whether that collaborative process occurs through the school's intervention team, between general and special educators, or as part of the program planning team. This emphasis is illustrated through the detailed discussions on IEP and IFSP development, parent partnerships, school-wide assistance teams, and inclusion.

Concept Reflection

A. What did I know about inclusion and collaboration in early childhood and elementary education before reading this chapter?	B. How did reading the chapter enhance or change what I already knew? (Relate this to Column A.)	C. What new information did I learn? (This may or may not be associated with your responses in A or B.)
1.	1.	1.
2.	2.	2.
3.	3.	3.
4.	4.	4.
5.	5.	5.

Keep the following questions in mind as you read this chapter.

3.1 Define inclusive education.
A.
B.

3.2 Describe the characteristics of effective inclusive schools.
A.
B.
C.
D.
E.

3.3 Define collaboration and identify its key characteristics.
A.
B.1
B.2
B.3

3.4 Why is it so important to provide early intervention services as soon as possible to young children at risk?
A.
B.
C.
D.

3.5 Identify the components of the Individualized Family Service Plan (IFSP).

A.

B.

C.

D.

E.

F.

G.

H.

3.6 Identify effective approaches for providing instruction for preschool-age children with disabilities

A.

B.

C.

D.

3.7 Describe the roles of special education and general education teachers in an inclusive classroom setting.

A.

B.

C.

D.

E.

3.8 Why are multilevel instruction, universal design for learning, direct instruction, assistive technology, and curriculum-based assessment considered effective practice in an inclusive classroom?

A.

B.

C.

D.

E.

Guided Review

Read – Matching Vocabulary

Following are a number of the key terms and concepts used in this chapter. Try to complete this matching exercise before you read the chapter. Match each term with the phrase that you think most closely describes or defines it.

A. Early intervention
B. Full inclusion
C. IFSP
D. Individualization

E. Intensity
F. Early intervention
G. Partial inclusion
H. Transdisciplinary teaming

3.9 _____ Comprehensive services for infants and toddlers who are disabled or acquiring a disability.

3.10 _____ An intervention plan for infants and pre-school children and their families.

3.11 _____ Preventive steps taken early in life to lessen the impact of a disability.

3.12 _____ Professionals from various disciplines develop instructional programs.

3.13 _____ The frequency and amount of time of a young child's engagement in intervention activities.

3.14 _____ A student-centered approach to instructional decision making.

3.15 _____ Model using a partnership of general and special educators providing services in the general education classrooms in the student's home school.

3.16 _____ Students with disabilities receive some of their instruction in a general education classroom with "pull out" to another instructional setting when appropriate to their individual needs

This exercise is intended to provide practice in recalling what you have just read. Try not to refer back to the chapter as you match the following items with their descriptions below. As you work through this exercise, consider how this new information relates to other knowledge, concepts, and/or principles you have learned before taking this course.

A. Collaboration
B. Cooperative learning
C. Curriculum-based assessments
D. Developmentally appropriate practices

E. Direct instruction
F. Functional assessment
G. Head Start
H. Universal design for learning

3.17 _____ Strategies that emphasize simultaneous/group learning.
3.18 _____ Program providing early enrichment experiences.
3.19 _____ Explicit teaching of academic, adaptive, and functional skills.
3.20 _____ One or more people working together to attain a common goal.
3.21 _____ Instructional approaches that use curriculum and learning environments consistent with the child's developmental level.
3.22 _____ Determination of a child's skills and the characteristics of the setting, as well as the family's needs, resources, and expectations.
3.23 _____ Instructional programs and environments that work for all students, to the greatest extent possible, without the need for adaptation or specialized design.
3.24 _____ The direct and frequent measurement of observable student behaviors toward progress within the curriculum.

Supply a word/phrase in each sentence in order to make sense out of the statement of a concept, definition, or principle that is otherwise incomplete or lacks closure. Several answers, other than those listed in the key, may be acceptable for an item. Focus on whether or not your answer is equivalent to the answer supplied and be prepared to explain why you completed the statement(s) as you did.

3.25 *Full inclusion* and *partial inclusion* describe the extent of _____ in the general education classroom.
3.26 It is the opinion of the authors of this text that the responsibility for ensuring a successful inclusive program lies with _____.
3.27 Everyone must feel _____ in order for collaboration to work.
3.28 Early childhood programs for children with disabilities cannot be successful without consistent family participation and _____ _____.
3.29 Three models of professional collaboration have been used to teach and support students with disabilities: multidisciplinary, interdisciplinary, and _____.
3.30 The first years of life are _____ to the overall development of children.

3.31   Early intervention services and support must be provided without lengthy _____.

3.32   The Individualized Family Service Plan (IFSP) is structured to include all members of the _____.

3.33   Early intervention programs should be based on _____ _____.

3.34   Early intervention programs that are family-centered address _____, _____, and _____ when determining program goals, supports needed, and services to be provided

3.35   _____ are used to plan a program that supports the preschool-age child in meeting the demands of the home, school, or community setting.

Review – True/False

Please indicate whether the statements are true (T) or false (F) by circling the corresponding letter. You should be able to briefly describe the rationale for your answer.

T   F   3.36   Though initially supported by research, Head Start has not been shown to be effective in preparing children for elementary school.

T   F   3.37   Meeting regularly is one way to enhance collaborative efforts among members of a team

T   F   3.38   Collaboration must sometimes be approached in a competitive manner.

T   F   3.39   If a professional believes that only he or she is qualified to provide instruction or support in particular areas of need, efforts to share successful strategies are inhibited.

T   F   3.40   Education of children with disabilities must be viewed as the primary responsibility of families.

T   F   3.41   Preschool-age children without disabilities learn to value and accept diversity through the practice of inclusion.

T   F   3.42   Cooperative learning is beneficial to all students from the highest achievers to those at risk of school failure.

T   F   3.43   Early intervention is most effective when delivered through a center-based model.

Chapter Review – Practice Test

In the following activity, select the most appropriate of the four answers provided for each item. Try to do this without looking at your text in order to get an idea of your comprehension level.

3.44 In order to identify the skills needed in the elementary school environment, a preschool transition plan should begin at least _____ prior to the child's actual move.
   A.   3 to 6 months
   B.   6 to 12 months
   C.   12 to 18 months
   D.   12 to 24 months

3.45 The current wave of reform in America's schools is centered on finding new and more effective ways to increase student learning by establishing
   A.   high standards for what should be taught.
   B.   high standards for specific guidelines for writing effective IFSPs and IEPs.
   C.   high standards for how performance will be measured.
   D.   A. and C.

3.46 All but which of the following are key characteristics in effective collaboration?
   A.   Promoting peer support and cooperative learning
   B.   Sharing responsibility
   C.   Viewing parents as partners
   D.   Developing IEPs that reflect curriculum goals

3.47 According to the United Nations Salamanca Statement, all but which of the following are true? Regular schools with inclusive orientation
   A.   are provided more supplies if they include students with disabilities.
   B.   are more efficient and cost effective.
   C.   are the most effective means of combating discriminatory attitudes.
   D.   provide an effective education to the majority of children.

3.48 One of the reasons the term *mainstreaming* has a negative connotation is because
   A.   inclusion is an easier term to remember.
   B.   additional support was not provided when it was instituted.
   C.   parents found the term offensive and confusing.
   D.   teachers did not agree with the concept it represented.

3.49 In order for early intervention to be effective, services must focus on
   A.   individualization.
   B.   intense interventions.
   C.   meeting the needs of the family.
   D.   All of the above.

3.50 The goal of general and special education teachers sharing responsibility in ensuring an appropriate educational experience for students with disabilities first came about
   A.   through Public Law 94-143.
   B.   through the Regular Education Initiative.
   C.   through the No Child Left Behind legislation.
   D.   through the Handicapped Children's Early Education Program (HCEEP).

3.51 The success of inclusion programs depends on
   A.   availability of a support network of education professionals.
   B.   access to a curriculum that meets the needs of each student.
   C.   strong belief in the value of inclusion on the part of professionals and parents.
   D.   All of the above.

3.52 It is generally agreed that schools are most successful in promoting students' achievement and valued post-school outcomes when they do all of the following, except:
    A. frequently monitor student progress.
    B. promote the values of diversity, acceptance, and belonging.
    C. ensure access to the general education curriculum.
    D. provide services and support in multi-age special education classrooms.

3.53 Effective inclusive schools provide students with disabilities
    A. transportation to and from school with other students with disabilities.
    B. informal opportunities to play on sports teams with their peers.
    C. formal and natural support networks.
    D. peers formally assigned to them to serve as social mentors.

3.54 Early stimulation is critical to the later development of
    A. language, intelligence, personality, and a sense of self worth.
    B. personality and an ability to read at an early age.
    C. relationships with family members and peers in preschool activities.
    D. parents' ability to develop appropriate IEP goals and objectives.

3.55 Meaningful participation in the general curriculum will necessitate the development and use of effective strategies, such as
    A. universally-designed curriculum, cooperative learning, and instructional adaptations.
    B. instructional adaptations, multilevel instruction, and assistive technology.
    C. All of the above.
    D. None of the above.

3.56 Collaboration among parents and educators is most effective when everyone
    A. shares in the responsibility and consequences for making a decision.
    B. signs the IEP when it is presented by the special education teacher.
    C. acknowledges that parents are the experts on their children.
    D. agrees that parents must accept full responsibility for their child's education.

3.57 The most important piece of legislation ever enacted on behalf of infants and preschool-age children with disabilities was
    A. Public Law 94-143.
    B. Public Law 99-457.
    C. the No Child Left Behind legislation.
    D. the Handicapped Children's Early Education Program (HCEEP).

3.58 The purpose for early intervention is all but which of the following?
   A. Minimize the likelihood of institutionalization of individuals with disabilities and maximize the potential for their living independently in society.
   B. Enhance the development of infants and toddlers with disabilities and minimize their potential for developmental delay.
   C. Reduce the educational cost to our society.
   D. Identify more individuals with developmental delays so that special education services will be prepared when they become school age.

3.59 Early intervention programs include intensive approaches which usually means how many hours of contact each week?
   A. 1 - 3 hours/2 - 3 times a week
   B. 3 - 4 hours/2 - 3 times a week
   C. 2 - 3 hours/4 - 5 times a week
   D. 4 - 5 hours/4 - 5 times a week

3.60 Coordination of early intervention services across disciplines and with the family is
   A. crucial if the goals of the program are to be realized.
   B. important if the goals of the program are to be realized.
   C. specific if the goals of the program are to be realized.
   D. generalized if the goals of the program are to be realized.

3.61 Circle all that apply to the statement, "Referrals for preschool services may be based on
   A. a child's perceived delays in physical development."
   B. a child's perceived delays in speech and language development."
   C. a child's perceived delays in excessive inappropriate behavior."
   D. a child's perceived delays in sensory difficulties."

3.62 In order for a preschool-age child with disabilities to be determined eligible for special education services, criteria must include which of the following?
   A. Concern by family members and friends that the child may be "slow" and needs to be taught in a direct and structured manner by a special education teacher.
   B. Recommendation by daycare workers and other professionals who believe the child would benefit from special education and related service providers.
   C. Developmental delays evident as measured by appropriate diagnostic instruments and procedures in one or more developmental area.
   D. Child appears to need occupational and/or physical therapy

3.63 The purpose for preschool programs for young children with disabilities is to
   A. provide a break for the families and friends.
   B. assist the students in living in and adapting to a variety of environmental settings.
   C. demonstrate a need for federal funding so that schools can be assured enough fiscal support to continue early intervention programs.
   D. allow the students an opportunity to adjust to the school environment and to make friends with other students.

3.64 Early childhood educators believe that emphasis should be placed on
    A. play and exploration.
    B. social interaction and inquiry.
    C. adults serving as guides.
    D. All of the above.

3.65 The National Association for the Education of Young Children (NAEYC) has
developed several guiding principles that include
    A. a caring community of learners.
    B. development of an IEP as soon as a child, age birth to three, is identified.
    C. enactment of laws that mandate full inclusion.
    D. parents actively working alongside their child.

3.66 Teachers must enter the classroom with a thorough understanding of child development
to support the inclusion of diverse learners. This is referred to as
    A. collaboration.
    B. reflective teaching.
    C. holistic view of child development.
    D. range of individualized supports and services.

3.67 Which of the following is not one of the 5 factors identified as being critical to
successfully serving young children with disabilities in inclusive, community-based
child care settings?
    A. Development of IEPs by a team before the parents and/or child agree to a setting
    B. Willingness to make inclusion work
    C. Access to emotional support and technical assistance from other professionals
    D. Realistic balance between resources needed and those available

Cryptogram

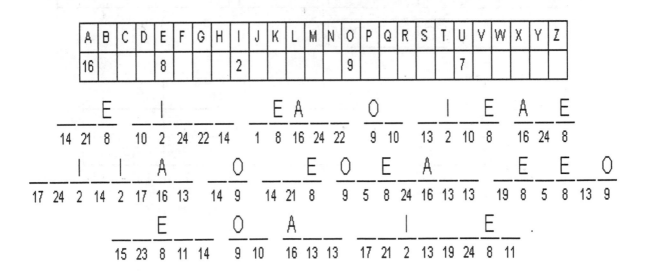

Double Puzzle

Unscramble each of the clue words. Copy the letters in the numbered cells to other cells with the same number.

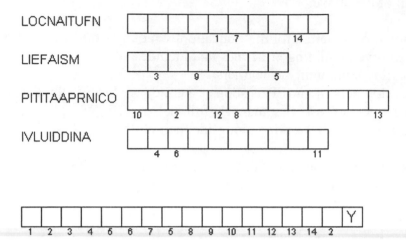

LOCNAITUFN

LIEFAISM

PITITAAPRNICO

IVLUIDDINA

Scramble

Unscramble the tiles to reveal a message.

A C C	E S O	I T Y ,	F D I	E P T A	B E L
F E C T		T H E	I V E	O T E	V E R S
O L S	S C H O	N G .	N C E ,	E F	V A L U
O N G I	A N D	P R O M			

Across

3. Intervention plan for infants and pre-school children and their families
5. Student-centered approach to instructional decision making

Down

1. When professionals from various disciplines develop instructional programs
2. _____ inclusion is when students with disabilities receive some of their instruction in a general education classroom with "pull out" to another instructional setting
4. _____ intervention is preventive steps taken early in life to lessen the impact of a disability
6. General and special educators providing services in the general education classrooms in the student's home school
7. Frequency and amount of time a young child is engaged in intervention activities.

Case Study

Jolie, a sweet 2 year old, was born with Down's syndrome. Her family recently moved from a Midwestern state to a small community several area codes away. Jolie has many of the physical characteristics of Down's syndrome: epicanthral folds of the eyes; an elongated tongue; straight, fine hair; short legs; and stubby fingers and toes. Her cognitive characteristics are less stereotypical. Jolie has some mild delays in speech and vocabulary, but the early intervention services provided through a home-based model were very effective. In fact, Jolie began receiving speech/language therapy and occupational therapy two times a week at age one month. Now her parents must navigate a new state system to obtain early intervention services for Jolie. Answer these questions based on your state's early intervention system.

1. What state and county services are available for Jolie? Who is responsible for providing those services? In what form will services be provided to Jolie?_____

_____

_____

_____

2. What is the process for obtaining those services for Jolie? What would the process be if Jolie hadn't already been receiving services from another state? _____

_____

_____

_____

3. What happens when Jolie celebrates her 3rd birthday 9 months from now? _____

_____

_____

_____

Community Activities

Contact the Early Intervention office at your State's Department of Education. Find out how early intervention/early childhood special education services are provided to infants and young children with developmental delays and disabilities. What did you discover?

_____

_____

_____

_____

Observe kindergarten round-up activities at a neighborhood school. What kinds of developmental differences were observed? How would you interpret those observations in terms of school-related expectations? _____

_____

_____

_____

Books

Negotiating the Special Education Maze by Winifred Anderson, Deidre Hayden, Stephen Chitwood. Available through Woodbine House.

The New Language of Toys: Teaching Communication Skills to Children with Special Needs by Sue Schwartz, Joan E. Miller, Joan E. Heller. Available through Woodbine House.

The Child with Special Needs: Encouraging Intellectual and Emotional Growth by Stanley I. Greenspan, Robin Simon, and Serena Weider. Available through Perseus Publishing.

Videos

Families, Friends, Futures, Comfort Media Concepts

I Belong Out There, Irene M. Ward & Associates

Small Differences, Braddock Films, Inc.

Bong and Donnell, Video Press

Special Needs Students in Regular Classrooms? Sean's Story, www.films.com

Websites

Circle of Inclusion Project: www.circleofinclusion.org

Learning Abled Kids: www.learningabledkids.com

Family Village: www.familyvillage.wisc.edu/index.html

Dictionary for Parents of Children with Disabilities: www.usd.edu/cd/dictionary

4

Transition and Adult Life

Children do not grow out of disabilities as they progress through their school career. In fact, many of the challenges they face as youngsters continue through their teen and young adult years. The field of special education has come to realize how important the secondary and post-secondary educational experiences are for students with disabilities. Thus, this chapter addresses important transition issues including transition planning and implementation, self-determination, and adult services.

Concept Reflection

A. What did I know about transition and adult life for individuals with disabilities before reading this chapter?	B. How did reading the chapter enhance or change what I already knew? (Relate this to Column A.)	C. What new information did I learn? (This may or may not be associated with your responses in A or B.)
1.	1.	1.
2.	2.	2.
3.	3.	3.
4.	4.	4.
5.	5.	5.

Keep the following questions in mind as you read this chapter.

4.1 What do we know about access to community living and employment for people with disabilities after they leave school?
A.
B.
C.
D.
4.2 What are the requirements for transition planning in IDEA?
A.
B.
C.
4.3 Identify the purpose of an ITP and the basic steps in its formulation.
A.
B.
C.
D.
E.
F.

4.4 Why is it important for students with disabilities to receive instruction in self-determination, academics, adaptive and functional life skills, and employment preparation during the secondary school years?

A.

B.

C.

D.

4.5 Describe government-funded and natural supports for people with disabilities.

A.

B.

C.

D.

E.

Read – Matching Vocabulary

Following are a number of the key terms and concepts used in this chapter. Try to complete this matching exercise before you read the chapter. Match each term with the phrase that you think most closely describes or defines it.

A. Adult service agencies
B. Individualized Transition Plan
C. Medicaid
D. Medicare
E. School to Work Act
F. Self-determination

4.6 _____ A statement about transition services within each student's IEP.

4.7 _____ A government-sponsored national insurance program for people over 65 years of age and eligible people with disabilities.

4.8 _____ Agencies providing services to adults with disabilities, accessing postsecondary education, participating in leisure activities, etc.

4.9 _____ The ability of a person to consider options and to make appropriate choices regarding residential life, work, and leisure time

4.10 _____ A government-sponsored health are program for people with disabilities.

4.11 _____ Legislation providing all students in the public schools with education and training to prepare them for first jobs.

Reflect – Matching Vocabulary

This exercise is intended to provide practice in recalling what you have just read. Try not to refer back to the chapter as you match the following items with their descriptions below. As you work through this exercise, consider how this new information relates to other knowledge, concepts, and/or principles you learned before taking this course.

A. Supported employment
B. Transition
C. Transition services
D. Vocational rehabilitation
E. Vocational Rehabilitation Act
F. Work Incentives Act of 1999

4.12 _____ Employment in an integrated setting provided for people with disabilities who need some type of continuing support and for whom competitive employment has traditionally not been possible.

4.13 _____ Legislation enabling people with disabilities to work and keep health care coverage.

4.14 _____ A program providing intensive, short-term support to people with disabilities who can undertake successful employment on their own.

4.15 _____ A federal mandate providing services for adults with disabilities through rehabilitation counselors in several areas.

4.16 _____ A term defined by Will (1984) as a "bridge between the security and structure offered by the school and adult life."

4.17 _____ A coordinated set of student activities that promote movement from school to post-school activities.

Supply a word/phrase in each sentence in order to make sense out of the statement of a concept, definition, or principle that is otherwise incomplete or lacks closure. Several answers, other than those listed in the key, may be acceptable for an item. Focus on whether or not your answer is equivalent to the answer supplied and be prepared to explain why you completed the statement(s) as you did.

4.18 More time to take tests, large print books, and interpreters are examples of _____.

4.19 A successful transition from school to adult years requires both _____ and _____ _____.

4.20 IDEA requires that beginning at age _____, and updated annually, a student's IEP must include a statement of the transition services that relate to various courses of study.

4.21 An Individualized Transition Plan (ITP) is based on an evaluation of student _____ and _____.

4.22 The purpose of the transition statement is to identify the type and range of transitional services and supports, and to establish _____ and _____ responsible for completing the plan.

4.23 _____ _____ _____ assist individuals with disabilities in accessing postsecondary education, employment, and/or leisure activities.

4.24 Research indicates that it is important for secondary schools to teach _____ _____ skills.

4.25 Students with disabilities have _____ drop out rates and _____ academic achievement.

4.26 Career education includes training in social skills development as well as _____ skills.

4.27 A common paradox for parents of a child with a disability is their struggle with their child's right to grow up and the need for continued _____.

4.28 Three of the most widely used models for residential living are foster family care, semi-independent homes/apartments, and _____ homes.

Please indicate whether the statements are true (T) or false (F) by circling the corresponding letter. You should be able to briefly describe the rationale for your answer.

T   F   4.29   Of the nearly half a million students who exit high school each year, only 61% of the students with disabilities leave with a diploma as compared to 90% of their peers without disabilities.

T   F   4.30   The family unit may be the single most powerful force in preparing the adolescent with disabilities for the adult years.

T   F   4.31   Transportation, telecommunication, employment, and public accommodations are often part of a student's transition plan.

T	F	4.32	As students enter adulthood they are not expected to function as independently as possible.
T	F	4.33	When a student has developed self-determination skills, he/she is more efficient in acquiring knowledge and solving problems.
T	F	4.34	The use of assistive technology is not recommended for students with disabilities.
T	F	4.35	In a longitudinal study (1996) many siblings believe that families should be responsible for the care of family members who are disabled.
T	F	4.36	All states have the same Medicaid service delivery regulations

Chapter Review – Practice Test

In the following activity, select the most appropriate of the four answers provided for each item. Try to do this without looking at your text in order to get an idea of your comprehension level.

4.37 Some of the challenging tasks related to inclusion for students in secondary settings
    A.   include selection of general education classes.
    B.   include selection of appropriate peer models.
    C.   include selection of challenging instructors.
    D.   include selection of colleges that support students with special needs.

4.38 In 1996 over _____ of the freshmen who reported having a disability were purported to have a learning disability.
    A.   15%
    B.   25%
    C.   35%
    D.   45%

4.39 Transition planning should culminate with
    A.   the transfer of support from the school to an adult service agency.
    B.   access to postsecondary education.
    C.   life as an independent adult.
    D.   All of the above.

4.40 Effective transition systems include
    A.   effective middle school and high school programs.
    B.   a cooperative system of transition planning.
    C.   availability of formal government-funded programs.
    D.   All of the above.

4.41 Greater opportunities for the employment of people with disabilities by allowing them to work and still keep critical health care coverage is possible through
    A.   Public Law 94-142.
    B.   the Ticket to Work and Work Incentives Improvement Act.
    C.   the Right to Work legislation.
    D.   All of the above.

4.42 Which of the following is not one of the three critical components about which parents and students must be educated in order to fully prepare to transition from school?
   A. Completing IEPs independently
   B. Current and potential opportunities for independent living
   C. Potential employment
   D. Characteristics of service agencies

4.43 A four-step problem-solving process includes which of the following steps?
   A. Role playing
   B. Identifying a leader
   C. Including students without disabilities in the process
   D. All of the above.

4.44 For students with moderate to severe disabilities, the purpose of academic learning may need to be
   A. academically oriented.
   B. more functional.
   C. less demanding.
   D. more inclusive.

4.45 The most notable difference between community-referenced instruction and work experience programs is that community-referenced instruction focuses on
   A. peer tutors who serve as models and mentors.
   B. development of isolated skills in the classroom.
   C. modeling skills taught through training tapes in the appropriate settings.
   D. activities to be accomplished at the work site.

4.46 Approximately _____ of adults with more severe disabilities of all ages live at home with their parents and/or siblings.
   A. 20%
   B. 40%
   C. 60%
   D. 80%

4.47 Supplemental Security Income (SSI) and Social Security Disability Insurance (SSDI)
   A. provide assistance at banking and financial institutions.
   B. provide basic economic assistance.
   C. provide training on how to manage money free of charge.
   D. All of the above.

4.48 The potential for locating and maintaining a job is enhanced greatly if the individual has
   A. a family who insists upon a job being provided.
   B. friends who are employed.
   C. expressed an interest in being employed.
   D. received training and experience during the school years.

4.49 Which of the following are present in the formulation of the ITP?
   A. Assessment data
   B. Updating of the ITP
   C. An ITP team
   D. All of the above.

4.50 For most of the twentieth century, federal support for residential living has been directed toward
   A. families.
   B. small group homes.
   C. large congregate care living.
   D. All of the above.

4.51 Effective transition planning includes the student's present levels of performance, annual goal(s), short term objectives, and
   A. practice in making decisions.
   B. an allowance that can be used for transportation.
   C. names of relatives that will help implement the plan.
   D. identification of needed transition services.

4.52 The transition planning process for students with disabilities should begin
   A. during the year the student is expected to graduate (ages 18 - 21).
   B. at age 14 and not later than age 16.
   C. immediately following graduation from high school.
   D. when the multidisciplinary team determines the student is ready for a job.

Cryptogram

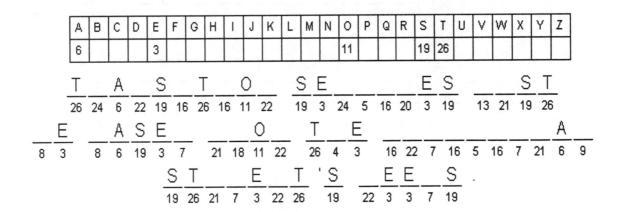

A	B	C	D	E	F	G	H	I	J	K	L	M	N	O	P	Q	R	S	T	U	V	W	X	Y	Z
6				3									11					19	26						

T A S T O _ S E _ _ _ E S _ _ S T
26 24 6 22 19 16 26 16 11 22   19 3 24 5 16 20 3 19   13 21 19 26

_ E _ A S E _ _ O _ T _ E _ _ _ _ _ _ _ A
8 3   8 6 19 3 7   21 18 11 22   26 4 3   16 22 7 16 5 16 7 21 6 9

S T _ _ E _ T ' S _ E E _ S .
19 26 21 7 3 22 26   19   22 3 3 7 19

Unscramble each of the clue words. Copy the letters in the numbered cells to other cells with the same number.

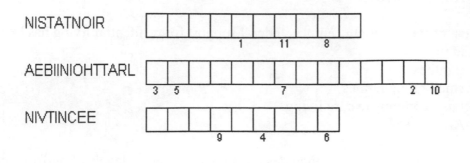

NISTATNOIR

AEBIINIOHTTARL

NIVTINCEE

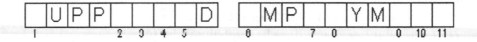

U	P	P				D

M	P		Y	M		

Unscramble the tiles to reveal a message.

T S W	I T H	B I L I	T H E	E N U	N D E R
M A T E	E S T I	T I E S	A R E	C A P A	B I L I
O F T	D I S A	T I E S	D .	A D U L	O F

Crossword Puzzle

Across

3. _____ homes are one model for residential living
5. Students with disabilities have _____ drop out rates
6. Government-sponsored health care program for people with disabilities.
7. The ability of a person to consider options and to make appropriate choices regarding residential life, work, and leisure time.
8. _____ plan is a statement about transition services within each student's IEP
9. More time to take tests

Down

1. Government-sponsored national insurance program for people over 65 and/or with disabilities
2. By age __ a student's IEP must include a statement of the transition services
4. Career education includes training in social skills development as well as _____ skills

Best Practices

Case Study

Anthony is 19 years old and is a senior in high school. Anthony, who has moderate mental retardation, is getting ready to attend a meeting with his transition team. This team, made up of the special education teacher, the civics teacher, Anthony's parents, the school counselor, the vocational coordinator, and the school principal, all work together to support Anthony as he moves into adulthood, work, and independence.

Today, the transition team is meeting to discuss Anthony's work assignments this semester, review data collected at the job site on Anthony's work habits, and to determine if the transition plan needs any modifications.

1. Describe the transition process. What is included in a transition plan? When is it prepared and implemented? Who is involved in the process? _____
_____
_____
_____
_____

2. What is the purpose of the transition process? _____
_____
_____
_____
_____

Community Activities

1. Visit a work program for adults with disabilities. What types of work are the participants learning about and doing? What are the work-related challenges for the participants? How does this program help their clients succeed in a work environment? _____
_____
_____
_____
_____

2. Visit a local vocational-technical school or program. What kinds of programs are available to young adults in the community? Does the school/program work with individuals with disabilities? What is the completion rate for the students who attend the program as compared to those with disabilities who attend? What is the employment rate for the students? _____
_____
_____
_____
_____

3. Shadow a school-based high school vocational coordinator for a day. What are examples of work-study experiences that are provided for students with disabilities? How often do the students work and for how long? What supports are needed by students with disabilities to have successful work experiences?_____
_____
_____
_____

50

Books

Life Beyond the Classroom: Transition Strategies for Young People with Disabilities, Third Edition, by Paul Wehman, Ph.D. Available from Paul H. Brookes Publishing Co.
Disability and the Family Life Cycle by Laura E. Marshak, Milton Seligman, and Fran Prezant. Published by Basic Books.
Laying Community Foundations: For Your Child With a Disability: How to Establish Relationships That Will Support Your Child After You're Gone by Linda J. Stengle. Available from Independent Publisher.

Videos

From Civil War to Civil Rights: A Century of Vocational Rehabilitation by Ability Today
Business as Usual by Sherry Kozak, www.fanlight.com
The Americans with Disabilities Act: New Access to the Workplace by Joel Marks/MTI Film & Video

Websites

Project Freedom: www.projectfreedom.org
Speaking For Ourselves: www.speaking.org
Federal Employment Office: www.opm.gov/disability

5

Multicultural and Diversity Issues

Schools reflect the complex and varied cultures in which they are located. Multicultural education, the belief that children and youth from backgrounds that differ from the majority culture have unique needs, is also a concern in special education. As schools see an increase in students born to immigrant parents or who are immigrants themselves, so does special education. In fact, special education has long struggled to address the disproportionate numbers of students with language, cultural, and socioeconomic differences.

This chapter addresses special education's response to cultural diversity in terms of major principles of IDEA, nondiscriminatory and multidisciplinary assessment, parent participation, individual education plans (IEP), and the least restrictive environment (LRE).

Concept Reflection

A. What did I know about multiculturalism and diversity before reading this chapter?	B. How did reading the chapter enhance or change what I already knew? (Relate this to Column A.)	C. What new information did I learn? (This may or may not be associated with your responses in A or B.)
1.	1.	1.
2.	2.	2.
3.	3.	3.
4.	4.	4.
5.	5.	5.

Keep the following questions in mind as you read this chapter.

5.1 Identify three ways in which the purposes of and approaches to general education in the United States sometimes differ from those of special education and multicultural education.
A.   B.   C.
5.2 Describe the population and trends among culturally diverse groups in the United States. How do they have an impact on the educational system?
A.   B.   C.
5.3 Identify two ways in which assessment may contribute to the overrepresentation of culturally diverse students in special education programs.
A.   B.
5.4 Identify three ways in which language diversity may contribute to assessment difficulties with students who are from a variety of cultures.
A.   B.   C.

5.5 Identify three ways in which differing socialcultural customs may affect the manner in which parents become involved in the educational process.
A.   B.   C.
5.6 Identify two areas that require particular attention when developing an individualized education plan (IEP) for a student from a culturally diverse background.
A.   B.
5.7 Identify two considerations that represent particular difficulties in serving children from culturally diverse backgrounds in the least restrictive environment (LRE).
A.   B.
5.8 Identify two ways in which poverty may contribute to the academic difficulties of children from culturally diverse backgrounds, often resulting in their referral to special education
A.   B.
5.9 Identify two ways in which migrancy among culturally diverse populations may contribute to academic difficulties.
A.   B.

5.10 Identify three conceptual factors that have contributed to heightened attention and concern regarding the placement of children from ethnic and cultural groups in special education.

A.

B.

C.

Read – Matching Vocabulary

Following are a number of the key terms and concepts used in this chapter. Try to complete this matching exercise before you read the chapter. Match each term with the phrase that you think most closely describes or defines it.

A. Cultural pluralism   E. Overrepresentation
B. Measurement bias   F. Prevalence
C. Multicultural education   G. Test bias
D. English   H. Justice

_____

5.11 _____ A situation in which one cultural group has a higher percentage of youngsters in special education than might be expected.

5.12 _____ The number of people in a given population who exhibit a condition, problem, or particular status.

5.13 _____ Many cultural subgroups living together in a manner that maintains cultural differences.

5.14 _____ Education that promotes learning about multiple cultures and values.

5.15 _____ Inaccuracy of assessment due to cultural background, sex, or race.

5.16 _____ The unfairness of a testing procedure or instrument which gives one group an advantage over another group.

5.17 _____ The number of children in the American education system who speak languages other than _____ is increasing.

5.18 _____ Social _____ should be of paramount importance in the design and delivery of curricula.

This exercise is intended to provide practice in recalling what you have just read. Try not to refer back to the chapter as you match the following items with their descriptions below. As you work through this exercise, consider how this new information relates to other knowledge, concepts, and/or principles you have learned before taking this course.

A. Acculturation process
B. Assessment tools
C. Impoverished environment
D. Nondiscriminatory assessment

E. Norm-based averages
F. Self-fulfilling prophecy
G. Special education
H. U.S. general education

_____

5.19 _____ Institution that provides an education for the masses.
5.20 _____ Field in which the basic purpose is dealing with differences.
5.21 _____ The instruments, or tests, used to evaluate students.
5.22 _____ The average performance scores of agemates.
5.23 _____ Home, neighborhood, or community lacking important resources.
5.24 _____ Socialization resulting from one's unique social/cultural environment.
5.25 _____ Testing that results in accurate reflections of ability.
5.26 _____ Prediction that an individual will become what he or she is labeled.

Supply a word/phrase in each sentence in order to make sense out of the statement of a concept, definition, or principle that is otherwise incomplete or lacks closure. Several answers, other than those listed in the key, may be acceptable for an item. Focus on whether or not your answer is equivalent to the answer supplied and be prepared to explain why you completed the statement(s) as you did.

5.27 The fundamental goal of education in the United States is to produce _____ citizens.

5.28 A complete education must include recognition of the many _____ of many people in shaping our country.

5.29 Contemporary multicultural education sees the school as a powerful tool for promoting _____ .

5.30 Four major elements of the Individuals with Disabilities Education Act (IDEA) include nondiscriminatory and multidisciplinary assessment, free and appropriate public education (FAPE) delivered through an Individualized Education Program (IEP), education in the least restrictive environment (LRE), and

_____ _____ .

5.31 Research indicates that thoughtfully developed early intervention programs have beneficial effects on poor children's academic performance, cognitive development, and general _____ .

5.32 There is an obvious link between special and multicultural education with issues such as _____ assessment.

5.33   Professionals need _____ training to help them see how easily bias can creep in to testing situations.

5.34   Some cultures have great difficulty accepting disabilities because of _____ beliefs.

Review – True/False

Please indicate whether the statements are true (T) or false (F) by circling the corresponding letter. You should be able to briefly describe the rationale for your answer.

T   F   5.35   Youngsters from minority backgrounds appear more frequently in disability categories than expected based on the proportion of culturally different people in the population.

T   F   5.36   Students who are white have a greater drop out rate than African Americans and/or Latinos.

T   F   5.37   In the U.S. over 21 million people 5 years of age or older speak English less than "very well."

T   F   5.38   Information about a child's home life can provide valuable insight to aid evaluators in interpreting the results of assessments.

T   F   5.39   There are times when it is appropriate to "pull out" a child for language instruction for a portion of the school day.

T   F   5.40   Conditions of poverty are rarely associated with homelessness and academic risk.

T   F   5.41   It is appropriate to place a child in special education even if the only apparent difficulty is the child's cultural background.

T   F   5.42   During teacher conferences cultural issues should be considered.

Chapter Review – Practice Test

In the following activity, select the most appropriate of the four answers provided for each item. Try to do this without looking at your text in order to get an idea of your comprehension level.

5.43   An IEP for a child from a culturally diverse background must include all but which one of the following items?
   A.   Type of language intervention needed
   B.   Language development
   C.   The proficiency of the speech-language therapist
   D.   Language dominance and proficiency

5.44   Proportionally, African Americans and Hispanics are found in poverty nearly _____ times as often as non-Hispanic Whites live at this level.
   A.   2
   B.   3
   C.   4
   D.   5

5.45 Multiculturalism has the goal of
    A.   teaching all students about different cultures.
    B.   teaching students from other culture about America.
    C.   teaching the general public about various cultures in the schools.
    D.   adopting cultural customs into the general education classrooms.

5.46 According to your text, multicultural and special education have this thing in common:
    A.   Children must all be at least 3 years of age to receive services.
    B.   Parents must agree to participate in all school activities.
    C.   In order to receive services, children must have an IEP.
    D.   They evolved because children's needs were not being appropriately met.

5.47 American education is aimed at the masses and performance is judged according to
    A.   special education teachers and psychologists.
    B.   general education teachers and principals.
    C.   individualized performances.
    D.   an average.

5.48 Which item is not cited as an assumption on which multicultural education is based?
    A.   Cultural differences have strength and value.
    B.   Homogenization of the population is of paramount importance.
    C.   Attitudes and values can be promoted in schools.
    D.   Educators working with families/communities must support multiculturalism.

5.49 The primary purpose of special education is to
    A.   focus on individual needs, strengths, and preferences.
    B.   support the families of students with special needs.
    C.   teach to the masses to "level the playing field."
    D.   teach topics similar to those of general education.

5.50 Factors associated with students *at risk* for academic failure include all but
    A.   poverty.
    B.   limited background in speaking English.
    C.   large families.
    D.   diverse cultural backgrounds.

5.51 A precedent set as a result of *Diana v. State Board of Education* was that
    A.   there can never be more females than males in special education classes.
    B.   assessments must be conducted in a child's native/primary language.
    C.   eligibility for special education must be offered to everyone.
    D.   special education teachers, with the written consent of the parents, can place a child in special education and waive the testing procedure.

5.52 The problem with measurement bias is that it
    A. fluctuates from child to child.
    B. slants the results of the testing in the child's favor so he/she will not qualify for special services.
    C. produces errors during testing, leading to inaccurate test results.
    D. identifies too many students from other cultures.

5.53 Standardized, norm-referenced instruments have been criticized because
    A. students score too high compared to students from this country.
    B. students score too low compared to students from this country.
    C. they are too easy for the students to complete.
    D. students are compared with norms developed from other populations.

5.54 Which two items identify revisions that were made to testing instruments so that cultural bias was reduced?
    A. Reduction of the amount of culture-specific language proficiency required to perform test tasks.
    B. Reduction in the amount of questions posed for younger children.
    C. Reduction in the amount of culture-specific content.
    D. Reduction in the number of adults allowed with the child at the time of the test.

5.55 According to your text, one of the best ways to ensure fair testing is to
    A. move the testing sessions to more comfortable and familiar surroundings.
    B. more adequately prepare those who give tests and interpret the results.
    C. teach to the tests.
    D. allow students from ethnic backgrounds to have a "practice" test before they are actually assessed by a professional.

5.56 A significant challenge in assessing students with diverse cultural backgrounds has always been
    A. a feeling of inferiority by the students.
    B. an overwhelming sense of confusion and apprehension by the parents.
    C. having enough interpreters available.
    D. taking into account the language differences.

5.57 Professional training challenges are often addressed unsuccessfully in all but
    A. intern classrooms.
    B. teacher education programs.
    C. psychology classes.
    D. related areas.

5.58 U.S. public education predominantly reflects the philosophy of the
    A. cultural minority.
    B. cultural majority.
    C. democratic party.
    D. teacher unions.

5.59 Effective educational programming for culturally diverse students requires
    A. a team effort among parents and professionals.
    B. at least one team member who is from the same country.
    C. a special education teacher.
    D. interpreters for the child, family, and teachers.

5.60 The teacher of an inclusive culturally diverse classroom must
    A. be extremely friendly to the families of students who represent diversity.
    B. learn the language of the children who represent diversity.
    C. be sensitive to cultural differences.
    D. establish rapport with the families before the children enter the class.

5.61 According to your text, an interruption in the continuity of schooling has an impact on all but which of the following?
    A. General academic progress
    B. Peer relationships
    C. Peer and teacher relationships
    D. Family relationships

5.62 Specialized instruction for students with disabilities from culturally diverse backgrounds must be based on
    A. the number of students already in the special education classroom.
    B. individual needs of the student.
    C. the amount of knowledge the teacher has about the child's background.
    D. how involved the parents agree to be in development of the child's IEP.

Cryptogram

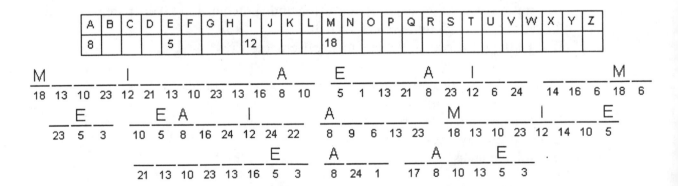

Scramble

Unscramble the tiles to reveal a message.

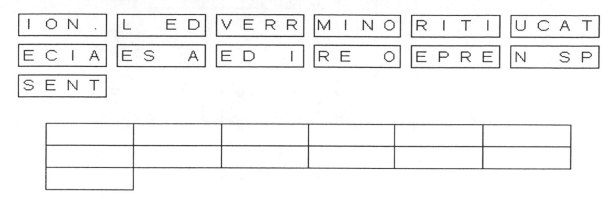

I O N .	L E D	V E R R	M I N O	R I T I	U C A T
E C I A	E S A	E D I	R E O	E P R E	N S P
S E N T

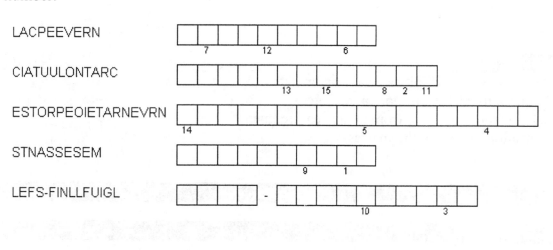

Double Puzzle

Unscramble each of the clue words. Copy the letters in the numbered cells to other cells with the same number.

LACPEEVERN

CIATUULONTARC

ESTORPEOIETARNEVRN

STNASSESEM

LEFS-FINLLFUIGL

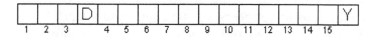

Crossword Puzzle

Across

    2. Students with and without disabilities in same classroom

    5. Education that is individualized

    6. To test

    7. Average performance of peers

    8. Skew

Down

    1. Population that exhibits a condition or status

    2. Community lacking important resources

    3. Socialization resulting from unique environment

    4. Education that is for the masses

Best Practices

Case Study

Debbie Cho is a model student in Mr. Wilson's 6th grade class. She is at school every day, follows the class and school rules, is courteous to her peers and teachers, and attends to instruction. However, despite these positive attributes and efforts, Debbie is not showing academic progress like her peers. Her reading and writing skills are several years behind her peers and this has affected her ability to read textbook material, complete the many writing assignments, and take tests.

Mr. Wilson has had contact with her parents several times, but communicating with them is difficult. Like Debbie, they speak English, but not as fluently as they speak Vietnamese. They often use Debbie as an interpreter. They seem very cooperative and tell him that they remind Debbie to work hard and listen to the teacher. Mr. Wilson has decided to refer Debbie to the teacher assistance team for help, but he is concerned about the parent's reaction to possible testing.

1. What are the diversity-related barriers for Debbie and her family? _____
_____
_____
_____

2. What could Mr. Wilson do to improve Debbie's school performance? _____
_____
_____
_____

3. What could Mr. Wilson do to help the Cho family be more successful in interacting with the school? _____
_____
_____
_____

Community Activities

1. Visit a school with a diverse student population and a school that is less diverse. Spend a few hours in one of their special education classrooms. Compare the classrooms in terms of the diversity observed, the social interactions that occurred between students and the teacher, and you. Compare the curriculum and teaching methods. _____
_____
_____
_____
_____
_____

2. Contact the state department of education in your state and obtain special education diversity information. Specifically, find out what exceptional student demographic information about gender, ethnicity, and socioeconomic status. Compare this to the two schools you visited. How are they similar and different? What impact do these differences have on the school's local reputation?_____
_____
_____
_____

3. Attend a class in a P-12 school for students with limited English proficiency. Describe the students in terms of their ability to communicate in an English environment. How does the teacher approach instruction for those students? _____

_____

_____

_____

_____

Resources

Books
Special Education Issues Within the Context of American Society by Susan McLean Benner and Susan Benner. Available from Wadsworth Publishers.
Dealing with Differences: Taking Action on Class, Race, Gender and Disability by Angele M. Ellis and Marilyn Llewelleyn. Available from Sage Publications.

Videos
Disability Culture Rap - Advocating Change Together
Crip Culture - www.fanlight.com

Websites
Disabilities Awareness: www.cqc.state.ny.us/disawhs.htm
The Alliance for People with Disabilities: www.afpwd.org
American Speech and Hearing Association: www.asha.org
Mantra Publishing House with a Global Reach: www.multicultural-childrens-books-cds-friezes.com
North Central Regional Educational Laboratory: www.ncrel.org

6

Exceptionality and the Family

This chapter discusses how raising children with disabilities affects parents, siblings, grandparents, and other extended family members. An array of issues related to families with children with disabilities are examined as well as the family as a social/ecological system. Of particular note is the impact the child with disabilities has on relationships – between that child and significant others and others' relationships with one another.

Concept Reflection

A. What did I know about exceptionality and its impact on the family before reading this chapter?	B. How did reading the chapter enhance or change what I already knew? (Relate this to Column A.)	C. What new information did I learn? (This may or may not be associated with your responses in A or B.)
1.	1.	1.
2.	2.	2.
3.	3.	3.
4.	4.	4.
5.	5.	5.

Keep the following questions in mind as you read this chapter.

6.1	Identify five factors that influence the ways in which families respond to infants with birth defects or disabilities.

A.

B.

C.

D.

E.

6.2	What three statements can be made about the stages parents may experience in responding to infants or young children with disabilities?

A.

B.

C.

6.3	Identify three ways in which a newborn child with disabilities influences the family social/ecological system.

A.

B.

C.

6.4	Identify three factors in raising a child with a disability that contribute to spousal stress.

A.

B.

C.

6.5 Identify four general phases that parents may experience in rearing a child with a disability.

A.

B.

C.

D.

6.6 Identify four factors that influence the relationship that develops between infants with disabilities and their mothers.

A.

B.

C.

D.

6.7 Identify three ways in which fathers may respond to their children with disabilities.

A.

B.

C.

6.8 Identify four ways in which siblings respond to a brother or sister with a disability.

A.

B.

C.

D.

6.9 **Identify three types of support grandparents and other extended family members may render to families with children with disabilities.**

A.

B.

C.

D.

6.10 **Describe five behaviors skilled collaborators exhibit when interacting and relating to families with children with disabilities.**

A.

B.

C.

D.

E.

6.11 **What are the five goals of family support systems?**

A.

B.

C.

D.

E.

6.12   What are five potential thrusts of parent training?

A.

B.

C.

D.

E.

Read – Matching Vocabulary

Following are a number of the key terms and concepts used in this chapter. Try to complete this matching exercise before you read the chapter. Match each term with the phrase that you think most closely describes or defines it.

A. Period of emotional disorganization
B. Realization
C. Acknowledgment
D. Social/ecological systems approach

E. Shock
F. Defensive retreat
G. Dyadic relationship
H. Family empowerment

6.13 _____   Stage in which parents may be forced to reassess the meaning of life and the reasons for their present challenges.

6.14 _____   Phase at which parents are able to mobilize their strengths to confront the conditions created by having an exceptional child.

6.15 _____   Phase at which parents attempt to avoid dealing with the anxiety-producing realities of their child's exceptionality.

6.16 _____   Phase at which parents may be anxious or fearful about their ability to cope with the demands of caring for a child with unique needs.

6.17 _____   A stage that may be distinguished by feelings of anxiety, guilt, numbness, confusion, and/or helplessness.

6.18 _____   Attachment that occurs between two people, particularly strong on occasion between a mother and her child with a disability.

6.19 _____   A theory that describes the interrelationships among family members and the effects family members have on one another.

6.20 _____   Enabling families to effectively meet both their needs and the child's needs.

Reflect – Matching Vocabulary

This exercise is intended to provide practice in recalling what you have just read. Try not to refer back to the chapter as you match the following items with their descriptions below. As you work through this exercise, consider how this new information relates to other knowledge, concepts, and/or principles you have learned before taking this course.

A. Respite care programs   E. Mirror
B. Lower   F. Parent training
C. Father-child relationship   G. Mother-child relationship
D. Spina bifida and Down syndrome   H. Hearing impairments and learning disabilities

6.21 _____ Relationship in which expectations and functions in nurturing play a significant role.

6.22 _____ Temporary care for disabled children so that parents have an opportunity to relax and renew their relationship.

6.23 _____ Relationship that often develops differently depending on the exceptional child's gender.

6.24 _____ Intervention that helps parents develop appropriate expectations for their child's current and future achievement.

6.25 _____ Relationships between siblings tend to be ambivalent in that the highs are higher and the lows are _____.

6.26 _____ Examples of conditions that are readily apparent at birth.

6.27 _____ Examples of conditions that are not evident until later in life.

6.28 _____ Children tend to _____ the attitudes and values of their parents.

Recite – Fill in the Blank

Supply a word/phrase in each sentence in order to make sense out of the statement of a concept, definition, or principle that is otherwise incomplete or lacks closure. Several answers, other than those listed in the key, may be acceptable for an item. Focus on whether or not your answer is equivalent to the answer supplied and be prepared to explain why you completed the statement(s) as you did.

6.29 Common reactions to the birth of an infant with disabilities include shock, disappointment, anger, depression, guilt, and _____.

6.30 Parents report experiencing feelings of numbness, unsureness, loneliness, fear, and anger _____ during the lifespan of their child with a disability.

6.31 Many mothers whose babies with abnormalities survive suffer more acute feelings of grief than mothers whose infants with defects _____.

6.32 During the _____ _____ parents attempt to avoid dealing with the anxiety-producing realities of their child's condition.

6.33 Factors such as reduction in time available for couple activities, financial burdens, and fatigue can cause _____ stress.

6.34 Parents are best able to receive and comprehend information concerning their child during the _____ stage.

6.35 A _____ _____ is often altered substantially within a family by the arrival of an infant with disabilities.

6.36 Spousal assistance with the burdens of caring for a child with a disability serves as a buffer, contributes to their partner's well-being, and is often predictive of couple _____.

Review – True/False

Please indicate whether the statements are true (T) or false (F) by circling the corresponding letter. You should be able to briefly describe the rationale for your answer.

T   F   6.37 Fathers often respond differently to their sons with disabilities than they do to their daughters with disabilities.

T   F   6.38 Family support services have reduced family stress and increased the capacity of family members to maintain arduous care routines.

T   F   6.39 Support groups for siblings of children with disabilities have not been shown to be especially helpful to adolescents.

T   F   6.40 During the stage of realization parents may spend considerable time in self-accusation.

T   F   6.41 Overprotection by the mother or care givers can be problematic in terms of the child becoming independent

T   F   6.42 Fathers are more likely to be involved if their child speaks or interacts with words and phrases.

T   F   6.43 The best way to help siblings of children with disabilities is to support the parents and families.

T   F   6.44 The most important role of grandparents is to provide transportation to their grandchildren with disabilities.

Chapter Review – Practice Test

In the following activity select the most appropriate of the four answers provided for each item. Try to do this without looking at your text in order to get an idea of your comprehension level.

6.45 Which factor most strongly influences the ways in which family members respond to an infant with a birth defect or disability?
  A. Employment status of the father
  B. The parents' occupations
  C. The severity of the disability
  D. The number of siblings in the family

6.46 Who is most likely to internalize feelings and become withdrawn?
   A. Father
   B. Mother
   C. Sibling
   D. Grandparent

6.47 The many emotions parents report having when a child is born with a disability have been likened to
   A. those experienced after the death of a loved one.
   B. those experienced by the professionals with whom they eventually work.
   C. an onset of depression that won't go away.
   D. losing all financial stability.

6.48 The immediate reaction of most parents to learning that their infant has a disability is
   A. acceptance.
   B. shock.
   C. fear.
   D. rejection.

6.49 Which statement is most accurate regarding the four stages that parents go through in accepting an exceptionality in an infant or young child (shock, realization, defensive retreat, acknowledgment)?
   A. The stages are generally the same among parents.
   B. Shock lasts the longest of the stages.
   C. The mother reaches acknowledgment first.
   D. The process of adjustment for parents is continuous and distinctly individual.

6.50 The ways in which parents react during the shock period depends on all but which of the following?
   A. Nature and severity of the disabling condition
   B. Psychological makeup
   C. The manner in which they are informed about their child's disability
   D. The types of assistance rendered

6.51 The stage when parents may be forced to reassess the meaning of life and the reasons for their present challenges is referred to as the period of
   A. reality confusion.
   B. emotional disorganization.
   C. emotional detachment.
   D. internal reflection.

6.52 During the _____ stage parents mobilize their strengths to confront the conditions crated by having a child with a disability.
 A. shock
 B. acknowledgment
 C. realization
 D. defensive

6.53 The first phase of the developmental cycle, when the parents try to determine if the child has a disability, is called the
 A. identification period.
 B. screening phase.
 C. diagnostic period.
 D. acknowledgment phase.

6.54 Training for professionals with regard to families focuses primarily on
 A. negotiation, assertiveness, and communication skills.
 B. relationship building, communication, and collaboration skills.
 C. problem solving, delegation, and negotiation skills.
 D. intervention, problem solving, and assertiveness skills.

6.55 From the list below, select the three most crucial factors identified as having an impact of the relationship between parents and children with disabilities.
 A. Socioeconomic status
 B. Seriousness of the disability
 C. Child's age and gender
 D. Reaction of siblings

6.56 Children whose fathers are involved in their education
 A. perform better in school.
 B. are less likely to exhibit delinquent behavior.
 C. A. and B.
 D. neither A. nor B.

6.57 _____ play an influential role in how parents respond to a child with a disability.
 A. Siblings
 B. Friends
 C. Neighbors
 D. Grandparents

6.58 Which does this chapter describe as a way in which a sibling is likely to react to an exceptional child?
 A. Run away from home
 B. Respond differently than the parents
 C. Respond the same way as the parents
 D. Never accept the exceptional child

6.59 Grandparents can give assistance to families of a child with a disability by
    A.   providing educational toys.
    B.   babysitting.
    C.   visiting only at pre-arranged times.
    D.   accepting some of the blame.

6.60 Which of the following statements does not apply to "effective collaboration"?
    A.   Provider is paid better than teachers.
    B.   Provider listens well.
    C.   Provider demonstrates sensitivity to family issues.
    D.   Provider shares information.

Cryptogram

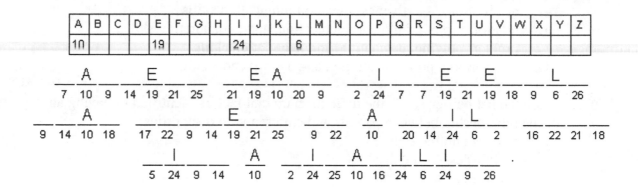

A	B	C	D	E	F	G	H	I	J	K	L	M	N	O	P	Q	R	S	T	U	V	W	X	Y	Z
10			19					24			6														

Scramble

Unscramble the tiles to reveal a message.

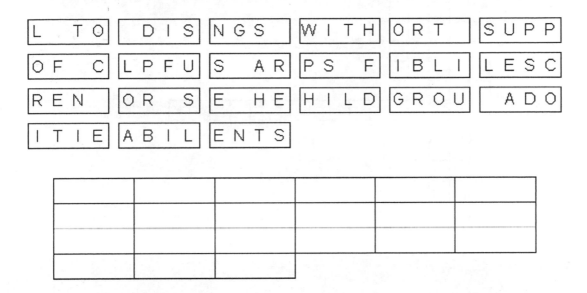

L TO	D I S	N G S	W I T H	O R T	S U P P
O F C	L P F U	S A R	P S F	I B L I	L E S C
R E N	O R S	E H E	H I L D	G R O U	A D O
I T I E	A B I L	E N T S			

Double Puzzle

Unscramble each of the clue words. Copy the letters in the numbered cells to other cells with the same number.

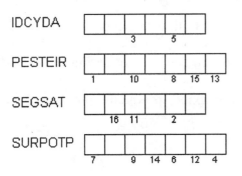

IDCYDA
— 3 — 5 —

PESTEIR
1 — 10 — 8 15 13

SEGSAT
— 16 11 — 2 —

SURPOTP
7 — 9 14 6 12 4

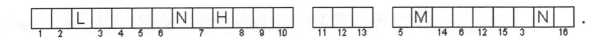

	L				N	H			
1	2	3	4	5	6	7	8	9	10

11	12	13

	M				N	
5	14	6	12	15	3	16

.

75

Crossword Puzzle

Across

3. _____ relationship is an attachment that occurs between two people
5. Parents mobilize their strengths to confront the conditions created by having an exceptional child
6. Stage that may be distinguished by feelings of anxiety and/or helplessness
7. _____ disorganization stage in which parents may be forced to reassess the meaning of life

Down

1. _____ empowerment enables families to effectively meet both their needs and the child's need.
2. Parents may be anxious about their ability to cope with the demands of caring for a child with unique needs
4. _____ retreat parents attempt to avoid dealing with the anxiety-producing realities of their child's exceptionality

Best Practices

Community Activities

1. Attend a parent support group meeting and the local school's PTA meeting. Listen to the parents' discussions. How are their discussions similar and how are they different? _____
_____
_____

2. Interview a parent with a child with a disability. How is parenting a child with a disability different than a child without a disability? How is it similar? What are the things that the parents find most challenging? What supports are available for the parents?_____

_____

Case Study

Mr. Williams, a CPA, and Mrs. Williams, a first grade teacher, met in high school and married after college. They have three children ages 8, 6, and 4. All of the children attend the elementary school where Mrs. Williams teaches; Brett is in 2nd grade, Michelle is in kindergarten, and Trey is in preschool. Their youngest son, Trey, was diagnosed with autism when he was 3 years old.

The Williams will tell you that they love all of their children equally but that raising them is not an equal experience and that sometimes they are not sure they are up to the challenges presented by Trey. Trey's autism is severe. He also has mental retardation and a seizure disorder. While he has received early intervention services since he was very young, his progress has been unpredictable and slow. At 4 years of age, Trey exhibits relatively typical gross motor patterns, but his cognitive and social/emotional skills are severely delayed. He does not have spoken language and uses gestures as his primary mode of communicating his demands. He is very socially withdrawn and, with the exception of his siblings and parents, does not tolerate physical contact well and can be physically aggressive to those who violate his personal space without his permission.

At home, the Williams family functions around Trey's needs. They schedule meals and activities around Trey's therapies and service appointments. Because Trey does not tolerate new situations well, Mrs. Williams stays home with him while Mr. Williams attends the other children's activities. On Sunday, the parents take turns going to church with Brett and Michelle so that one of them can stay home with Trey. They don't know how long they can keep this up.

1. How has Trey's disability affected the family? The siblings? _____

_____

_____

_____

_____

_____

2. What kind of supports could this family use? How do they access those supports?_____

_____

_____

_____

_____

_____

_____

3. What national supports are available to families with children with disabilities? What kinds of support do they provide?_____

_____

_____

_____

_____

Resources

Books

After the Tears: Parents Talk about Raising a Child with a Disability by Robin Simons. Available from Harvest Books.

Independence Bound by Jaquelyn Altman. Available from www.independencebound.com

From the Heart: On Being the Mother of a Child with Special Needs by J. Marsh, Available from Woodbine House.

Uncommon Fathers: Reflections on Raising a Child with a Disability by D.J. Meyer. Available from Woodbine House.

Nobody's Perfect: Living and Growing with Children Who Have Special Needs by N.B. Miller. Available from Paul H. Brookes.

Videos

When Parents Can't Fix It by Virginia Cruz and Sharon Thompson. www.fanlight.com

Disability and Motherhood. www.films.com

Family Caregivers. www.films.com

Websites

Beach Center on Disability: www.beachcenter.org

Family Village: A Global Community of Disability-Related Resources: www.familyvillage.edu

Kid Source Online: www.kidsource.com

Parent Advocacy Coalition for Educational Rights (PACER Center): www.pacer.org

Technical Assistance Alliance for Parent Centers: www.taalliance.org

7

Learning disabilities, the largest and fastest growing category in special education, represents a diverse group of individuals with mild to severe learning problems. Because of this, the field of LD has long been associated with confusion and controversy. The definition of LD allows for tremendous variability in interpretation, assessment, and identification, thus, the relatively unchecked increase in the numbers of children and youth identified with this learning difference.

Nearly all children with LD are educated in the general education classroom with their same-age peers. Collaboration and consultation between general and special educators is important to provide support to the student with learning disabilities. An understanding of this field is important for all teachers because they will be responsible for teaching children with LD.

Concept Reflection

A. What did I know about learning disabilities before reading this chapter?	B. How did reading the chapter enhance or change what I already knew? (Relate this to Column A.)	C. What new information did I learn? (This may or may not be associated with your responses in A or B.)
1.	1.	1.
2.	2.	2.
3	3.	3.
4.	4.	4.
5.	5.	5.

Keep the following questions in mind as you read this chapter.

7.1 Identify four reasons why definitions of learning disabilities have varied.
A.
B.
C.
D.
7.2 Identify three ways in which classification has been used with people having learning disabilities and state how research evidence supports them.
A.
B.
C.
7.3 Identify two current estimated ranges for the prevalence of learning disabilities.
A.
B.

7.4 Identify seven characteristics attributed to those with learning disabilities and explain why it is difficult to characterize this group.

A.

B.

C.

D.

E.

F.

G.

H.

7.5 Identify four causes thought to be involved in learning disabilities.

A.

B.

C.

D.

7.6 Identify four questions that are addressed by screening assessment in learning disabilities.

A.

B.

C.

D.

7.7 Identify three types of intervention or treatment employed with people diagnosed as having learning disabilities.

A.

B.

C.

7.8 How are the services and supports for adolescents and adults with learning disabilities different from those used with other children?

A.

B.

C.

Following are a number of the key terms and concepts used in this chapter. Try to complete this matching exercise before you read the chapter. Match each term with the phrase that you think most closely describes or defines it.

A.	Samuel Kirk	E.	Learning disabilities
B.	Overused	F.	Cognition
C.	Depression	G.	Mirror writing
D.	Comorbidity	H.	Figure-ground discrimination

7.9 _____ A condition in which one or more of the basic psychological processes in understanding or using language are deficit.

7.10 _____ The term "specific learning disabilities" was first introduced by _____.

7.11 _____ Some professionals and parents believe that the learning disabilities category is being _____ to avoid the stigma associated with other labels.

7.12 _____ Writing backwards from right to left while producing backwards letters is known as _____.

7.13 _____ Stage of "What's the use?"

7.14 _____ The act of thinking, knowing, or processing information.

7.15 _____ Distinguishing an object from its background.

7.16 _____ Situation in which multiple conditions occur together.

This exercise is intended to provide practice in recalling what you have just read. Try not to refer back to the chapter as you match the following items with their descriptions below. As you work through this exercise, consider how this new information relates to other knowledge, concepts, and/or principles you have learned before taking this course.

A.	Phonemic	E.	Composition
B.	Retarded	F.	Lifelong
C.	Brief	G.	Hyperactivity
D.	Context	H.	Read

7.17 _____ In the past, many children now identified as having specific learning disabilities would have been labeled as children who were _____.

7.18 _____ Individuals with reading disabilities often have difficulty using _____ to determine meaning.

7.19 _____ Instruction that combines _____ awareness and specific skill instruction may serve students with reading disabilities better than single-focused methods.

7.20 _____ Individuals with learning disabilities often have difficulty with handwriting, spelling skills, and _____.

7.21 _____ Learning disabilities are _____ problems.

7.22 _____ Verbal instructions should be simple and _____.

7.23 _____ This is not a universal characteristic of individuals with learning disabilities.

7.24 _____ In general, children who write spontaneously also seem to _____ spontaneously

Supply a word/phrase in each sentence in order to make sense out of the statement of a concept, definition, or principle that is otherwise incomplete or lacks closure. Several answers, other than those listed in the key, may be acceptable for an item. Focus on whether or not your answer is equivalent to the answer supplied and be prepared to explain why you completed the statement(s) as you did.

7.25 _____ _____ has been endorsed by the Division of Learning Disabilities are being an effective instructional approach.

7.26 Learning disabilities is an umbrella label that includes a variety of conditions and behavioral and performance _____.

7.27 The IDEA and Joint Committee definitions (1990) provided a _____ focus for the provision of services in the public schools.

7.28 Mastery of _____ quantitative concepts is vital to learning more abstract and complex mathematics.

7.29 _____ function is centrally involved in language skills and development and an area of challenge for many children with learning disabilities.

7.30 Being unable to identify the difference between the words set and sat is known as _____ discrimination.

7.31 Recalling information presented orally is known as _____ memory.

7.32 Nearly _____% of the individuals identified with disabilities have learning disabilities.

Please indicate whether the statements are true (T) or false (F) by circling the corresponding letter. You should be able to briefly describe the rationale for your answer.

T   F   7.33   People with learning disabilities usually have average or near-average intelligence.

T   F   7.34   Most individuals with learning disabilities struggle throughout life and are rarely successful or leaders.

T   F   7.35   According to your text, assessment and accountability for all students is essential.

T   F   7.36   The most prevalent disabilities identified in the U.S. are specific learning disabilities.

T   F   7.37   When parents are in the shock stage, teachers should employ active listening.

T   F   7.38   Assistive technology is proving more harmful than helpful in assisting students with writing problems.

T   F   7.39   A child can be identified as having a specific learning disability if the severe discrepancy between ability and achievement is primarily the result of economic disadvantage.

T   F   7.40   ADHD is always present in individuals with learning disabilities.

In the following activity, select the most appropriate of the four answers provided for each item. Try to do this without looking at your text in order to get an idea of your comprehension level.

7.41 Learning disabilities came to be recognized in the
    A. 1920s.
    B. 1940s.
    C. 1960s.
    D. 1980s.

7.42 People with learning disabilities usually achieve at low levels in
    A. interpersonal skills and reading.
    B. math and physical ability.
    C. social skills and reading.
    D. reading and math.

7.43 A common practice in education is to describe individuals with learning disabilities on the basis of
    A. what they are not.
    B. intelligence quotients (IQ).
    C. reading and writing abilities.
    D. math scores.

7.44 Adolescents with learning disabilities need to be encouraged to
    A. get a job after school hours.
    B. make plans for the years after high school.
    C. practice driving a long time before they take their driving test.
    D. learn a musical instrument so they can express themselves more fully.

7.45 One element that has not emerged as a classification scheme is
    A. heterogeneity.
    B. severity.
    C. exclusion.
    D. discrepancy.

7.46 Students with reading disabilities experience substantial difficulty with the process of
    A. determining when is the best time for them to read.
    B. generalizing reading from one topic to another.
    C. generalizing letter patterns and drawing analogies.
    D. reading aloud to their peers.

7.47 Adults with learning disabilities need to be encouraged to
    A. devise ways of compensating.
    B. quit making excuses for their lack of success.
    C. make new friends who can do some of their work for them.
    D. rely on family members to provide the support they need.

7.48 According to your text, strategies that can help students with reading disabilities include organizing and summarizing, problem solving, relational thinking, and
   A. alphabet charts.
   B. agendas and calendars.
   C. peers they can tutor.
   D. mnemonics.

7.49 Some individuals with poor handwriting have not mastered
   A. grasping a pen or pencil.
   B. reading enough to know what to write.
   C. selection of the right size pencil.
   D. enough spelling words.

7.50 For many students with severe handwriting problems, age and practice will
   A. make the problem go away.
   B. not make the problem go away.
   C. make the problem worse.
   D. will have no effect on the problem.

7.51 Some researchers view the handwriting, writing, and composition skills of students with learning disabilities as closely related to their _____ ability.
   A. creative
   B. math
   C. reading
   D. spelling

7.52 Your text suggests that if a student is having trouble taking notes from a lecture for a test in the general education classroom, the teacher could encourage him to
   A. sit at the front of the classroom.
   B. try harder.
   C. go to bed earlier so he is not too tired to write.
   D. use a tape recorder.

7.53 Differences between students with behavior disorders and those with specific learning disabilities have been defined based on
   A. learner characteristics and reading scores.
   B. reading and math scores.
   C. social skills and math scores.
   D. social skills and learner characteristics.

7.54 _____ are often associated with individuals with learning disabilities.
   A. Short attention spans
   B. Long term memories
   C. Intellectualized memories
   D. Sporadic memory skills

7.55 Services and supports for children focus primarily on
    A. developing abstract thinking skills.
    B. building the most basic skills.
    C. improving the coping skills of the parents.
    D. increasing the tolerance level of their peers.

7.56 Specific learning disabilities are the most _____ disability in the U.S.
    A. obvious
    B. harmful
    C. prevalent
    D. female-dominated

Cryptogram

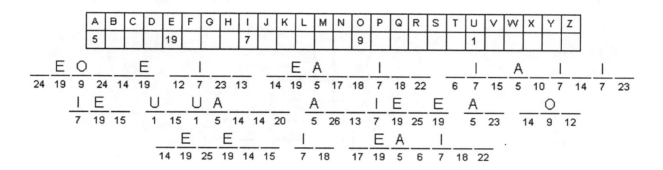

A	B	C	D	E	F	G	H	I	J	K	L	M	N	O	P	Q	R	S	T	U	V	W	X	Y	Z
5				19				7						9						1					

```
_  E  O  _  E  _  I  _     _  E  A  _  I  _  _     _  I  _  A  _  I  _  I  _
24 19 9 24 14 19   12 7 23 13   14 19 5 17 18 7 18 22   6 7 15 5 10 7 14 7 23

_  I  E  _     U  _  U  A  _  _     _  A  _  I  E  _  E  A  _     _  O  _
7 19 15   1 15 1 5 14 14 20   5 26 13 7 19 25 19   5 23   14 9 12

_  E  _  E  _  _     I  _     E  A  _  I  _  _ .
14 19 25 19 14 15   7 18   17 19 5 6 7 18 22
```

Double Puzzle

Unscramble each of the clue words. Copy the letters in the numbered cells to other cells the same number.

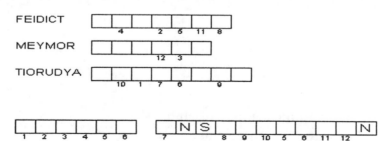

FEIDICT   □□□□□□□ (4 2 5 11 8)

MEYMOR   □□□□□□ (12 3)

TIORUDYA   □□□□□□□□ (10 1 7 6 9)

□□□□□□ (1 2 3 4 5 6)   N S □□□□□ N (7 8 9 10 5 6 11 12)

Scramble

Unscramble the tiles to reveal a message.

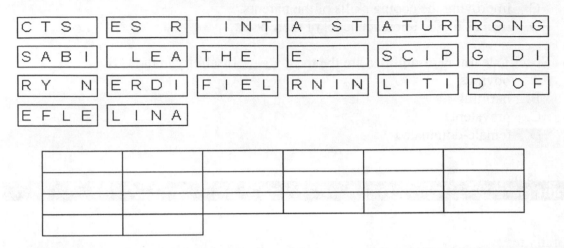

C T S	E S R	I N T	A S T	A T U R	R O N G
S A B I	L E A	T H E	E .	S C I P	G D I
R Y N	E R D I	F I E L	R N I N	L I T I	D O F
E F L E	L I N A				

Crossword Puzzle

Across
2. Introduced the term "specific learning disabilities"
5. Learning disabilities are _____ problems
6. Discrepancy between academic achievement and the student's assessed ability and age
7. In the past, many children now identified as having specific learning disabilities would have been labeled as _____ children.
8. Some professionals and parents believe that the learning disabilities category is being _____ to avoid the stigma associated with other labels

Down

1. Verbal instructions should be simple and _____
3. Hyperkinetic behavior is also known as _____
4. Thinking, knowing, or processing information
5. _____ disabilities is a condition in which one or more of the basic psychological processes in understanding or using language are deficit

Best Practices

Case Study

Malcolm, 18, is in 11th grade. Malcolm is a very shy and reserved young man who rarely speaks in class or participates in class discussions. He was identified as having a learning disability in 4th grade.

Malcolm orally reads on the 5th grade level; but when given a listening comprehension test he scored on the 8th grade level. In class he does not volunteer to participate but does sit quietly during class. He does not always seem to be attending during presentations and often needs directions repeated. His in-class work is often cursory without much detail and is of poor quality with the exception of math calculation skills, which he mastered with ease.

Malcolm struggles to write. His handwriting is illegible and his spelling extremely poor. In group activities where the students must work together to prepare a written product, Malcolm contributes to the ideas but cannot serve as scribe. Although most students do not clamor to have Malcolm in their group, he does get along with all of the students.

He has difficulty communicating in class. Whether he is having a conversation or is trying to answer a question, Malcolm can't seem to find the right words to express himself. The other day, his social studies teacher asked him to express his opinion about the possible war in Iraq. Malcolm responded, "Well, you know the president, he, well, he thinks it is a good thing and you know, well, that's why."

At home Malcolm is an important and active member of the family. He completes home chores and spends his free time building models. He and his dad have been building a ship in a bottle for the past two months. In addition, he is an active member of 4 H and earned a blue ribbon for his steer last month.

1. What characteristics of a learning disability does Malcolm exhibit? _____
   _____
   _____

2. What are Malcolm's greatest barriers to academic success? _____
   _____
   _____

3. What are Malcolm's greatest barriers to social success?_____

_____

_____

4. What accommodations would need to be provided for Malcolm to be successful in your classroom? _____

_____

_____

Community Activities

1. Arrange with local school to observe in a special education classroom that serves children with learning disabilities. Observe the children with learning disabilities. What are some of the learning characteristics? How does the teacher address those differences? How successful is the child in this environment? _____

_____

_____

2. Arrange with local school to observe in a general education classroom that has a child or children with learning disabilities. Observe the child with learning disabilities. What are some of his/her learning characteristics? How does the general education teacher address those differences? How successful is the child in this environment? _____

_____

_____

3. Observe the child with the learning disability in settings other than the classroom such as in the cafeteria or during art, physical education, and music. How does the child compare to his/her peers in terms of participation and attention? _____

_____

_____

Resources

Books
The Misunderstood Child by Larry B. Silver, M.D. Available from Three Rivers Press.
All Kinds of Minds by Mel Levine. Available from Educators Publishing Service.
How Many Days until Tomorrow? by Caroline Janover. Available from Woodbine House.

Videos
When the Chips are Down by Richard Lavoie. Available from PBS.
How Difficult Can This Be: The F.A.T. Workshop by Richard Lavoie. Available from PBS.
Last One Picked, First One Picked On by Richard Lavoie. Available from PBS.

Websites
SmartKids with Learning Disabilities. www.smartkidswithld.org
LD On Line. www.ldonline.org
Learning Disabilities Association of America. www.ldanatl.org

8

Attention-Deficit/Hyperactivity Disorder (ADHD)

Preview

In Chapter Eight you will learn about Attention-Deficit/Hyperactivity Disorder (ADHD). This disorder is a lifelong condition for many, with characteristics that may include impulsivity, attentional differences, and high levels of activity. While ADHD seems to be a relatively new disorder, descriptions of persons with this disorder can be found in historical writing as early as a century ago.

ADHD can be identified in the early developmental years and is often a result of difficulties with the child's behavior at home or in a educational environment. ADHD is often treated from both a medical and psychological perspective. That is, for individuals with serious ADHD, treatment recommendations are likely to include a central nervous system stimulant and behavioral counseling.

Concept Reflection

A. What did I know about ADHD before reading this chapter?	B. How did reading the chapter enhance or change what I already knew? (Relate this to Column A.)	C. What new information did I learn? (This may or may not be associated with your responses in A or B.)
1.	1.	1.
2.	2.	2.
3.	3.	3.
4.	4.	4.
5.	5.	5.

Keep the following questions in mind as you read this chapter.

8.1   Identify three behavioral symptoms commonly associated with ADHD.
A.
B.
C.
8.2   Identify two ways the behavior of children with ADHD detrimentally affects instructional settings.
A.
B.
8.3   Identify four other areas of disability that are often found to be comorbid with ADHD.
A.
B.
C.
D.
8.4   Identify the three major types of ADHD according to the *DSM-IV*.
A.
B.
C.
8.5   Identify two prevalence estimates for ADHD that characterize the difference in occurrence by gender.
A.
B.

8.6 **Identify the two broad categories of assessment information useful in diagnosing ADHD.**

A.

B.

8.7 **Identify three areas of characteristics that present challenges for individuals with ADHD.**

A.

B.

C.

8.8 **Identify three possible causes of ADHD.**

A.

B.

8.9 **Identify two approaches to intervention that appear to show positive results with individuals having ADHD.**

A.

B.

Read – Matching Vocabulary

Following are a number of the key terms and concepts used in this chapter. Try to complete this matching exercise before you read the chapter. Match each term with the phrase that you think most closely describes or defines it.

A. Impulsivity
B. Structure
C. Cerebellum
D. Impulse control

E. Executive function
F. Explicitly
G. Referral
H. Comorbidity

8.10 _____ Hallmark symptoms of ADHD include (1) inattention, (2) distractibility, (3) emotional instability before age 7, and (4) _____.

8.11 _____ The _____ process begins with the educational and psychological data-gathering process.

8.12 _____ Effective instructional settings for children with ADHD consistently include a good deal of _____.

8.13 _____ Students with ADHD do best when information is _____ demonstrated rather than explained.

8.14 _____ The literature on ADHD increasingly reflects attention to _____ and thinking about the consequences of one's actions.

8.15 _____ People with ADHD seem to exhibit brain abnormalities in three areas. One of these is the _____.

8.16 _____ Conditions occurring together.

8.17 _____ The ability to monitor and regulate one's own behavior.

Reflect – Matching Vocabulary

This exercise is intended to provide practice in recalling what you have just read. Try not to refer back to the chapter as you match the following items with their descriptions below. As you work through this exercise, consider how this new information relates to other knowledge, concepts, and/or principles you learned before taking this course.

A. Conduct disorders
B. Inclusion
C. Strengths
D. Hyperactivity

E. Multimodal
F. Psychostimulants
G. Frontal lobes
H. Listen

8.18 _____ _____ treatments are more effective for children with ADHD.

8.19 _____ The behavior of approximately 80% of children with ADHD improves when they take _____.

	8.20 _____	People with ADHD seem to exhibit brain abnormalities in the basal ganglia, cerebellum, and _____.
	8.21 _____	The environment should be structured to take advantage of the child's _____.
	8.22 _____	A child with ADHD often does not seem to _____ when spoken to directly.
	8.23 _____	_____ are sometimes found to be comorbid with ADHD.
	8.24 _____	Adherence to the _____ model is crucial for students with ADHD.
	8.25 _____	This is a primary characteristic of ADHD.

Recite – Fill in the Blank

Supply a word/phrase in each sentence in order to make sense out of the statement of a concept, definition, or principle that is otherwise incomplete or lacks closure. Several answers, other than those listed in the key, may be acceptable for an item. Focus on whether or not your answer is equivalent to the answer supplied and be prepared to explain why you completed the statement(s) as you did.

8.26 ADHD is often viewed as a symptom of other conditions such as emotional-behavior disorders and _____ _____.

8.27 The assessment of ADHD requires evidence directly obtained from _____/ _____ and _____

8.28 _____ twins have a higher degree of coincidence of ADHD than _____ twins.

8.29 Two broad categories for interventions include behavioral and _____.

Review – True/False

Please indicate whether the statements are true (T) or false (F) by circling the corresponding letter. You should be able to briefly describe the rationale for your answer.

T   F   8.30   ADHD is a lifelong condition for approximately 25% of those who have been diagnosed as having it

T   F   8.31   It appears that people with the symptoms of ADHD may have been around as early as 100 years ago.

T   F   8.32   ADHD is actually a variety of physical processes interacting with social, psychological, or environmental factors.

T   F   8.33   Researchers are in agreement as to why there are more boys than girls identified with ADHD.

T   F   8.34   In order to be considered truly hyperactive, the behavior must create maladaptive problems for the individual.

T   F   8.35   Research indicates that substance abuse is closely associated with ADHD.

T   F   8.36   Due to their social nature, most individuals with ADHD have a number of close friends.

T   F   8.37   In recent years the number of children under the age of 4 who take Ritalin has decreased.

In the following activity, select the most appropriate of the four answers provided for each item. Try to do this without looking at your text in order to get an idea of your comprehension level.

8.38 A condition characterized by motor or verbal tics that cause the person to make repetitive movements, emit strange involuntary sounds, or say words or phrases that are inappropriate for the context is known as
   A. Tourette's syndrome.
   B. Cerebral palsy.
   C. ADHD.
   D. All of the above.

8.39 Which of the following is not true relevant to being diagnosed with ADHD?
   A. Some impairment from the symptoms must be present in at least 2 settings such as home and school.
   B. There must be clear evidence of interference with developmentally appropriate social, academic, or occupational functioning.
   C. Some symptoms that cause impairment must have been present before age 7.
   D. The individual must exhibit symptoms of learning disabilities.

8.40 According to the DSM-IV definition of ADHD, blurting out answers, difficulty waiting turns, and interrupting others can be symptoms of
   A. emotional disturbance.
   B. hyperactivity.
   C. inattention.
   D. .iImpulsivity.

8.41 Assessment and diagnostic information for ADHD falls into two broad categories. These include data that provide information about educational, behavioral, and contextual circumstances as well as information that is
   A. medical in nature.
   B. readily available from experts.
   C. available through school records.
   D. reported by the student with suspected ADHD.

8.42 All but which of the following are instruments used to assess ADHD?
   A. Behavior Assessment System for Children–Teacher Rating Scales (BASE-TRS)
   B. Child Behavior Checklist (CBCL)
   C. Assessment Protocol for Individuals with Suspected ADHD (APIS)
   D. School Situations Questionnaire (SSQ)

8.43 A structured interview designed for use by trained psychologists or lay interviewers is known as the
   A. School Situations Questionnaire (SSQ).
   B. Diagnostic Interview Schedule for Children (DISC-IV).
   C. Behavior Assessment System for Children-Teacher Rating Scales (BASE-TRS)
   D. Child Behavior Checklist (CBCL).

8.44 One of the defining factors regarding hyperactivity is that it
   A. occurs in inappropriate settings.
   B. is always present in group activities.
   C. is especially obvious to peers.
   D. almost always allergy related.

8.45 Academic performance for students with ADHD tends to suffer due to
   A. specific memory problems.
   B. a general lack of interest.
   C. impulsivity.
   D. reduced effort.

8.46 Individuals with ADHD often do not
   A. enjoy reading.
   B. graduate from high school.
   C. attain a driver's license.
   D. excel in sports.

8.47 Your text states that in academic environments that adapt instruction to individual student needs and abilities, students with ADHD can
   A. give in to their active nature.
   B. provide support for other students with ADHD.
   C. improve their self-management.
   D. determine their own IEP goals.

8.48 The actual cause of ADHD is
   A. unknown.
   B. genetic.
   C. biological.
   D. environmental.

8.49 All but which of the following place developing embryos and infants at high risk for serious learning and developmental delays?
   A. Exposure to tobacco smoke
   B. Alcohol abuse by the pregnant mother
   C. Lead exposure
   D. High fat diet for the pregnant mother

8.50 If parents and/or siblings have ADHD, youngsters appear to have a good chance of
   A. having ADHD.
   B. having no symptoms of ADHD.
   C. having ADHD to a lesser degree.
   D. having ADHD to a greater degree.

8.51 Control of hyperactive and impulsive behavior appears to be most effectively accomplished with
   A. increased behavior modification.
   B. increased parental pressure.
   C. medication.
   D. allergy treatments.

8.52 Further investigation into the side effects of medication given for ADHD is
   A. not needed.
   B. dependent upon the recipient.
   C. overrated.
   D. warranted.

8.53 _____ can be effective in helping students listen to directions when they are given.
   A. Threats
   B. Bribes
   C. Medication
   D. Cuing

8.54 Instruction may be more effective if reinforcement is combined with
   A. modeling.
   B. increased practice.
   C. Both of the above.
   D. Neither of the above.

8.55 The National Institutes of Health consensus report (1998) noted that communication is often poor between
   A. educational and health-related services.
   B. academic and recreational services.
   C. special and general educators.
   D. educational systems and parents.

8.56 According to your text, instruction for adolescents with ADHD is more effective when they can employ learning strategies such as
   A. palm pilots and additional time for activities.
   B. mnemonics and conceptual organizers.
   C. peer tutoring and attentional cueing.
   D. classroom assistants and tutors.

8.57 The main reason more boys than girls are diagnosed with ADHD is that
   A. the genetic makeup of boys makes them more susceptible.
   B. girls manifest the symptoms differently.
   C. parents expect it from boys so are more open to the diagnosis.
   D. girls are usually in their teens before the symptoms become obvious.

A	B	C	D	E	F	G	H	I	J	K	L	M	N	O	P	Q	R	S	T	U	V	W	X	Y	Z
7	5		8					16					17							22					

```
 B  E     A     I  O        O  I     I  A     I  O        I
 5  8  1  7 20 16 17 18   9 17 19 16  2 16 24  7 21 16 17 11  16 25

 A     E     E     I     E  A        O  A           I
 7 11  8  2  2  8 24 21 16 20  8   7  6  6 18 17  7 24  1   4 16 21  1

          U     E           I        A
       25 21 22 19  8 11 21 25   4 16 21  1   7 19  1 19  .
```

Unscramble the tiles to reveal a message.

G E T I	I T Y ,	U S A	I N A B	T E R I	L S I V
A N D	F O C	A D H	N C H	D .	Y T O
F I D	O M M O	N G ,	A R A C	S O F	I L I T
S T I C	I M P U	R E C

Double Puzzle

Unscramble each of the clue words. Copy the letters in the numbered cells to other cells with the same number.

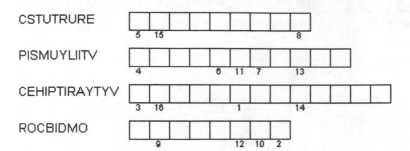

CSTUTRURE — ⬜⬜⬜⬜⬜⬜⬜⬜⬜
5 15 8

PISMUYLIITV — ⬜⬜⬜⬜⬜⬜⬜⬜⬜⬜⬜
4 6 11 7 13

CEHIPTIRAYTYV — ⬜⬜⬜⬜⬜⬜⬜⬜⬜⬜⬜⬜⬜
3 16 1 14

ROCBIDMO — ⬜⬜⬜⬜⬜⬜⬜⬜
9 12 10 2

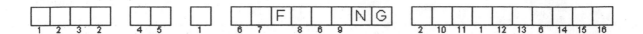

⬜⬜⬜⬜ ⬜⬜ ⬜ ⬜⬜ F ⬜ ⬜ N G ⬜⬜⬜⬜⬜⬜⬜⬜⬜⬜⬜
1 2 3 2   4 5   1   6 7   8 6 9   2 10 11 1 12 13 6 14 15 16

Crossword Puzzle

Across

3. Effective instructional setting for children with ADHD
4. Hallmark symptom of ADHD
5. Process that begins with the educational and psychological data-gathering process
6. _____ twins have a higher degree of coincidence of ADHD than fraternal twins
7. Conditions occurring together
8. _____ ability to monitor and regulate one's own behavior

Down

1. A primary characteristic of ADHD
2. _____ abuse is closely associated with ADHD
6. Adherence to the _____ model is crucial for students with ADHD

100

Case Study

Francisca is one of the most popular 4th graders in her class. Her classmates think she is smart, friendly, and funny, but they will also tell you that she can be a little strange, like forgetting what she is talking about in the middle of a story, knocking over books and things on their desks, or yelling out answers during class. Francisca's desk looks like a tornado struck and she is often found looking for a pencil, paper, or her assignment. The teacher must frequently repeat directions for Francisca, redirect her back to the assignment during independent work, and allow her to turn assignments in past the due date. Francisca's teacher will tell you that she is an average student who would do better in class if she were more organized and focused.

At home, Francisca's bedroom looks like a jungle of clothes, books, toys, and other abandoned objects on the floor, bed, dresser, and desk. Francisca's mother will smile and call Francisca her "messy monkey" and describe all that she does at home to try to manage the chaos of Francisca's room. However, she admits that she has concerns about Francisca's disorganization at home and school.

1. What behaviors of Francisca are associated with those characteristics of someone with ADHD?

_____
_____
_____
_____

2. What could the teacher do to help Francisca be more successful in the classroom? _____
_____
_____
_____

3. How could Francisca's mother help her daughter at home? _____
_____
_____
_____

Community Activities

1. Arrange with local school to observe in a special education classroom that serves children with attention deficit disorder. Observe the children with attention deficit disorder. What are some of the student's characteristics? How does the teacher address those differences? How successful is the child in this environment?_____
_____
_____
_____

2. Arrange with local school to observe in a general education classroom that has a child or children with attention deficit disorder. Observe the child with attention deficit disorder. What are some of his/her characteristics? How does the general education teacher address those differences? How successful is the child in this environment?_____

_____

_____

_____

3. Observe the child with the attention deficit disorder in settings other than the classroom, such as in the cafeteria or during art, physical education, and music. How does the child compare to his/her peers in terms of participation and attention?_____

_____

_____

_____

Resources

Books

Taking Charge of ADHD – The Complete, Authoritative Guide for Parents by Russell A. Barkley. Available from Woodbine House.
Understanding ADHD: A Practical Guide for Teachers and Parents by William N. Bender. Available from Prentice Hall.
Eddie Enough! by Debbie Zimmett. Available from Woodbine House.

Videos

A New Look at ADHD – Inhibition, Time and Self-Control by Russell A. Barkley
ADHD – What Can We Do? by Russell A. Barkley.

Websites

Children and Adults with Attention Deficit-Hyperactivity Disorder. www.chadd.org
A.D.D. WareHouse. www.addwarehouse.com
Attention Deficit Disorder Links Project. www.attentiondeficitdisorder.ws

9

Emotional/Behavioral Disorders

This chapter introduces five factors that influence the ways in which behavior may be evaluated. The authors explain why emotional or behavioral disorders are difficult to study, discussing variables that affect many different types of behavior that may be exhibited or suppressed when an individual has a behavior disorder. Typically, definitions of EBD refer to behavior in terms of frequency and contexts.

The authors describe the characteristics of people with emotional or behavioral disorders – including intelligence, adaptive and social behavior, and academic achievement. The causes of disorders are reviewed from five perspectives: biophysical, psychoanalytical, behavioral, phenomenological, and sociological-ecological. The chapter includes an overview of assessment and intervention programs that are implemented during early childhood, elementary school years, and the adolescent years. Issues involved with placing students with behavior disorders in inclusion programs are briefly discussed. The chapter closes by summarizing promising practices for addressing chronic behavior problems.

Concept Reflection		
A. What did I know about emotional and behavioral disorders before reading this chapter?	B. How did reading the chapter enhance or change what I already knew? (Relate this to Column A.)	C. What new information did I learn? (This may or may not be associated with your responses in A or B.)
1.	1.	1.
2.	2.	2.
3.	3.	3.
4.	4.	4.
5.	5.	5.

Keep the following questions in mind as you read this chapter.

9.1   Identify six essential parts of the definition describing emotional/behavioral disorders.
A.
B.
C.
D.
E.
F.
9.2   Identify five factors that influence the ways in which others' behaviors are perceived.
A.
B.
C.
D.
E.
9.3   Identify three reasons why classification systems are important to professionals who identify, treat, and educate individuals with E/BD.
A.
B.
C.
9.4   What differentiates externalizing disorders from internalizing disorders?
A.
B.

9.5 **Identify five general characteristics (intellectual, adaptive, social, and achievement) of children and youth with E/BD.**

A.

B.

C.

D.

E.

9.6 **What can be accurately said about the causes of E/BD?**

A.

9.7 **What four important outcomes are achieved through a functional behavioral assessment?**

A.

B.

C.

D.

9.8 **What five guiding principles are associated with systems of care?**

A.

B.

C.

D.

E.

9.9 **What five factors should be considered in placing a child or youth with E/BD in general education settings and related classes?**

A.

B.

C.

D.

E.

9.10 **What are several promising practices for dealing with challenging behavior in children and youth?**

A.

B.

C.

D.

E.

F.

G.

H.

I.

J.

K.

L.

M.

Read – Matching Vocabulary

Following are a number of the key terms and concepts used in this chapter. Try to complete this matching exercise before you read the chapter. Match each term with the phrase that you think most closely describes or defines it.

A. Tourette's   E. ADHD
B. Elimination   F. Abnormal
C. Pica   G. Tic
D. Internalized   H. Autism

_____

9.11 _____ What may be viewed as normal by some may be viewed by others as _____.
9.12 _____ Withdrawal, depression, shyness, and phobias are example of _____ behaviors.
9.13 _____ Pervasive developmental disorders include Rett's disorder, childhood disintegration disorder, Asperger's disorder, and _____.
9.14 _____ An example of a tic disorder that is involuntary, rapid, and recurrent over time is _____ disorder.
9.15 _____ Recent research studies suggest that as many as 40% to 70% of students with E/BD exhibit symptoms of _____.
9.16 _____ The Diagnostic and Statistical Manual of Mental Disorders (DSM-IV) identifies _____ disorder as one of the ten major groups of disorders for infants through adolescents.
9.17 _____ Encopresis and enuresis are examples of _____ disorder.
9.18 _____ The persistent eating of nonnutritive materials for at least one month.

Reflect – Matching Vocabulary

This exercise is intended to provide practice in recalling what you have just read. Try not to refer back to the chapter as you match the following items with their descriptions below. As you work through this exercise, consider how this new information relates to other knowledge, concepts, and/or principles you learned before taking this course.

A. Socialized aggression   E. Reactive attachment
B. Emotional/behavioral   F. Elective mutism
C. Positive behavioral support G. Behavior intervention
D. Treatment   H. Functional behavior

_____

9.19 _____ Gang activities, cooperative stealing truancy, and participation in a delinquent subculture known as _____.

9.20 _____ A persistent refusal to talk in typical social, school, and work environments is known as _____.

9.21 _____ Early identification leads to early _____, which may reduce the overall impact of the E/BD on the individual and family.

9.22 _____ The purpose of the _____ assessment is to identify the functions of a student's behavior in relationship to various school, home, or community settings.

9.23 _____ A _____ plan may include new curricular and instructional approaches tailored to the student's learning needs and preferences.

9.24 _____ _____ disorder appears as a result of grossly inadequate care.

9.25 _____ Children reared in low-income families bear increased risks for high rates of _____ problems.

9.26 _____ Prereferral interventions and _____ hold great promise for helping students from diverse backgrounds remain and succeed in less restrictive settings and in general education classrooms.

Recite – Fill in the Blank

Supply a word/phrase in each sentence in order to make sense out of the statement of a concept, definition, or principle that is otherwise incomplete or lacks closure. Several answers, other than those listed in the key, may be acceptable for an item. Focus on whether or not your answer is equivalent to the answer supplied and be prepared to explain why you completed the statement(s) as you did.

9.27 The IDEA definition for E/BD has been criticized for its lack of clarity, _____ and exclusion of individuals described as social maladjusted.

9.28 The eligibility decision must be based on _____ sources of data about the individual's behavioral or _____ functioning.

9.29 Classification systems are important to professionals who identify, treat, and educate individuals with E/BD because they provide a _____ language.

9.30 Pica, anorexia nervosa, bulimia, and _____ disorder are examples of feeding and eating disorders.

9.31 Approximately _____% of children with E/BD show clinically significant language deficits.

9.32 Difficulties identified in children who have been neglected or abused often include poor peer relationships, depression, and low _____ _____.

9.33 Once a referral has been appropriately processed and parental permission for testing and evaluation has been obtained, assessment team members observe and assess a child's present levels of _____.

9.34 In order to be considered identified, E/BD must be exhibited in at least two different settings with one of them being _____ related.

Please indicate whether the statements are true (T) or false (F) by circling the corresponding letter. You should be able to briefly describe the rationale for your answer.

T   F   9.35   E/BD is the most common diagnosis represented in the school systems of the U.S.

T   F   9.36   More than 40% of the youth with disabilities in correctional facilities are youngsters with identified E/BD.

T   F   9.37   About half of the students with E/BD drop out of school before they finish the tenth grade.

T   F   9.38   Many professionals agree that the causes of behavior disorder are usually multimodal.

T   F   9.39   Few states require prereferral interventions before referrals may be received and processed by school personnel.

T   F   9.40   In the system-of-care, the child and family become the focus of the delivery system.

T   F   9.41   Bullying others can be a symptom of conduct disorder.

T   F   9.42   Children with disruptive E/BD rarely destroy other people's property.

In the following activity, select the most appropriate of the four answers provided for each item. Try to do this without looking at your text in order to get an idea of your comprehension level.

9.43 Special classes for children with moderate to severe disorders are most effective when
    A.   they have only students with special needs in them.
    B.   they have a high degree of structure and specialized instruction.
    C.   they have highly trained specialists serving as their teachers.
    D.   they have a high number of adults available to support them.

9.44 For youth who have been incarcerated, immediate school placements
    A.   improve their interest in school.
    B.   reduce their chances of being suspended.
    C.   reduce their chances of reentry into youth correctional facilities.
    D.   aggravate already volatile situations.

9.45 According to your text, key elements of the prevention process include all but which of the following?
    A.   Improved nutrition
    B.   Early identification
    C.   Home-based interventions
    D.   Collaborative teaming

9.46 The definition for emotional disturbance proposed by the Council for Exceptional Children specifically addresses educational performance in all but what area?
   A. Physical abilities
   B. Self-care
   C. Personal adjustment
   D. Classroom behavior

9.47 According to your text, factors that influence the types of behavior that individuals with E/BD exhibit or suppress include all but which of the following?
   A. Responses of siblings and peers
   B. Parents' management styles
   C. Educational background of the parents
   D. Academic characteristics

9.48 Your text states that externalized symptoms may include
   A. noncompliance.
   B. phobias.
   C. shyness.
   D. fears.

9.49 Most students with E/BD
   A. spend time in correctional facilities before they graduate.
   B. are educated in general education settings.
   C. are served through an inclusion model.
   D. are served in separate settings.

9.50 Overt aggression, disruptiveness, negativism, irresponsibility, and defiance of authority are characteristics of
   A. internalized symptoms.
   B. anxiety-withdrawal.
   C. anxiety.
   D. conduct disorders.

9.51 The most distinguishing feature of anorexia nervosa is
   A. the lackluster appearance of the individual's skin and eyes.
   B. bodyweight that is 15% below the norm.
   C. loss of bone density.
   D. bodyweight that fluctuates dramatically over a 6-month period of time.

9.52 An excessive fear of leaving home or being separated from persons to whom the child is attached is known as
   A. pervasive developmental disorder.
   B. attention deficit disorder.
   C. separation anxiety disorder.
   D. oppositional defiance disorder.

9.53 During their school years, children and youth with minimal personal and social skills are more likely than other youth with disabilities to be
A. shy.
B. victimized.
C. bored.
D. poor students.

9.54 Nightmares, loss of energy, excessive feelings of guilt, and inability to concentrate can be manifestations of
A. depression.
B. anxiety.
C. fear.
D. fatigue.

9.55 All but which of the following statements complete this sentence accurately? "Students with E/BD _____."
A. fail more classes
B. are absent more often
C. are retained more frequently
D. are extremely social

9.56 The individual who is credited with promoting the notion that behavior could be explained in terms of subconscious phenomena or early traumatic experiences was
A. Samuel Kirk.
B. William Jensen.
C. Sigmund Freud.
D. Bernard Rimland.

9.57 According to your text, home environments that are devoid of consistent rules and consequences for child behavior, reinforce aggressive behavior, and lack parental supervision produce children who are at-risk for developing
A. depression.
B. phobia disorders.
C. conduct disorders.
D. aggressive disorders.

9.58 The three-stage process of the Systematic Screening for Behavior Disorders (SSBD) includes all but which of the following steps?
A. General education teacher nominations
B. Special education teacher nominations
C. A ranking within the group according to severity and frequency of behaviors
D. Systematic observations of most highly ranked students

9.59 If the functional behavioral assessment is done well, it gives rise to _____ that may be used to assist the child or youth in developing more adaptive behaviors.
   A. behavior intervention plans
   B. individualized education programs
   C. 504 documents
   D. classroom assistants

9.60 The Behavior and Emotional Rating Scale (BERS) is used to develop
   A. deficit-centered IEPs for children and youth with E/BD.
   B. family-centered IFSPs for children and youth with E/BD.
   C. peer-centered IEPs for children and youth with E/BD.
   D. strength-centered IEPs for children and youth with E/BD.

9.61 Care that provides comprehensive services to youth and their families, addressing individual and family needs through flexible approaches coordinated through a team of professionals and paraprofessionals, is known as
   A. intervention teams.
   B. wraparound process.
   C. referral teams.
   D. comprehensive services.

9.62 To be effective the system of care should be all but
   A. community based.
   B. child centered and family focused.
   C. government funded.
   D. culturally competent.

Cryptogram

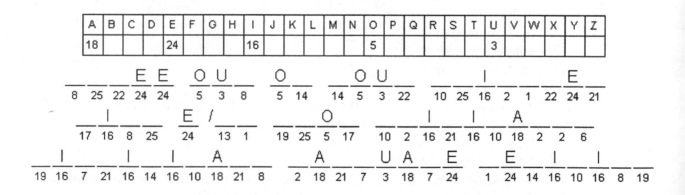

Scramble

Unscramble the tiles to reveal a message.

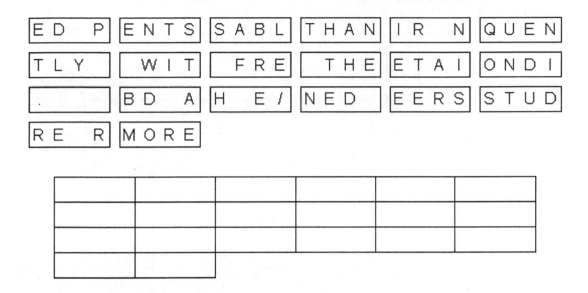

ED P	ENTS	SABL	THAN	IR N	QUEN
TLY	WIT	FRE	THE	ETAI	ONDI
.	BD A	H E /	NED	EERS	STUD
RE R	MORE				

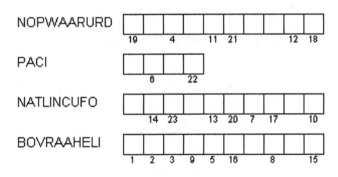

Double Puzzle

Unscramble each of the clue words. Copy the letters in the numbered cells to other cells with the same number.

NOPWAARURD
19 4 11 21 12 18

PACI
6 22

NATLINCUFO
14 23 13 20 7 17 10

BOVRAAHELI
1 2 3 9 5 16 8 15

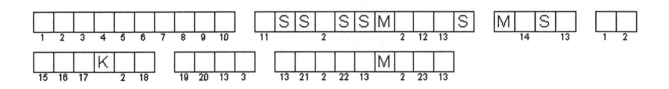

1 2 3 4 5 6 7 8 9 10   11   S S   S S M   2 12 13   S   M   S   14   13   1 2

15 16 17   K   2 18   19 20 13 3   13 21 2 22 13   M   2 23 13

Crossword Puzzle

Across

2. Three out of _____ children with E/BD show clinically significant language deficits
7. _____ aggression, such as in gangs and truancy
9. Rapid and recurrent movement
10. Behavior problems that are frequently internal in nature

Down

1. Pervasive developmental disorder that is increasing in prevalence
3. Therapy that is a critical component of effective programs for antisocial children
4. Attachment disorder that occurs as a result of grossly inadequate care
5. Persistent eating of nonnutritive material
6. Comprehensive services for youth and their families
8. _____ identification leads to early treatment

Case Study

Jerome is a 5th grader at Eisenhower Elementary School. He is in the general 5th grade classroom for most of the day, but also spends 45 minutes a day in the resource room to get help with his behavior problems. Jerome was identified as having an emotional/behavioral disorder in 3rd grade. His 3rd grade teacher referred him to the building pre-referral team because of his low tolerance for frustration and explosive outbursts. For example, if Jerome was given assignments that seemed very difficult or very long, Jerome would tantrum. His tantrums were loud and long, often with crying or yelling and physical responses such as kicking his desk or running around the room. During the comprehensive assessment process, it was observed that Jerome had a very difficult time handling unpredictable environments, had problems with planning and managing his effort and time, and had an unusually low tolerance for frustration. Because these problems were interfering with his school performance, Jerome was identified as having an emotional/behavioral disorder and given special education services.

1. If you were the special education teacher, what behaviors would you want to work on improving? _____

_____

_____

_____

_____

2. If you were Jerome's 5th grade teacher, what would you want to do to help increase his success in your class? _____

_____

_____

_____

_____

3. In what ways could the 5th grade teacher and the special education teacher work together to help Jerome? _____

_____

_____

_____

_____

Community Activities

1. Arrange with local school to observe in a special education classroom that serves children with emotional/behavioral disorders. While observing the classroom and the interactions that occur, answer the following questions: What are some of the student's characteristics? How does the teacher address those differences? How successful is the child in this environment?

_____

_____

_____

_____

_____

2. Arrange with a local school to observe in a general education classroom that has a child or children with emotional/behavioral disorders. While observing the classroom and the interactions that occur, answer the following questions. What are some of his/her characteristics? How does the general education teacher address those differences?   How successful is the child in this environment?_____

_____

_____

_____

_____

3. Observe the child with the emotional/behavioral disorder in settings other than the classroom such as in the cafeteria or during art, physical education, and music. How does the child compare to his/her peers in terms of positive social interaction, compliance with teacher requests, attention, and task completion? _____

_____

_____

_____

_____

Resources

Books
Growing Up Sad by Leon Cytryn, Donald H. McKnew, and Jerry M. Wiener. Available from W.W. Norton & Company.
The Depressed Child: A Parent's Guide for Rescuing Kids by Riley A. Douglas. Available from Taylor Publishing.
Your Anxious Child by John S. Dacey, Lisa B. Fiore, and George T. Ladd. Available from Jossey-Bass.

Videos
I Love You Like Crazy by the Mental Illness Education Project, Inc., www.miep.org/
The Bonnie Tapes by the Mental Illness Education Project, Inc., www.miep.org/

Websites
The National Mental Health Association: www.nmha.org
About our Kids: www.aboutourkids.org
The Child Advocate: www.childadvocate.net

10

Mental Retardation (Intellectual Disabilities)

According to the American Association on Mental Retardation (AAMR), mental retardation is defined in relation to three components: intelligence, adaptive skills, and age of onset. In order to more clearly represent the diversity of functional levels and characteristics of persons with mental retardation, four classification systems are explained in the chapter: severity of condition, educability expectations, medical descriptors, and level of needed support.

This chapter details the characteristics of mental retardation in seven areas: learning and memory, self-regulation, adaptive skills, academic achievement, motivation, speech-language development, and physical characteristics. Possible causes of mental retardation that are discussed include sociocultural influences, biomedical factors, metabolic and nutritional factors, behavioral factors, and unknown prenatal influences. Recent preventive measures have focused on immunizing against disease, monitoring maternal nutritional habits during pregnancy, providing appropriate prenatal care, and screening for genetic disorders at birth.

The importance of early childhood education is stressed. Educational programming for elementary school age children is concerned with decreasing dependence on others (motor development, self-care, and functional academics) and teaching adaptation to the environment (social skills and communication). The goals of educational programming for adolescents include increasing personal independence and enhancing opportunities for participation in the local community, as well as preparing for employment and successful transition into adulthood.

Concept Reflection

A. What did I know about mental retardation before reading this chapter?	B. How did reading the chapter enhance or change what I already knew? (Relate this to Column A.)	C. What new information did I learn? (This may or may not be associated with your responses in A or B.)
1.	1.	1.
2.	2.	2.
3.	3.	3.

Keep the following questions in mind as you read this chapter.

10.1 Identify the major components of the AAMR definition of mental retardation.
A.
B.
C.
D.
10.2 Identify four approaches to classifying people with mental retardation.
A.
B.
C.
D.
10.3 What is the prevalence of mental retardation?
A.
B.
C.
10.4 Identify intellectual, self-regulation, and adaptive skills characteristics of individuals with mental retardation.
A.
B.
C.

10.5	**Identify the academic, motivational, speech and language, and physical characteristics of children with mental retardation.**

A.

B.

C.

D.

E.

F.

G.

H

10.6	**Identify the causes of mental retardation.**

A.

B.

10.7	**Why are early intervention services for children with mental retardation so important?**

A.

B.

10.8	**Identify five skills areas that should be addressed in programs for elementary-age children with mental retardation.**

A.

B.

C.

D.

E.

10.9 Identify four educational goals for adolescents with mental retardation.

A.

B.

C.

D.

10.10 Why is the inclusion of students with mental retardation in general education settings to an appropriate educational experience?

A.

Guided Review

Read – Matching Vocabulary

Following are a number of the key terms and concepts used in this chapter. Try to complete this matching exercise before you read the chapter. Match each term with the phrase that you think most closely describes or defines it.

A. Support
B. Metacognitive
C. Intellectual
D. Neurofibromatosis

E. Normalization
F. Metabolic
G. Functional
H. Galactosemia

10.11 _____ Thinking abstractly, learning quickly and from experience, planning, solving problems, and reasoning are all examples of _____ reasoning.

10.12 _____ The principle of _____ emphasizes the need to make the conditions of everyday life as close to the norm of mainstream society as possible.

10.13 _____ A _____ reading program is one in which students are able to develop a useful vocabulary that will facilitate inclusion.

10.14 _____ The body's inability to process certain substances that can become poisonous and damage the central nervous system are known as _____ disorders.

10.15 _____ Inherited disorder that results in multiple tumors in the skin and peripheral nerve tissue.

10.16 _____ The four approaches to defining mental retardation include severity, educability, medical, and _____.

10.17 _____ The inability to process lactose.

10.18 _____ The process that helps a person plan how to solve a problem.

This exercise is intended to provide practice in recalling what you have just read. Try not to refer back to the chapter as you match the following items with their descriptions below. As you work through this exercise, consider how this new information relates to other knowledge, concepts, and/or principles you learned before taking this course.

A. Medical
B. Learning
C. Biomedical
D. Williams

E. Anencephaly
F. Self-regulation
G. Unmotivated
H. Functioning

10.19 _____ A condition in which the individual has a partial or complete absence of cerebral tissue is known as _____.

10.20 _____ AAMR indicates that the _____ level for people with mental retardation is significantly affected by physical and mental health.

10.21 _____ Metabolism, nutrition, postnatal brain disease, and chromosomal abnormalities are all known as _____ factors.

10.22 _____ Fetal alcohol syndrome and Down syndrome are common _____ descriptors.

10.23 _____ Individuals with mental retardation develop _____ sets at a slower rate than nonretarded peers.

10.24 _____ The ability to mediate one's own behavior.

10.25 _____ Learned helplessness can make a person appear _____.

10.26 _____ An example of a chromosomal abnormality is _____ syndrome.

Supply a word/phrase in each sentence in order to make sense out of the statement of a concept, definition, or principle that is otherwise incomplete or lacks closure. Several answers, other than those listed in the key, may be acceptable for an item. Focus on whether or not your answer is equivalent to the answer supplied and be prepared to explain why you completed the statement(s) as you did.

10.27 People with _____ retardation often depend on others to maintain their most basic life functions.

10.28 The six major dimensions of the AAMR definition of mental retardation include (1) intellectual abilities; (2) participation, interactions, and social roles; (3) health; (4) environmental context; (5) age of onset; and (6) _____ behavior.

10.29 The four levels of support recognized by the AAMR include pervasive, extensive, limited, and _____.

10.30 According to the U.S. Census Bureau (2000), people with mental retardation constitute about _____ million people in the U.S.

10.31 Possible causes of mental retardation include sociocultural influences, biomedical and behavioral factors, as well as unknown _____ factors.

10.32 Mental retardation that is attributable to both sociocultural and genetic factors is known as _____-_____ retardation.

10.33 Fragile-X syndrome is a _____ abnormality.
10.34 The most common speech difficulties for individuals with mental retardation include articulation problems, voice problems, and _____.

Review – True/False

Please indicate whether the statements are true (T) or false (F) by circling the corresponding letter. You should be able to briefly describe the rationale for your answer.

T F 10.35 Until PL 94-142 (1975) many children who were labeled trainable could not get a free public education.

T F 10.36 Nearly 5% of students with mental retardation attend public special schools.

T F 10.37 For most people with mental retardation, memory capabilities are significantly below average

T F 10.38 The overriding goal of language intervention is to increase the functional communication of students

T F 10.39 The greater the retardation, the greater the language difficulty and related physical problems.

T F 10.40 A significantly lower percentage of children with mental retardation come from low socioeconomic backgrounds in comparison to peers without disabilities.

T F 10.41 All states require mandatory screening for PKU.

T F 10.42 Most people with mild mental retardation are identified at birth.

Chapter Review – Practice Test

In the following activity, select the most appropriate of the four answers provided for each item. Try to do this without looking at your text in order to get an idea of your comprehension level.

10.43 Most people with moderate to severe mental retardation are capable of learning
    A. adaptive skills with ongoing support.
    B. to drive within a few years of turning sixteen.
    C. to read within a few months of their same-age peers without disabilities.
    D. to socialize on the same level as their peers without disabilities.

10.44 The term *mental retardation* is a term
    A. that will always be used because it is so well understood by most people.
    B. that will probably be replaced in the years to come.
    C. that should never be used in the presence of family members.
    D. a term that is rarely used in respected professional publications.

10.45 Practical examples of adaptive skills include all but which of the following?
A. Following rules
B. Preparing meals
C. Managing money
D. Using the telephone

10.46 Mental retardation originates prior to ____ years of age.
A. 3
B. 14
C. 18
D. 21

10.47 When a child's IQ is defined as anywhere from 55 to about 70, it is generally expected
that he/she will
A. always need significant support.
B. never hold a job.
C. learn primarily self-care skills and mostly functional academics.
D. learn academics up to approximately the second to fifth-grade level.

10.48 Approximately ____ of all students with disabilities between the ages of 6 and 21
have mental retardation
A. < 1%
B. 2%
C. 11%
D. 25%

10.49 For individuals with mental retardation, the academic area that is generally
considered the weakest is
A. math.
B. reading.
C. social studies.
D. writing .

10.50 According to your text, in order to help a child overcome feelings of learned
helplessness, professionals and family members should focus on providing
A. additional leisure time.
B. less opportunities to be involved .
C. more friends.
D. more opportunities with high chances for success.

10.51 Speech and language pathologists are able to correct minor speech differences for
____ students with mental retardation.
A. all
B. most
C. a few
D. no

10.52 People with cultural-familial retardation are often described as having all but
   A. large families.
   B. one parent or sibling with retardation.
   C. low socioeconomic status.
   D. mild retardation.

10.53 Characteristics commonly associated with individuals with Down syndrome include
   A. severe mental retardation and physical disabilities.
   B. broad feet with short toes and high-set ears.
   C. excessive ability to extend the joints and a flat bridge of the nose.
   D. many creases across the palm of one or both hands.

10.54 The intelligence of individuals with fragile X syndrome
   A. can range from normal IQ to severe retardation.
   B. is usually in the severely retarded range.
   C. cannot be determined due to limited language ability.
   D. is usually unaffected by presence of the condition.

10.55 Congenital rubella has been shown
   A. to effect the fetus only during the last trimester.
   B. to cause blindness, cerebral palsy, and seizures.
   C. to have no effect on the fetus if the mother is otherwise healthy.
   D. to effect only male fetuses.

10.56 Maternal substance abuse is associated with gestation disorders involving
   A. prematurity and small heads.
   B. low birthweight and fluid on the brain.
   C. extremely small hands and feet as well as low birthweight.
   D. prematurity and low birthweight.

10.57 An individual who scores more than _____ standard deviations below 100 on an intelligence test meets the criteria for being considered mentally retarded.
   A. 1
   B. 2
   C. 3
   D. None of the above.

10.58 Instruction and support for children with mental retardation focuses on
   A. teaching academic skills that are known to be easy.
   B. teaching adaptive skills that "everyone" can do.
   C. teaching independence by individualizing programs.
   D. teaching dependence by identifying specialists.

10.59 A language board with pictures is an example of
  A. low expectations for communication.
  B. high expectations for communication.
  C. low tech assistive device.
  D. high tech assistive device.

10.60 Goals for employment
  A. have shifted away from sheltered workshops.
  B. have shifted away from community employment.
  C. have shifted toward sheltered workshops.
  D. have shifted toward community employment.

10.61 Articulation problems are defined as primarily including all but
  A. delayed language development.
  B. distortions of words.
  C. word substitutions.
  D. omissions of sounds.

10.62 Early intervention that provides an infant with an array of visual, auditory, and
physical stimuli to promote development are known as
  A. special education preschools.
  B. Head Start.
  C. infant stimulation.
  D. sensory integration.

Cryptogram

A	B	C	D	E	F	G	H	I	J	K	L	M	N	O	P	Q	R	S	T	U	V	W	X	Y	Z
23												10		14						9					

```
___ ___ ___    _A_ _U_ ___ ___    _O_ ___    _M_ ___ ___ ___    ___ ___ ___ _A_ ___ ___ _A_ ___ ___ _O_
22  20  6      11  23  9   25  6   14  13     10  8   26  17     18  6   22  23  18  17  23  22  8   14  19

       ___ ___    ___ ___ ___ ___ _A_ ___ ___ ___    _U_ ___ ___ _O_ ___ .
        8   25     4   6   19  6   18  23  26  26  24   9   19  1   19  14  12  19
```

Scramble

Unscramble the tiles to reveal a message.

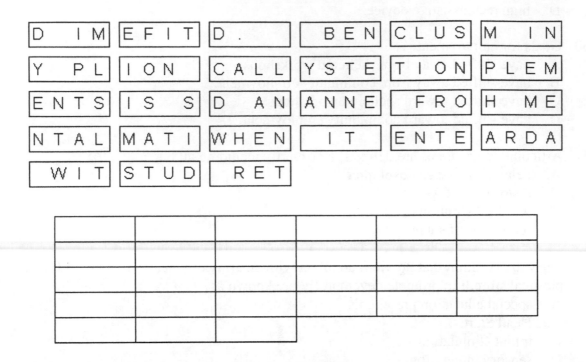

D I M	E F I T	D .	B E N	C L U S	M I N
Y P L	I O N	C A L L	Y S T E	T I O N	P L E M
E N T S	I S S	D A N	A N N E	F R O	H M E
N T A L	M A T I	W H E N	I T	E N T E	A R D A
W I T	S T U D	R E T			

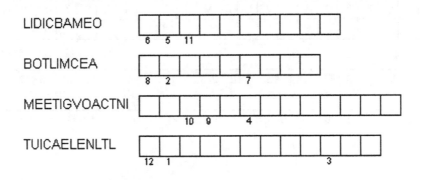

Double Puzzle

Unscramble each of the clue words. Copy the letters in the numbered cells to other cells with the same number.

LIDICBAMEO

6 5 11

BOTLIMCEA

8 2 7

MEETIGVOACTNI

10 9 4

TUICAELENLTL

12 1 3

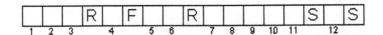

_ _ R _ F _ R _ _ _ S _ S
1 2 3 4 5 6 7 8 9 10 11 12

126

Crossword Puzzle

Across

1. Most people with mental retardation are identified at _____
4. Normalization emphasizes the need to make the conditions of everyday life as close to the _____ as possible
6. The _____ the retardation, the greater the related physical problems
9. Support, severity, educability, and _____ are approaches used to define mental retardation
10. Most people with mental retardation have significantly below average _____ capabilities

Down

2. Weakest area for individuals with mental retardation
3. Speech and language pathologists are able to correct minor speech differences for _____ students with mental retardation
5. Level for people with retardation is significantly affected by physical and _____ health
7. Congenital _____ causes blindness, seizures, and cerebral palsy
8. Number of deviations below 100 on an IQ test that meets the criteria for mental retardation

Case Study

Chloe is 15 years old. She is a typical teenager in many respects. Her ears are double-pierced, she loves jewelry, and she likes to wear makeup. Her mother will tell you that Chloe is on the telephone all the time with her friends, Debbie and Koree. The three girls have been inseparable since they were 4 years old when they met in the early intervention program at their neighborhood elementary school. Eleven years and hundreds of hours of ballet and ice skating lessons later, they are still best friends and attend Garfield High School together.

Chloe will tell you she is "slower" than her friends. Chloe's academic skills are not at the same level as her peers. Recent assessments show her reading, writing, and math skills at the 5th grade level. Chloe always sits in the front row near the teacher with Debbie or Koree near. However, Chloe's motivation to do well in school and her willingness to work is very high.

Chloe is eligible for special education services, but her parents have waived those services, preferring to keep her out in the general classroom and address her needs through out-of-school services, like tutoring. She does have a 504 Plan that provides classroom accommodations. Chloe's parents believe that because of their decision to keep her out of special education, she is viewed as one of the kids and not given negative labels often associated with special education.

1. What kind of learning characteristics is Chloe likely to demonstrate? _____
_____
_____
_____
_____

2. Identify instructional accommodations that would be effective for supporting Chloe in the general classroom. _____
_____
_____
_____
_____

3. Do you think Chloe's parents made the right decision to keep her out of special education? What are the benefits and drawbacks of their decision? _____
_____
_____
_____
_____

1. Arrange with local school to observe in a special education classroom that serves children with mental retardation. While observing in the classroom think, about the following questions: What are some of the students' characteristics? How does the teacher address those differences? How successful is the child in this environment? _____

_____

_____

_____

_____

2. Arrange with local school to observe in a general education classroom that has a child or children with mental retardation. While observing in the classroom, think about the following questions: What are some of his/her characteristics? How does the general education teacher address those differences?   How successful is the child in this environment? _____

_____

_____

_____

_____

3. Observe the child with the mental retardation in settings other than the classroom such as in the cafeteria or during art, physical education, and music. How does the child compare to his/her peers in terms of social interaction, class participation, and attention? _____

_____

_____

_____

_____

Resources

Books
Retarded Isn't Stupid, Mom! By Sandra Z. Kaufman. Published by Brookes Publishing.
Nobody's Perfect:Living and Grown with Children who have Special Needs by Nancy Miller, with Susie Burmester, Diane G. Callahan, Janet Deterle, and Stephanie Niedermeyer.
The Child Who Never Grew by Pearl S. Buck. Published by Woodbine House.

Videos
I am Dekel: Portrait of a Life with Down's Syndrome. Published by Films For The Humanities & Sciences.
Sean's Story: A Lesson in Life. Available from Films for the Humanities & Sciences.

Websites
American Association for Mental Retardation. www.aamr.org.
The Arc of the United States. www.thearc.org.
Best Buddies. www.bestbuddies.org.

This chapter addresses two major interrelated components of communication: speech and language. Speech is the audible production of language, and language is the intended message contained in speech. Problems in either can significantly affect a person's daily life.

Language disorders occur when individuals experience a serious disruption in the language process: a breakdown in the ability to understand or express ideas in the communication system that is being used. The authors address both *receptive* and *expressive* problems, as well as aphasia, which may include elements of both. Receptive and expressive problems are often intertwined, thus causation is difficult to determine. Treatment of language disorders must consider both the nature of the problem and the manner in which an individual is affected.

The authors define a speech disorder as a behavior that is sufficiently deviant from normal speaking patterns that communication is impaired. Speech disorders are discussed under the categories of fluency disorders, delayed speech, articulation disorders, and voice disorders. The chapter explains some of the features of each category, including characteristics, causes, intervention strategies, and prevalence estimates.

Concept Reflection

A. What did I know about communication disorders before reading this chapter?	B. How did reading the chapter enhance or change what I already knew? (Relate this to Column A.)	C. What new information did I learn? (This may or may not be associated with your responses in A or B.)
1.	1.	1.
2.	2.	2.
3.	3.	3.
4.	4.	4.
5.	5.	5.

Keep the following questions in mind as you read this chapter.

11.1 Identify four ways in which speech, language, and communication are interrelated.
A.
B.
C.
D.
11.2 Identify two ways in which language delay and language disorder are different.
A.
B.
11.3 Identify three factors thought to cause language disorders.
A.
B.
C.
11.4 Describe two ways in which treatment approaches for language disorders generally differ for children and for adults.
A.
B.
11.5 Identify three factors thought to cause stuttering.
A.
B.
C.

11.6 Identify two ways in which learning theory and home environments relate to delayed speech.
A.
B.
11.7 Identify two reasons why some professionals are reluctant to treat functional articulation disorders in young school children.
A.
B.

Read – Matching Vocabulary

Following are a number of the key terms and concepts used in this chapter. Try to complete this matching exercise before you read the chapter. Match each term with the phrase that you think most closely describes or defines it.

A. Malocclusion

B. Semantics

C. Functional

D. Stuttering

E. Pragmatics

F. Aphasia

G. Expressive

H. Neurological

11.8 _____ A speech disorder that occurs when the flow of speech is abnormally interrupted by repetitions, blocking, or prolongations of sounds, syllables, words, or phrases.

11.9 _____ An acquired language disorder caused by brain damage and characterized by complete or partial impairment of language comprehension, formulation, and use.

11.10 _____ A component of language that represents the rules that govern the reason(s) for communicating.

11.11 _____ The understanding of language that is sometimes unique to a particular individual.

11.12 _____ Difficulty with formulating and using spoken or written language is representative of an _____ language disorder.

11.13 _____ _____ articulation disorders are likely a result of environmental or psychological influences.

11.14 _____ Physical trauma can cause _____ damage which can cause language disorders.

11.15 _____ An abnormal fit between the upper and lower dental structures.

This exercise is intended to provide practice in recalling what you have just read. Try not to refer back to the chapter as you match the following items with their descriptions below. As you work through this exercise, consider how this new information relates to other knowledge, concepts, and/or principles you learned before taking this course.

A. Cleft palate
B. Augmentative
C. Delayed speech
D. Hoarseness

E. Temperament
F. Speech
G. Language
H. Emphysema

_____

11.16 _____ A deficit in speaking proficiency whereby the individual performs like someone much younger.

11.17 _____ A gap in the soft palate and roof of the mouth, sometimes extending through the upper lip.

11.18 _____ A serious disruption of the language acquisition may result in this type of disorder.

11.19 _____ Communication, language, and _____ overlap to some degree in their development

11.20 _____ An ILP is designed based on an individual's strengths, limitations, developmental level, age, mono/bilingual background, literacy, and _____.

11.21 _____ Abnormally low voice intensity may result from _____.

11.22 _____ Children with voice disorders often speak with _____.

11.23 _____ Forms of communication that employ nonspeech alternatives.

Recite – Fill in the Blank

Supply a word/phrase in each sentence in order to make sense out of the statement of a concept, definition, or principle that is otherwise incomplete or lacks closure. Several answers, other than those listed in the key, may be acceptable for an item. Focus on whether or not your answer is equivalent to the answer supplied and be prepared to explain why you completed the statement(s) as you did.

11.24 _____ aphasia is a term used with children, while aphasia in adults is commonly referred to as _____ language disorder.

11.25 Language consists of pragmatics, semantics, phonology, syntax, and _____.

11.26 The distinction between _____ and _____ disorders is like the difference between a sound of a word and the meaning of a word.

11.27 Articulation problems that tend to cease to exist for many children after the age of 5 include _____, _____, or _____.

11.28 _____ and _____ diminish speech disorders considerably.

11.29 When both parents are deaf, a child's _____ development is delayed.

Please indicate whether the statements are true (T) or false (F) by circling the corresponding letter. You should be able to briefly describe the rationale for your answer.

T	F	11.30	Language delay is defined as the sequence of development being intact, but the rate interrupted.
T	F	11.31	Assistive communication devices are being shown to be effective when selected with the individual in mind.
T	F	11.32	The amount of language modeled in the home does not appear to have a direct bearing on the language development of the child.
T	F	11.33	The only treatment that is shown to consistently be effective in increasing the fluency rate of a person who stutters is biofeedback.
T	F	11.34	An infant's initial verbal output is primarily crying.
T	F	11.35	Some components of communication involve language but not speech.
T	F	11.36	In order to have language, one must have speech.
T	F	11.37	Articulation problems are common among young children.

Chapter Review – Practice Test

In the following activity select the most appropriate of the four answers provided for each item. Try to do this without looking at your text in order to get an idea of your comprehension level.

11.38 Over _____ of the children (6 - 21 years old) with disabilities who were served under federal law during 1999 - 2000 had speech and language difficulties.
   A. 9%
   B. 19%
   C. 29%
   D. 39%

11.39 An individualized language plan (ILP) must include all but which of the following?
   A. Long-range, annual goals
   B. Description of evaluation methods
   C. Positions and names of evaluators
   D. Beginning and ending dates of the ILP

11.40 Turn-taking, initiating, maintaining, and ending a conversation are processes that represent _____.
   A. morphology
   B. semantics
   C. syntax
   D. pragmatics

11.41 For most children strings of two and three words that resemble sentences typically begin between
  A. 9 and 14 months.
  B. 18 and 24 months.
  C. 36 and 40 months.
  D. 40 and 48 months.

11.42 While speech disorders include problems related to verbal production, language disorders represent serious difficulties in
  A. applying the sounds to the letters they represent.
  B. learning how to position one's tongue and lips.
  C. establishing necessary eye contact and staying engaged with the listener.
  D. understanding and expressing ideas.

11.43 A child may have a language impairment when he/she exhibits difficulty in all but which of the following?
  A. Requesting needs
  B. Interpreting humor
  C. Mispronouncing words
  D. Comprehending new words

11.44 Remediation of adults with aphasia is more likely to progress if
  A. direct services are received in their own home/familiar surroundings.
  B. direct therapeutic instruction is implemented.
  C. they are allowed to observe other adults with aphasia as they speak first.
  D. indirect services are provided through skilled case managers.

11.45 One common theme among definitions of speech disorders is that they
  A. always include language disorders as a by-product.
  B. generally address only disorders in young individuals.
  C. involve deviations of sufficient magnitude to interfere with communication.
  D. All of the above.

11.46 Spontaneous recovery of adults with aphasia may occur during the first 6 months after an accident, but waiting beyond _____ months to start treatment may seriously delay recovery.
  A. 1
  B. 2
  C. 4
  D. 5

11.47 It is theorized that stuttering is caused by all but which of the following?
  A. Neurological problem
  B. Emotional disturbance
  C. Peer modeling
  D. Learned behavior

11.48 Males who stutter outnumber females who stutter
   A. 5:1.
   B. 4:1.
   C. 3:1.
   D. 2:1.

11.49 When an individual speaks like a much younger person, he/she is said to have
   A. delayed speech.
   B. language disorder.
   C. immature speech.
   D. impaired speech.

11.50 Individuals with aphasia resulting from injury to the back part of the brain
   A. have poor articulation skills.
   B. comprehend better than they speak.
   C. have speech that lacks content.
   D. have difficulty finding words.

11.51 When defective learning is the primary cause of delayed speech, treatment is likely to
   A. focus on articulation skills.
   B. focus on relaxation therapy and biofeedback.
   C. focus on biological and medical causes.
   D. focus on basic principles of learned behavior.

11.52 Articulation disorders are
   A. the least common of all speech problems.
   B. the most common of all speech problems.
   C. more damaging to self-image than other speech problems.
   D. less damaging to self-image than other speech problems.

11.53 Most problems encountered by speech clinicians involve
   A. articulation disorders.
   B. receptive disorders.
   C. language delay.
   D. pervasive developmental delay.

11.54 In most cases, by the time a child is _____, articulation problems that are likely to improve will have done so.
   A. 5 - 6 years of age
   B. 7 - 8 years of age
   C. 9 - 10 years of age
   D. 11 - 12 years of age

11.55 Unusual acoustical qualities in the sounds made when a person speaks are
    A. known as articulation errors.
    B. a result of abnormal neurological transmissions.
    C. referred to as voice disorders.
    D. causal factors of language disorders.

11.56 What percentage of students in kindergarten through fourth grade are identified with speech disorders?
    A. <1%
    B. 3% to 5%
    C. 8% to 10%
    D. 12% to 15%

11.57 During the early stages of speech development, everyone
    A. stutters.
    B. models peers.
    C. exhibits degrees of language delay.
    D. demonstrates receptive disorders.

Cryptogram

A	B	C	D	E	F	G	H	I	J	K	L	M	N	O	P	Q	R	S	T	U	V	W	X	Y	Z
			23								15		16	20		17									

D _ R P _ D L R _ _ _ O P P O R _ _ _ _ _ _
23 1 10 17 7 20 22 18 23   15 18 21 17 2 1 2 13   16 20 20 16 17 22 7 2 1 22

_ _ _ _ _ _ _ _ _ _ P R O _ L _ _ _ _ _ _ _
1 18 10   19 21 2   19 21 7 10 18   20 17 16 4 15 18 9 10   24 1 22 12

L _ _ _ _ _ _ _ .
15 21 2 13 7 21 13 18

137

Scramble

Unscramble the tiles to reveal a message.

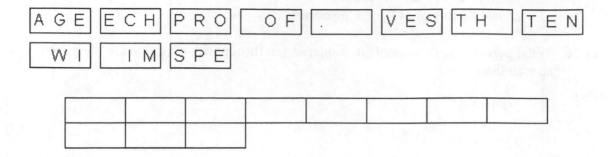

| A G E | E C H | P R O | O F | . | | V E S | T H | T E N |

| W I | | I M | S P E |

Double Puzzle

Unscramble each of the clue words. Copy the letters in the numbered cells to other cells with the same number.

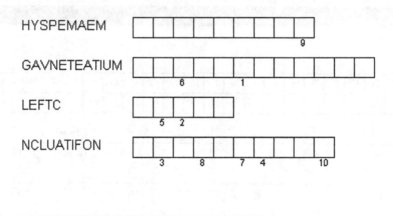

HYSPEMAEM

GAVNETEATIUM

LEFTC

NCLUATIFON

Across

1. Language consists of pragmatics, semantics, phonology, _____, and morphology
5. Damage which can cause language disorders
7. Aphasia in adults is commonly referred to as an _____ language disorder
8. Speech patterns of a person much younger than the speaker
9. One of three articulation problems that tend to cease to exist after the age of 5

Down

1. Understanding of language that is sometimes unique to an individual
2. Interruption in the flow of speech
3. Rules that govern the reason(s) for communicating
4. Type of sound individuals with voice disorders often make when speaking
6. Gap in the soft palate and roof of the mouth

Case Study

Derrick is a very shy and quiet young man. He rarely speaks in class, and when he does his responses are very short and often monosyllabic. Derrick is a very accomplished student with high marks across the curriculum. He is clearly very bright and competent in an academic environment. On his grade reports, teachers lavish praise on him for his academic prowess, but always comment that he needs to speak up in class, take more leadership opportunities, and spend more time with his peers.

While Derrick is confident in his academic knowledge and skills, he is unwilling to take his teachers' advice. Derrick has a serious stuttering problem and he does not like to speak when he is not confident about it. Derrick has received speech-language therapy for many years to help with his stuttering. While it has reduced the stuttering's frequency, when Derrick is anxious his stuttering becomes very obvious. In addition, there are some words that Derrick simply cannot say without stuttering. For some reason, those words just don't come out smoothly.

1. What strategies might a teacher use to encourage Derrick to participate more fully in the classroom? _____
_____
_____
_____
_____

2. What are the possible consequences for Derrick's decision to be a quiet spectator in the classroom? _____
_____
_____
_____
_____

Community Activities

1. Arrange with local school to observe in a program that serves children with communication disorders. While observing in the classroom think about the following questions: What are some of the student's characteristics? How does the teacher address those differences? How successful is the child in this environment? _____
_____
_____
_____
_____
_____

2. Arrange with local school to observe in a general education classroom that has a child or children with communication disorders. While observing in the classroom think about the following questions: What are some of his/her characteristics? How does the general education teacher address those differences? How successful is the child in this environment? _____

_____

_____

_____

_____

3. Observe the child with the communication disorders in settings other than the classroom such as the cafeteria, during art, physical education, and music. How does the child compare to his/her peers in terms of social interaction, class participation and attention? _____

_____

_____

_____

_____

Resources

Books
The Late Talker: What to Do if Your Child Isn't Talking Yet by Marilyn C. Agin, Lisa F. Geng, and Malcolm Nicholl. Published by St. Martin's Press.
Does My Child Have a Speech Problem? by Katherine L. Martin. Published by Chicago Review Press.
Childhood Speech, Language and Listening Problems by Patricia McAleer Hamaguchi. Published by John Wiley & Sons.

Videos
Unlocking Language. Available through Films for the Humanities & Sciences.
No Words to Say. Available from Amick Holzman Company

Websites
Kaufman's Children's Center for Speech, Language, and Sensory Disorders, Inc. www.kidspeech.com.
The American Speech-Language-Hearing Association: www.asha.org
Teaching Resources and information: www.schooltrain.info

Severe and Multiple Disabilities

This chapter presents several definitions of severe and multiple disabilities. Information regarding the prevalence and causation of severe and multiple disabilities is also presented.

The characteristics of people with severe and multiple disabilities, including their intelligence and academic achievement, adaptive skills, speech and language skills, physical and health attributes, and vision and hearing abilities are described. Assessment, both traditional and functional, as it relates to people with severe and multiple disabilities, is explained.

Services and supports for people with severe and multiple disabilities at various life stages are presented. Emphasis is given to the features that characterize quality programs. Key features of effective services and supports for individuals through the duration of educational program are described.

Concept Reflection

A. What did I know about severe and multiple disabilities before reading this chapter?	B. How did reading the chapter enhance or change what I already knew? (Relate this to Column A.)	C. What new information did I learn? (This may or may not be associated with your responses in A or B.)
1.	1.	1.
2.	2.	2.
3.	3.	3.
4.	4.	4.

Keep the following questions in mind as you read this chapter.

12.1 What are the three components of the TASH definition of severe disabilities?
A.
B.
C.

12.2 Define the terms *multiple disabilities* and *deaf-blindness* as described in IDEA.
A.
B.

12.3 Identify the estimated prevalence and causes of severe and multiple disabilities.
A.
B.
C.

12.4 What are the characteristics of persons with severe and multiple disabilities?
A.
B.
C.
D.
E.

12.5 Identify three types of educational assessments for students with severe and multiple disabilities.
A.
B.
C.

12.6	Identify the features of effective services and supports for children with severe and multiple disabilities during the early childhood years.

A.

B.

C.

D.

12.7	Identify the features of effective services and supports for children with severe and multiple disabilities during the elementary school years.

A.

B.

C.

D.

12.8	Describe four outcomes that are important in planning for the transition from school to adult life for adolescents with severe and multiple disabilities.

A.

B.

C.

D.

12.9	Describe four features that characterize successful inclusive education for students with severe and multiple disabilities.

A.

B.

C.

D.

12.10	Describe four bioethical dilemmas that can affect people with severe disabilities and their families.

A.

B.

C.

D.

Read – Matching Vocabulary

Following are a number of the key terms and concepts used in this chapter. Try to complete this matching exercise before you read the chapter. Match each term with the phrase that you think most closely describes or defines it.

A. Hypotonia   E. Athetosis
B. Respite care   F. Epilepsy
C. Spasticity   G. Bioethics
D. Genetic testing   H. Gastronomy

_____

12.11 _____ Poor muscle tone.
12.12 _____ Constant, contorted twisting motions in the wrists and fingers.
12.13 _____ Involuntary contractions of various muscle groups.
12.14 _____ Brief disturbances in the normal electrical functions of the brain.
12.15 _____ Study of ethics in medicine.
12.16 _____ The process of feeding through a rubber tube that is inserted into the stomach is known as _____ tube feeding.
12.17 _____ Assistance provided by individuals outside the family that allows family members time away from the child with the disability for a recreational event.
12.18 _____ The search for genes in the human body that are predisposed to disease.

This exercise is intended to provide practice in recalling what you have just read. Try not to refer back to the chapter as you match the following items with their descriptions below. As you work through this exercise, consider how this new information relates to other knowledge, concepts, and/or principles you learned before taking this course.

A. Adaptive
B. Accommodations
C. Dual
D. Child-centered

E. Authentic
F. Family-centered
G. Functional
H. Adjustment

12.19 _____ Identification of both serious emotional problems and mental retardation in the same individual constitutes provision of a _____ diagnosis.

12.20 _____ Parental involvement can be a powerful predictor of post-school _____ for students with severe and multiple disabilities.

12.21 _____ Picture cards, communication boards, gestures, and signs are examples of _____ communication systems.

12.22 _____ Assessments that focus on valued skills to promote independence and quality of life in natural settings are referred to as _____ assessments.

12.23 _____ Large-print text, testing in a separate setting, and extended time are examples of _____.

12.24 _____ _____ skills involve both personal independence and social interaction.

12.25 _____ Holistic approach that involved the child as a member of the family unit.

12.26 _____ Approach focused on identifying and meeting individual needs of the child.

Supply a word/phrase in each sentence in order to make sense out of the statement of a concept, definition, or principle that is otherwise incomplete or lacks closure. Several answers, other than those listed in the key, may be acceptable for an item. Focus on whether or not your answer is equivalent to the answer supplied and be prepared to explain why you completed the statement(s) as you did.

12.27 When a mechanical aid is used to supply oxygen to an individual with breathing problems, it is known as _____ _____.

12.28 A condition characterized by vision and hearing sensory impairments (deaf-blindness) is known as _____ _____ impairments.

12.29 Three components of the TASH definition of severe disabilities include (1) relationship of the individual with the environment, (2) extensive ongoing support, and (3)_____.

12.30 Giving students the opportunity to communicate their needs and preferences enhances autonomy, problem-solving skills, self-efficacy expectations, and _____.

12.31 Effective educational programs include opportunities for interaction between students with severe and multiple disabilities and _____ without disabilities.

12.32 One of the major concerns surrounding genetic counseling focuses on the _____ of the counselor.

Review – True/False

Please indicate whether the statements are true (T) or false (F) by circling the corresponding letter. You should be able to briefly describe the rationale for your answer.

T   F   12.33 A functional skill will have frequent and meaningful use across multiple environments.

T   F   12.34 Deaf-blindness is not included in the IDEA definition of multiple disabilities.

T   F   12.35 Educational supports and services should begin by the third birthday for individuals with severe and multiple disabilities.

T   F   12.36 All students with and without disabilities must take the standard statewide or districtwide assessments of achievement.

T   F   12.37 IDEA mandates that when a student's disabilities are very severe, they can be assessed using alternate means.

T   F   12.38 Alternate assessments must involve normative performance standards.

T   F   12.39 The term "severe disabilities" is not defined by IDEA.

T   F   12.40 Most individuals who are deaf-blind are severely retarded.

Chapter Review – Practice Test

In the following activity, select the most appropriate of the four answers provided for each item. Try to do this without looking at your text in order to get an idea of your comprehension level.

12.41 Approximately _____ individuals in the United States are identified as deaf-blind.
   A. 1,400
   B. 14,000
   C. 140,000
   D. 1,400,000

12.42 The definitions of severe and multiple disabilities focus on the
   A. importance of the individual's IQ.
   B. importance of an education.
   C. need for substantial support from others.
   D. importance of full lives.

12.43 Most people with severe and multiple disabilities have a primary condition of
   A. speech language disorder.
   B. learning disabilities.
   C. deaf-blindness.
   D. mental retardation.

12.44 Academic learning should be
    A. taught in the context of daily living.
    B. made a low priority in school.
    C. made a high priority in school.
    D. taught by family members .

12.45 Being able to communicate one's needs and preferences as well as listen and respond appropriately are known as _____ skills.
    A. listening
    B. adaptive
    C. social
    D. assertiveness

12.46 A person with severe and multiple disabilities will acquire and use appropriate speech and language if these skills are taught and applied
    A. by members of the medical profession.
    B. in the individual's home.
    C. by speech pathologists in the classroom.
    D. in natural settings.

12.47 _____ is an international advocacy association of people with disabilities, their family members, other advocates, and people who work in the disability field.
    A. TASH
    B. Human Genome Project
    C. CEC
    D. DB-LINK

12.48 The purpose of an assessment is to determine
    A. a child's IQ and write an IEP.
    B. which teachers are most qualified to educate the student.
    C. what supports are necessary for the child to be successful.
    D. how each student is doing compared to his peers.

12.49 The most effective way to prepare a student to participate in the community is
    A. through video modeling.
    B. to learn the necessary skills in the natural setting.
    C. to have him/her practice the skills in the classroom first.
    D. to have him/her role play in the classroom with a peer.

12.50 The greater the degree of mental retardation, the greater the degree of
    A. family involvement.
    B. physical disabilities.
    C. speech and language deficits and delays.
    D. community resources available.

12.51 Effective early intervention programs for infants and toddlers are characterized as
    A.   being family- and child-centered.
    B.   being child- and sibling-centered.
    C.   being classroom- and student-centered.
    D.   being inclusive- and team-oriented.

12.52 In addition to self-determination, identify three more features of quality programs for elementary-age students with severe and multiple disabilities.
    A.   Parental involvement
    B.   Functional skills
    C.   Community involvement
    D.   Augmentative communication

12.53 In your text Drew and Hardman (2004) suggest that a functional approach teaches academic skills in the context of
    A.   a small pupil-teacher ratio.
    B.   a family-centered meaning.
    C.   environmental cues.
    D.   general education expectations.

12.54 Wheelchairs, scooters, laser canes, seating and positioning devices, watch alarms, and touch talkers are all examples of
    A.   assistive technology.
    B.   modifications.
    C.   child-centered devices.
    D.   family-centered devices.

12.55 Four important considerations when transitioning from school to adult life include networking, using community resources, established independence, and
    A.   communicating with family members.
    B.   getting to know a case manager well.
    C.   being able to utilize public transportation.
    D.   securing a paid job.

12.56 Genetic engineering, screening for genetic disease, abortion, and life-sustaining medical treatment are examples of
    A.   family issues.
    B.   bioethical issues.
    C.   medical issues.
    D.   social issues.

12.57 The ultimate purpose of the Human Genome Project is to
    A.   conquer disease.
    B.   identify the 80,000 genes in human DNA.
    C.   develop tools for data analysis.
    D.   determine the sequences of 3 billion chemical base pairs in human DNA.

12.58 Most severe and multiple disabilities are evident
    A. during the mother's pregnancy.
    B. at birth.
    C. immediately following the birth.
    D. as infants become toddlers.

12.59 Blissymbols include all but which of the following symbols?
    A. Map
    B. Relational
    C. Abstract
    D. Pictographic

12.60 The purpose of family-centered intervention is to
    A. acquaint the family with the school personnel.
    B. develop an individualized family service plan.
    C. enable family members to initially cope and become empowered.
    D. let the family gain knowledge regarding their child's disability.

Cryptogram

A	B	C	D	E	F	G	H	I	J	K	L	M	N	O	P	Q	R	S	T	U	V	W	X	Y	Z
21		7				22								17											

```
___ ___ ___   G__ _A_ ___ ___ ___   ___ ___ ___   ___ ___ _A_   _D_ _A_ ___ ___ ___ _O_ ___  ,
12  20  6     22 3 6 21 12 6 3       12  20  6     3   6   12 21  3   7   21 12  11 17  15

___ ___ ___   G__ _A_ ___ ___ ___   ___ ___ ___   ___ ___ ___ ___ ___ ___   _A_ ___ _D_
12  20  6     22 3 6 21 12 6 3       12  20  6     25  9   6   6   10  20      21  15  7

      _A_ ___ ___ G__ ___ _A_ G__ ___   ___ ___ ___ _D_ ___  .
      19  21  15  22  8   21  22  6      15  6   6   7   25
```

Unscramble the tiles to reveal a message.

N C E	.	E N T I	W I T H	O R T A	T I E S
S O F	E A R L	F O R	V I D U	I N D I	O N I
E R E	D I S A	Y I N	B I L I	I M P	A L S
S E V	K E Y	T E R V			

(empty grid)

Unscramble each of the clue words. Copy the letters in the numbered cells to other cells with the same number.

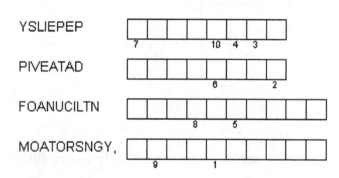

YSLIEPEP   □□□□□□□□□
                7   10 4 3

PIVEATAD   □□□□□□□□
                      6   2

FOANUCILTN   □□□□□□□□□□
                    8   5

MOATORSNGY,   □□□□□□□□□□□
                  9   1

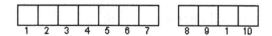

□□□□□□□   □□□□
1 2 3 4 5 6 7   8 9 1 10

Crossword Puzzle

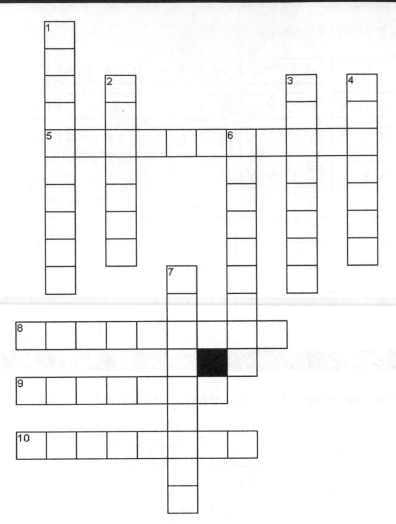

Across

5. Primary condition of most people with severe/multiple disabilities
8. Poor muscle tone
9. Type of care that allows family members recreation time away from individual with disabilities
10. Personal independence and social interaction skills

Down

1. Tube feeding through stomach
2. Setting in which most skills should be taught
3. Brief disturbances in the normal electrical functions of the brain
4. Type of testing that searches for genes that are predisposed to disease
6. Constant, contorted twisting motions in the wrists and fingers
7. Study of medical ethics

Bart is a 10-year old boy with severe cerebral palsy and mental retardation. Bart's disabilities are the result of trauma during birth. Today, Bart uses a wheelchair, is able to point to pictures on the table top of his wheelchair to communicate, and is fed through a gastro-intestinal tube because of swallowing difficulties. His significant physical limitations are accompanied by severe mental retardation. Bart's curriculum focuses on developing basic living skills such as identifying shapes, colors, and numbers; identifying money and using money to make purchases; telling time, etc. He works on these skills in the special education classroom, but also goes to the 4th grade classroom during art and social studies. In addition, he goes to recess and lunch with the 4th grade class and considers it his homeroom.

Bart is a very happy young man. He enjoys country music and likes to listen to his favorite CD when he is receiving physical therapy each day. Bart also receives speech-language therapy to help him develop more vocabulary. The speech-language therapist is also working with Bart to see if he might be able to use a computer synthesizer one day to communicate.

1. What environmental, social, and instructional challenges would Bart face in school? _____
_____
_____
_____
_____

2. What environmental changes would be needed to support Bart's participation in the classroom? _____
_____
_____
_____
_____

3. What social and instructional modifications would be needed to support Bart's participation in the classroom? _____
_____
_____
_____
_____

1. Arrange with local school to observe in a special education classroom that serves children with severe multiple disabilities. While observing in the classroom think about the following questions: What are some of the student's characteristics? How does the teacher address those differences? How successful is the child in this environment? _____

_____

_____

_____

2. Arrange with local school to observe in a general education classroom that has a child or children with severe multiple disabilities. While observing in the classroom think about the following questions: What are some of his/her characteristics? How does the general education teacher address those differences?   How successful is the child in this environment? _____

_____

_____

_____

3. Observe the child with the severe multiple disabilities in settings other than the classroom, such as in the cafeteria or during art, physical education, and music. How does the child compare to his/her peers in terms of social interaction, class participation and attention? _____

_____

_____

_____

Resources

Books
Backyards and Butterflies: Ways to Include Children with Disabilities in Outdoor Activities by Doreen Greenstein. Published by Brookline Books.
Including Students With Severe and Multiple Disabilities in Typical Classrooms: Practical Strategies for Teachers by June E. Downing, Joanne Eichinger, & Maryann Demchak. Published by Paul H. Brookes.

Videos
Ready to Live. Available through Films for the Humanities & Sciences.
Without Barriers or Borders. Available through Films for the Humanities & Sciences.

Websites
The Ragged Edge Magazine: www.ragged-edge-mag.com.
ABLEDATA – Assistive Technology: www.abledata.com.
I Can!: www.ican.com

Preview

Autism was first recognized as a disability in 1990 by IDEA (Individuals with Disabilities Education Act). Autism is considered one of the most disruptive of all childhood diseases with most cases becoming evident before age 2½ to 3 and diagnosis usually occurring before age 5. More males than females are diagnosed with autism. Its prevalence is estimated by the American Psychological Association to be about 5 cases in 10,000.

Four areas of functional challenge often found in children with autism include language, interpersonal skills, emotional or affective behaviors, and intellectual functioning. In addition to discussion in this chapter relevant to these four areas, information will be presented regarding six characteristics commonly associated with the condition of autism. Additionally, causal factors and four treatment approaches commonly used will be presented. A final component will address the impact a child with autism has on his or her family.

Concept Reflection

A. What did I know about autism before reading this chapter?	B. How did reading the chapter enhance or change what I already knew? (Relate this to Column A.)	C. What new information did I learn? (This may or may not be associated with your responses in A or B.)
1.	1.	1.
2.	2.	2.
3.	3.	3.
4.	4.	4.
5.	5.	5.

Keep the following questions in mind as you read this chapter.

13.1 Identify four areas of functional challenge often found in children with autism.
A.
B.
C.
D.
13.2 What is the general prevalence estimated for autism?
A.
13.3 Identify six characteristics of children with autism.
A.
B.
C.
D.
E.
F.
13.4 Identify the two broad theoretical views regarding the causes of autism.
A.
B.
13.5 Identify four major approaches to the treatment of autism.
A.
B.
C.
D.

Guided Review

Read – Matching Vocabulary

Following are a number of the key terms and concepts used in this chapter. Try to complete this matching exercise before you read the chapter. Match each term with the phrase that you think most closely describes or defines it.

A. Vermis
B. Cues
C. Asperger's syndrome
D. Psychodynamic

E. Alcohol
F. LSD
G. Echolalia
H. Language

13.6 _____ A repetition or imitation of words that have been spoken
13.7 _____ Structured verbal and visual _____ are being used to facilitate smoother transitions from one activity to another.
13.8 _____ Two theories about the causes of autism include biological and _____.
13.9 _____ Part of the cerebellum that may be related to cognitive malfunctions found in autism.
13.10 _____ _____ abuse has been associated with autism.
13.11 _____ Medication once used with individuals with autism that is now regarded as highly controversial.
13.12 _____ A condition that has certain features of unusual social interactions and behaviors associated with autism but typically no general language delay.
13.13 _____ Functional challenges often found in children with autism include interpersonal skills, emotional behaviors, intellectual functioning, and _____.

Reflect – Matching Vocabulary

This exercise is intended to provide practice in recalling what you have just read. Try not to refer back to the chapter as you match the following items with their descriptions below. As you work through this exercise, consider how this new information relates to other knowledge, concepts, and/or principles you learned before taking this course.

A. Least
B. Independence
C. Splinter skills
D. Autism

E. Fragile X
F. Flat
G. Psychodynamic
H. Observation

13.14 _____ Areas of ability in which performance levels are unexpectedly high compared to those of other domains of functioning.
13.15 _____ A suspected cause of autism because it does damage to the chromosomal structure.
13.16 _____ In most cases, the ultimate goal is to prepare individuals with autism to live in their home community and in the _____ restrictive environment.
13.17 _____ IEPs must focus on individual strengths and skills required for maximum _____.

13.18 _____ Presumably faulty relationship between the child and his/her parents.

13.19 _____ Behavior management for individuals with autism requires a statement of precise operational definition, _____, and recording of data on behaviors.

13.20 _____ Children who are diagnosed with serious emotional disturbance cannot be diagnosed with _____.

13.21 _____ The tonal quality of speech in students with autism is often _____.

Recite – Fill in the Blank

Supply a word/phrase in each sentence in order to make sense out of the statement of a concept, definition, or principle that is otherwise incomplete or lacks closure. Several answers, other than those listed in the key, may be acceptable for an item. Focus on whether or not your answer is equivalent to the answer supplied and be prepared to explain why you completed the statement(s) as you did.

13.22 Though autism is regarded as a low-incidence disability, the American Psychiatric Association estimates the prevalence of autism as about _____ cases in 10,000.

13.23 Echolalic behavior is sometimes misinterpreted as an indicator of _____ intellectual abilities.

13.24 Self-injurious behavior is most commonly found in students who are _____-functioning.

13.25 Children with autism seem to have more frequent _____ problems.

13.26 Community integration for children with autism has been effectively facilitated through _____ intervention.

13.27 A procedure that emphasizes typed communication through the use of a facilitator is known as _____ _____.

13.28 Autism was first recognized as a disability _____ category in the IDEA in 1990.

13.29 In the movie *Rain Man*, the individual with autism demonstrated narrow islands of high performance, sometimes referred to as _____-_____ characteristics.

Review – True/False

Please indicate whether the statements are true (T) or false (F) by circling the corresponding letter. You should be able to briefly describe the rationale for your answer.

T F 13.30 Autism is never diagnosed after age 3.

T F 13.31 More males than females are diagnosed with autism.

T F 13.32 One thing that makes it easier to teach students with autism is that they all have the same educational, communication, and social needs.

T F 13.33 Research has shown conclusive results that the primary cause of autism is vaccinations for measles, mumps, and rubella given at one time.

T F 13.34 The research literature supports early intervention as an important element in promoting growth for children with autism.

T F 13.35 It is vital that IEPs have a central component of communication and social skills.

T	F	13.36	Electroconvulsive shock has recently been shown to be effective in treating autism.
T	F	13.37	Speech therapy combined with medications has been shown to be the most effective method for treating autism.

Chapter Review – Practice Test

In the following activity, select the most appropriate of the four answers provided for each item. Try to do this without looking at your text in order to get an idea of your comprehension level.

13.38 Autism is a childhood disorder that is generally evident prior to _____ months.
   A. 6
   B. 12
   C. 24
   D. 36

13.39 Autism is characterized it as a "_____disability significantly affecting verbal and nonverbal communication and social interaction."
   A. communication
   B. social
   C. emotional
   D. developmental

13.40 Which of the following characteristics may suggest to parents that their child has autism?
   A. Intense need for physical contact
   B. Extreme staring at others
   C. Unresponsive when held
   D. Excessive random crying

13.41 Often children with autism who develop language have a limited speaking repertoire and they fail to use _____ when speaking directly to another person.
   A. adjectives
   B. pronouns
   C. verbs
   D. nouns

13.42 An activity/behavior that is self-satisfying is
   A. self-stimulation.
   B. echolalia.
   C. perseveration.
   D. facilitated communication.

13.43 Echolalia refers to speech patterns in which the youngster
   A. repeats back only what has been said to him/her.
   B. responds to questions which have been repeated several times.
   C. responds to individuals seen often.
   D. emotionally echoes words in a high-pitched voice.

13.44 About _____ of children with autism have measured IQs below 70.
   A. 20%
   B. 35%
   C. 60%
   D. 75%

13.45 Approximately _____ of those identified with autism exhibit splinter skills.
   A. 10 to 15%
   B. 10 to 25%
   C. 25 to 50%
   D. 25 to 80%

13.46 Individuals with autism often experience difficulty interacting with teachers and other students because of their inability to understand
   A. eye contact.
   B. social cues.
   C. large words.
   D. picture communication cards.

13.47 The abilities of students with autism may be described as
   A. uneven within and between skill areas.
   B. Consistent.
   C. focused on generalization of concepts.
   D. relying on changes in routine.

13.48 Inclusion options may be limited for some students with autism due to all but
   A. stereotypic self-stimulation.
   B. resistance to change.
   C. advanced socialization skills.
   D. communication responses.

13.49 Many high-functioning students with autism who have some language interpret speech literally; therefore, it is important for teachers to avoid
   A. telling or reading fairy tales.
   B. expressing strong emotions.
   C. ethnic jokes.
   D. slang, idioms, and sarcasm.

13.50 When an individual with autism demonstrates *resistance to change* he
   A. enjoys selecting different clothes for each activity.
   B. is bothered by loose change in his pocket.
   C. enjoys transitioning from one activity to another.
   D. prefers familiar routines.

13.51 A "safe place" and a "safe person" are important for a child with autism to be able to identify
    A. in case of dangerous weather.
    B. in case the child becomes confused or upset.
    C. in case there is a stranger in the school.
    D. in case the child encounters a change in routine.

13.52 An approach that focuses on enhancing appropriate behaviors and decreasing inappropriate behaviors is known as a
    A. educational intervention.
    B. medical intervention.
    C. behavioral intervention.
    D. psychodynamic intervention.

13.53 Facilitated communication is not identified as a legitimate strategy because
    A. researchers have not been able to obtain results supporting its effectiveness.
    B. it reveals too much about the home life of students with autism.
    C. it is regarded as an invasion of privacy.
    D. it interferes with behavior interventions.

13.54 Living with a child with autism challenges the family in all but which way?
    A. Strained relationships
    B. Food selection
    C. Social isolation
    D. Fatigue

13.55 Four major approaches to the treatment of autism include psychological interventions, behavioral interventions, educational interventions, and _____ interventions.
    A. sibling
    B. physical
    C. medical
    D. parental

13.56 This disorder includes a range of functioning in the multiple skill areas of communication and language, intelligence and social interaction.
    A. Emotional disturbance
    B. Asperger's syndrome
    C. Fragile X
    D. Autism Spectrum Disorder

13.57 The wide variation in the prevalence of autism may change over time as
    A. a greater consensus is achieved about what constitutes autism.
    B. less vaccines are given to infants.
    C. more teachers become better prepared to teach students with autism.
    D. data is more accurately gathered and analyzed.

A	B	C	D	E	F	G	H	I	J	K	L	M	N	O	P	Q	R	S	T	U	V	W	X	Y	Z
	17						6	21			20			15	25		8	2	22						

```
 T  _  O    B  R  O  _  _      T  H  _  O  R  T  I  _  _  L      _  _  _  _  S
22  1 15   17  8 15 10 18     22  6 13 15  8 13 22 21  7 10 20  16 21 13  1  2

 R  _  R  I  _  _  _  _      T  H      _  _  S  S  O      _  _      _  _  T  I  S  _
 8 13 12 10  8 18 21  5 12  22  6 13   7 10  9  2 13  2  15 14    10  9 22 21  2  4

 I  _  _  L  _  _  _      P  S  _  _  _  H  O  _  _  L  _  T  I  _  L
21  5  7 20  9 18 13     25  2 26  7  6 15 10  5 10 20 26 22 21  7 10 20

 _  _  _      B  I  O  L  O  _  I  _  _  L
10  5 18     17 21 15 20 15 12 21  7 10 20
```

Unscramble the tiles to reveal a message.

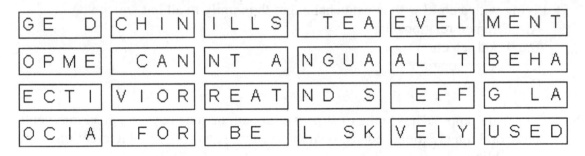

GE D	CHIN	ILLS	TEA	EVEL	MENT
OPME	CAN	NT A	NGUA	AL T	BEHA
ECTI	VIOR	REAT	ND S	EFF	G LA
OCIA	FOR	BE	L SK	VELY	USED

Unscramble each of the clue words. Copy the letters in the numbered cells to other cells with the same number.

CILDEAM

□□□□□□
4 13   11

CULDEONAAIT

□□□□□□□□□□
19 2   15 6

CYCTAYHAPLOLNISL

□□□□□□□□□□□□□□□□
8 14   12 9 7 20   16   5

VIERAAHOBL

□□□□□□□□□□
17 10   1 3 18

F□□□ □□J□□ □□□□□□□□□□□□ □□ □□□□□□□□□□
1 2 3 4 5 6 3 7 8 8 3 9 10 11 12 13 14 15 1 16 3 17 18 15 4 19 20 15

Across
4. Applying learned concepts from one situation to another
6. Tonal quality of speech in students with autism
8. Number of cases identified
9. A form of autism that does not include language delays

Down
1. Change from one activity to another
2. Legislation that ensures education for children with disabilities
3. _____ impairment – extreme difficulty relating to others
5. _____ goal is to live in the least restrictive environment in home community
7. _____ contact – a skill many people with autism lack

Michael is 10 years old with high functioning autism. He has below average intellectual ability and limited language skills. Intelligence testing showed that his intellectual functioning is in the mental retardation range. He uses multiple means of communication, including about 50 spoken words, 10 ASL signs, and a few written words. Michael's academic skills are below his grade placement, particularly in reading. His math skills are on level and he is able to understand most concepts, particularly when they are presented using visual demonstrations and manipulatives. His reading skills are at the emergent level with Michael now able to read a primer and identify key characters in the story. His written language skills are also below grade level but are showing improvement, particularly when he is given fill-in-the blank tasks.

Michael is currently placed in a 3rd grade class and receives 2 hours of special education daily and weekly speech/language services. In the 3rd grade class Michael is given a modified curriculum and goes to the special education classroom to work on reading and social skills. In speech/language, he works on building vocabulary and responding to questions.

Michael is a well-behaved and gentle young man. His classmates are very kind to him and see him as part of their class. They go out of their way to include Michael in class activities and projects. While he does not initiate conversations or interactions directly he does respond well and positively to his peers' social interactions and has benefited from the inclusive placement.

1. What would be the benefits of Michael's placement in the general classroom rather than a full-time special education assignment?_____

_____

_____

_____

2. Based on the information above, what kinds of instructional modifications would Michael need to succeed in the 3rd grade class?_____

_____

_____

_____

3. What unique challenges would the teacher have with Michael in his class?_____

_____

_____

_____

4. What might be an instructional priority for Michael? What should be taught first to him?

_____

_____

_____

1. Attend a special education advocacy group event. This may be hosted by a group such as PTA (www.pta.org), the Autism Society of America (autism-society.org), or the State Department of Education. While you are at the meeting, pay particular attention to issues related to the parenting challenges, working with school and other education professionals to design appropriate educational experiences, and efforts parents must make to integrate their child in the community.

2. Visit a classroom for children with autism. Contact the special education director of a local school district or the principal of a neighborhood school to schedule an appointment. During your visit in the classroom watch for how:
   A. the students respond to a visitor in the classroom,
   B. the teacher addresses the need for routines and predictability for the students,
   C. the teacher manages student behavior,
   D. the children interact with one another, and
   E. the curriculum and instruction compares in this classroom to that in the general education classroom.

3. Interview a special education teacher who serves children with autism. Ask the teacher to identify:
   A. what instructional resources she/he uses to teach students with autism,
   B. what professional development activities/classes that have been most effective in acquiring the skills needed for teaching children with autism, and
   C. how the teacher collaborates with the parent/guardians and other interested persons in providing a comprehensive educational experience for the child.

Books
Children with Autism: A Parent's Guide (2nd Ed.) by M. D. Powers. Available through Woodbine House
Educating Children and Youth with Autism: Strategies for Effective Practice by R. L. Simpson and B. S. Myles. Published by PRO-ED.
Thinking in Pictures and Other Reports From My Life by T. Grandin. Published by Doubleday.

Videos
Asperger's Syndrome: Diagnosis and Support by T. Attwood. Available through www.amazon.com..
Breaking the Silence Barrier (1996) by Thirteen/WNET. Available through Films for the Humanities and Sciences at 1-800-257-5126 or http://www.films.com.
Social Stories and Comic-Strip Conversations: Unique Methods to Improve Social Understanding by C. Gray. Available through www.amazon.com.

Websites
Autism Research Institute: www.autism.com/ari/main.html
Division TEACCH: Treatment and Education of Autistic and Related Communication
Handicapped Children: www.teacch.com/mainpage.htm
Online Asperger Syndrome Information and Support O.A.S.I.S: www.udel.edu/bkerby/asperger
Tony Attwood's website: www.tonyattwood.com.au/introduction.html
Yale Child Study Center: Developmental Disabilities Clinic: info.med.yale.edu

Traumatic Brain Injury

This chapter begins with medical and educational definitions (IDEA) of traumatic brain injury (TBI) and an explanation of acquired brain injury (ABI). The prevalence of these conditions is then reported.

The most salient characteristics of individuals with TBI are presented along with the various types of educational supports and services for people with traumatic brain injury or acquired brain injury. The chapter also provides an explanation of medical and psychological services available to individuals with TBI.

Concept Reflection

A. What did I know about Traumatic Brain Injury (TBI) before reading this chapter?	B. How did reading the chapter enhance or change what I already knew? (Relate this to Column A.)	C. What new information did I learn? (This may or may not be associated with your responses in A or B.)
1.	1.	1.
2.	2.	2.
3.	3.	3.
4.	4.	4.
5.	5.	5.

Keep the following questions in mind as you read this chapter.

| **14.1   Identify three key elements of traumatic brain injury.** |
| A. |
| B. |
| C. |

| **14.2   Identify four general characteristics of individuals with traumatic or acquired brain injury.** |
| A. |
| B. |
| C. |
| D. |

| **14.3   Identify the most common causes of brain injury in children, youth, and adults.** |
| A. |
| B. |
| C. |

| **14.4   Describe the focus of educational interventions for individuals with traumatic or acquired brain injuries.** |
| A. |
| B. |
| C. |

| **14.5   Identify four common types of head injuries.** |
| A. |
| B. |
| C. |
| D. |

14.6 Describe five important elements of medical treatment for individuals with traumatic or acquired brain injuries.
A.
B.
C.
D.
E.

Read – Matching Vocabulary

Following are a number of the key terms and concepts used in this chapter. Try to complete this matching exercise before you read the chapter. Match each term with the phrase that you think most closely describes or defines it.

A. Concussion

B. Skull fracture

C. Computed tomography (CT)

D. Contusion

E. Epidural hematoma

F. Magnetic resonance imaging (MRI)

14.7 _____ An imaging technique in which computers create cross-sectional images of specific body areas or organs.

14.8 _____ Impaired brain functioning derived from brutal shaking, violent blows, or other serious impacts to the head.

14.9 _____ Collection of blood between the skull and covering of the brain which puts pressure on vital brain structures.

14.10 _____ Break, crack, or split of the skull resulting from a violent blow or other serious impact to the head.

14.11 _____ A technique of x-ray imaging by which computers create cross-sectional images of specific body areas of organs.

14.12 _____ The brain is bruised as a result of a severe hit or blow.

This exercise is intended to provide practice in recalling what you have just read. Try not to refer back to the chapter as you match the following items with their descriptions below. As you work through this exercise, consider how this new information relates to other knowledge, concepts, and/or principles you learned before taking this course.

A. Aphasia   E. Expressive aphasia
B. Reducing   F Prevent
C. Neuromotor   G. Coma
D. Judgment   H. Concentrate

_____

14.13 _____ An acquired language disorder caused by brain damage that is characterized by complete or partial impairment of language comprehension, formulation, and use.

14.14 _____ An inability to verbally express one's own thoughts and desires.

14.15 _____ Helmets, seat belts, and child restraints could _____ many TBI accidents.

14.16 _____ Reduced stamina and impaired balance represent _____ problems.

14.17 _____ Following a TBI, it may be difficult to ____.

14.18 _____ _____ may be impaired due to a TBI.

14.19 _____ The first signs of brain injury often manifest themselves in a _____.

14.20 _____ Appropriate teaching of a child with TBI includes _____ antecedents that elicit challenging behaviors.

Supply a word/phrase in each sentence in order to make sense out of the statement of a concept, definition, or principle that is otherwise incomplete or lacks closure. Several answers, other than those listed in the key, may be acceptable for an item. Focus on whether or not your answer is equivalent to the answer supplied and be prepared to explain why you completed the statement(s) as you did.

14.21 _____ Tearing of nerve fibers, bruising of brain tissue against the skull, brain stem trauma, and swelling can result in _____ _____ _____.

14.22 _____ Epidural and subdural hematomas both have to do with the collection of _____.

14.23 _____ Concentration problems, slowed information processing, vision problems, memory loss, headaches, and _____ are just a few of the potential problems associated with TBI.

14.24 _____ Generally, individuals with TBI need services and supports in (1) social and behavioral skills, (2) physical functioning, (3) speech and language, and (4)_____.

170

Please indicate whether the statements are true (T) or false (F) by circling the corresponding letter. You should be able to briefly describe the rationale for your answer.

T	F	14.25	Life-long disabilities result from TBI for approximately 2% to 5% of the children involved.
T	F	14.26	Individuals with traumatic brain injury often know an answer but are unable to express it.
T	F	14.27	Insensitivity to others and low thresholds for inconvenience are common behavior characteristics of individuals with TBI.
T	F	14.28	IDEA's definition of TBI includes congenital brain injuries induced by birth trauma.
T	F	14.29	Memory loss is a common symptom in people with TBI.
T	F	14.30	Whiplash can cause TBI.
T	F	14.31	Social behaviors are rarely impacted by TBI.
T	F	14.32	TBI is the second most common cause of acquired disabilities.

Chapter Review – Practice Test

In the following activity, select the most appropriate of the four answers provided for each item. Try to do this without looking at your text in order to get an idea of your comprehension level.

14.33 A collection of blood between the covering of the brain and the brain itself that results in pressure on vital brain structures is known as
   A. an arterial wall.
   B. a venal network.
   C. an epidural hematoma.
   D. a subdural hematoma.

14.34 Anoxic injuries, strokes, and severe blood loss can result in
   A. intracranial pressure.
   B. magnetic resonance imaging (MRI).
   C. acquired brain injury (ABI).
   D. epidural hematoma.

14.35 An estimated _____ million Americans live with disabilities from TBI.
   A. 5.3
   B. 4.7
   C. 3.1
   D. 1.2

14.36 Rapid acceleration or deceleration of the brain may cause tearing of nerve fibers in the brain which can result in
A. seizures.
B. headaches.
C. vision problems.
D. All of the above.

14.37 Damage that develops over time as the brain responds to the original trauma is
A. acquired brain damage.
B. primary brain damage.
C. secondary brain damage.
D. delayed brain damage.

14.38 According to IDEA's definition of TBI, a student
A. can have brain damage and not necessarily receive special services.
B. must have primary and secondary brain damage in order to receive services.
C. with TBI must demonstrate that it is adversely affecting his/her education.
D. must be able to demonstrate abilities from before the brain damage.

14.39 The definition of acquired brain injury (ABI) does not include
A. strokes and other vascular accidents.
B. brain injuries induced by birth trauma.
C. encephalitis and meningitis.
D. toxic products ingested or inhaled into the body.

14.40 Approximately _____ of all head injuries that occur involve children.
A. 20%
B. 30%
C. 40%
D. 50%

14.41 Reasons TBIs increase in individuals between the ages of 15 and 24 include all but which of the following?
A. Greater use of automobiles
B. Increased hormonal changes
C. More use of mountain bikes
D. Exposure to firearms

14.42 TBI incidences increase in individuals
A. below 5, between 15 and 24, and over 70 years of age.
B. below 1, between 15 and 24, and over 84 years of age.
C. between 15 and 24, between 50 and 62, and over 78 years of age.
D. between 15 and 24 and over 70 years of age.

14.43 Half of those who die from TBI do so within the first _____ hours following the accident/insult to the brain.
   A. 2
   B. 4
   C. 12
   D. 24

14.44 _____ account for more traumatic brain injuries for all ages than any other.
   A. Drugs
   B. Sports
   C. Automobiles
   D. Strokes

14.45 Your text states that the eventual outcomes of a trauma to the brain are a function of
   A. the location and degree of the injury.
   B. the size of the brain in relation to the skull.
   C. the mental state of the individual following the incident.
   D. the reaction and support of the family members to the incident.

14.46 In returning the child with TBI to school, educational supports must focus on
   A. writing an IEP that includes physical activity specific to the child's needs.
   B. environmental changes and critical transition issues.
   C. educating the families as to what they can expect from the transition.
   D. securing an educational specialist in the area of TBI.

14.47 When a child with TBI returns to school, priorities for the teacher must include all but
   A. language and writing skills.
   B. general behavior skills.
   C. social skills.
   D. teacher reactions.

14.48 Individuals with TBI usually experience the most gain during
   A. the first six to eight weeks following the incident.
   B. the first six months following the incident.
   C. the first year following the incident.
   D. the first two years following the incident.

14.49 The IEP of a student returning to school with TBI should be reviewed
   A. annually.
   B. every six months.
   C. every few weeks, initially.
   D. each week, initially.

14.50 The most common causes for brain injury in high school students is/are
   A.   automobiles and sports-related injuries.
   B.   drugs.
   C.   physical abuse.
   D.   pedestrian accidents.

14.51 Critical factors for those with TBI who move on to postsecondary education include
   A.   social and personal support systems.
   B.   career/vocational training and placement.
   C.   living arrangements.
   D.   All of the above.

14.52 Universal use of bicycle helmets could prevent
   A.   four deaths and one brain injury every day.
   B.   two deaths every day and four brain injuries every two minutes.
   C.   one death every day and two brain injuries every four minutes.
   D.   one death every day and one brain injury every four minutes.

Cryptogram

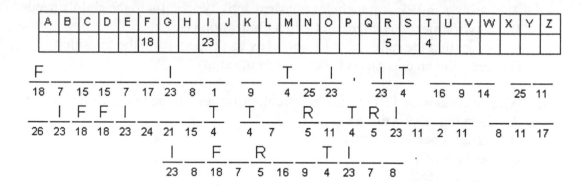

Unscramble the tiles to reveal a message.

I N J U	I O R S	Q U E N	A L B	A R E	T L Y
F R E	S O C I	R Y .	C T E D	M A T I	E H A V
T R A U	C B R	A I N	I M P A	B Y

<table>
<tr><td></td><td></td><td></td><td></td><td></td><td></td></tr>
<tr><td></td><td></td><td></td><td></td><td></td><td></td></tr>
<tr><td></td><td></td><td></td><td></td><td></td></tr>
</table>

Double Puzzle

Unscramble each of the clue words. Copy the letters in the numbered cells to other cells with the same number.

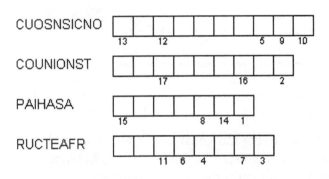

CUOSNSICNO ⬚⬚⬚⬚⬚⬚⬚⬚⬚⬚
            13 12   5 9 10

COUNIONST   ⬚⬚⬚⬚⬚⬚⬚⬚⬚
               17   16 2

PAIHASA   ⬚⬚⬚⬚⬚⬚⬚
            15   8 14 1

RUCTEAFR   ⬚⬚⬚⬚⬚⬚⬚⬚
            11 6 4   7 3

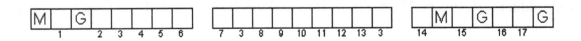

M		G			
1	2	3	4	5	6

7	3	8	9	10	11	12	13	3

M		G			G
14	15	16	17

Crossword Puzzle

Across

2. Acquired language impairment relevant to comprehension, formulation, and use
7. _____ problems are representative of reduced stamina and impaired balance
8. One of the first signs of brain injury often manifested in this manner
9. Type of aphasia in which there is an inability to verbally express one's own thoughts
10. Epidural and subdural hematomas have to do with collection of this substance

Down

1. Split of the skull due to a violent blow to the head
3. Item that could prevent many TBI accidents
4. Bruising of the brain as a result of a severe blow
5. May be impaired due to a TBI
6. Impaired brain functioning derived from brutal shaking

Case Study

Angela was a typical 2nd grade student before she fell from her bicycle and struck her forehead on the pavement. Her standardized achievement test scores placed her in the 65th percentile in academics. Her teacher, Mr. Paul described her as an able student with a sharp memory and a particular fondness for memorizing and reciting children's poems and songs for her classmates. Socially, Angela was outgoing and exubcrant. She was funny and well-liked.

The accident affected Angela cognitively and emotionally. Her thought processes have been altered in many ways, impairing her ability to solve logical problems, handle directions involving sequences, and reason through complex situations. Her concentration has weakened dramatically, limiting her to short 10-minute bursts of focused attention on a given task. Her academic skills diminished considerably; Angela's reading comprehension has slipped to a mid-first grade level, while her decoding skills have remained high second grade. Her ability to accurately perform basic arithmetic operations like addition and subtraction has remained, but her capabilities in figuring word problems or in following a sequence of operations have been reduced significantly.

In addition, Angela is frustrated and critical of herself. She has a strong awareness of her sudden loss of ability and this has caused much anger. Angela suffers from depression, often crying for long periods. She is irritable and angry to her parents and peers. Her overall temperament has changed from happy and playful to gloomy and angry.

1. Based on the information provided about Angela, what challenges does she face in a classroom? _____
_____
_____
_____

2. What environmental and instructional strategies would provide Angela with supports that would improve her academic functioning? _____
_____
_____
_____

3. What could the teacher do to address Angela's social/behavioral concerns? _____
_____
_____
_____

1. Arrange with local school to observe in a special education classroom that serves children with traumatic brain injury. While observing in the classroom, think about the following questions: What are some of the student's characteristics? How does the teacher address those differences? How successful is the child in this environment? _____

_____

_____

_____

2. Arrange with local school to observe in a general education classroom that has a child or children with traumatic brain injury. While observing in the classroom, think about the following questions: What are some of his/her characteristics? How does the general education teacher address those differences? How successful is the child in this environment? _____

_____

_____

_____

3. Observe the child with the traumatic brain injury in settings other than the classroom, such as in the cafeteria or during art, physical education, and music. How does the child compare to his/her peers in terms of social interaction, class participation and attention? _____

_____

_____

_____

_____

Resources

Books
Children with Traumatic Brain Injury: A Parent's Guide by Lisa Schoenbrodt. Published byWoodbine House.
Over My Head by Claudia L. Osborn. Published by Andrews McMeel Publishing
Brain Repair by Donald G. Stein, Simon Brailowsky & Bruno Will. Published by Oxford Press.

Videos
Regarding Henry. Produced by Paramount Studios.

Websites
The Brain Injury Association of Washington: www.biawa.org
The Perspectives Network: www.tbi.org
Traumatic Brain Injury Resource Guide: www.neuroskills.com

This chapter covers characteristics, causes, and assessment and intervention strategies for individuals with hearing loss. The authors supply definitions and classifications of hearing loss, along with statistics associated with the prevalence of hearing impairments. The hearing process is described, including details of the outer, middle, and inner ear.

The authors explain general characteristics of people with hearing loss: intelligence, speech and language skills, educational achievement, and social development. Because they experience difficulty in learning speech and language, people with severe hearing loss must overcome many barriers in order to communicate with the hearing world. Adjustment to the hearing world, and the deaf culture, are also discussed.

The causes of hearing loss are examined and explained under two general classification approaches: (1) congenital or acquired and (2) central or peripheral. Peripheral hearing loss, the most common, is further classified into conductive, sensorineural, or mixed hearing loss.

Common approaches to teaching communication skills are explained, and a rationale for each approach is presented. The chapter also describes the professionals involved in assessment and intervention, and it explains the services of the medical, social, and educational fields.

Concept Reflection

A. What did I know about hearing loss before reading this chapter?	B. How did reading the chapter enhance or change what I already knew? (Relate this to Column A.)	C. What new information did I learn? (This may or may not be associated with your responses in A or B.)
1.	1.	1.
2.	2.	2.
3.	3.	3.
4.	4.	4.

Keep the following questions in mind as you read this chapter.

15.1 Describe how sound is transmitted through the human ear.

A.

B.

C.

D.

15.2 Distinguish between the terms *deaf* and *hard of hearing*.

A.

B.

C.

15.3 Why is it important to consider age of onset and anatomical site when defining a hearing loss?

A.

B.

C.

15.4 What are the estimated prevalence and causes of hearing loss?

A.

B.

C.

D.

E.

F.

G.

15.5	Describe the basic intelligence, speech and language skills, educational achievement, and social development associated with people who are deaf or hard of hearing.
A.	
B.	
C.	
D.	
E.	

15.6	Identify four approaches to teaching communication skills to persons with a hearing loss.
A.	
B.	
C.	
D.	

15.7	Describe the uses of closed-caption television, computers, and the Internet for people with a hearing loss.
A.	
B.	
C.	
D.	

15.8	Why is the early detection of a hearing loss so important?
A.	

15.9	Distinguish between an otologist and an audiologist.
A.	
B.	
C.	

15.10	**Identify factors that may affect the social inclusion of people who are deaf in the hearing world.**
A.	
B.	

Guided Review

Read – Matching Vocabulary

Following are a number of the key terms and concepts used in this chapter. Try to complete this matching exercise before you read the chapter. Match each term with the phrase that you think most closely describes or defines it.

A.	Eustachian	E.	Hertz
B.	Ossicular chain	F.	Otologist
C.	Atresia	G.	Tinnitus
D.	Audition	H.	Otosclerosis

15.11 _____ A tube that extends from the throat to the middle-ear cavity and controls air flow into the cavity.

15.12 _____ A unit that measures the frequency of sound in terms of the number of cycles that vibrating molecules complete per second.

15.13 _____ A disease of the inner ear that results in high-pitched throbbing or ringing sounds in the ear.

15.14 _____ A disease of the ear characterized by destruction of the capsular bone in the middle ear and the growth of a weblike bone that attaches to the stapes.

15.15 _____ The malleus, incus, and stapes bones that transmit vibrations through the middle-ear cavity to the inner-ear.

15.16 _____ The absence or malformation of the external auditory canal.

15.17 _____ The act or sense of hearing.

15.18 _____ A person who is involved in the study of the ear.

This exercise is intended to provide practice in recalling what you have just read. Try not to refer back to the chapter as you match the following items with their descriptions below. As you work through this exercise, consider how this new information relates to other knowledge, concepts, and/or principles you learned before taking this course.

A. Deaf
B. Pinna
C. Audiogram
D. Bicultural-bilingual

E. Meatus
F. Tympanic
G. Audiologist
H. Vestibular

15.19 _____ A culture in which people are bonded through the commonality of language, customs, and heritage.
15.20 _____ A cartilage structure on the side of the head whose function is to collect sounds.
15.21 _____ The concave membrane that vibrates freely when struck by sound waves.
15.22 _____ When ASL is provided as the primary language and English as the second, it is known as the _____ approach.
15.23 _____ A record obtained from an audiometer that graphs the levels of sound a person is able to hear in each ear.
15.24 _____ The outer ear canal whose function is to secrete cerumen.
15.25 _____ A specialist in the assessment of a person's hearing ability.
15.26 _____ The mechanism in the inner ear where balance is controlled.

Supply a word/phrase in each sentence in order to make sense out of the statement of a concept, definition, or principle that is otherwise incomplete or lacks closure. Several answers, other than those listed in the key, may be acceptable for an item. Focus on whether or not your answer is equivalent to the answer supplied and be prepared to explain why you completed the statement(s) as you did.

15.27 A hearing impairment that occurs at any age following speech development is known as a _____ loss.
15.28 In the U.S., the languages used more than American Sign Language are _____ and _____.
15.29 The _____ translates vibrations into nerve impulses that are sent directly to the brain.
15.30 When hearing is so limited that a child is impaired in the processing of linguistic information through hearing, with or without amplification, which adversely affects educational performance, the child is said to be _____.
15.31 Three types of peripheral hearing loss include (1) conductive, (2) sensorineural, and (3)_____.

15.32   Hearing loss _____ with age and is more likely to occur in _____.
15.33   The four approaches to teaching communication skills to students with a hearing loss include (1) auditory, (2) _____, (3) manual, and (4) total communication.
15.34   The four signed systems used in the U.S. include Seeing Essential English, Signing Exact English, Linguistics of Visual English, and _____ _____.

Review – True/False

Please indicate whether the statements are true (T) or false (F) by circling the corresponding letter. You should be able to briefly describe the rationale for your answer.

T   F   15.35   Nearly 17 million people in the U.S. have a significant irreversible hearing loss.
T   F   15.36   A recent study found that people who engage in target shooting have a higher risk for high-frequency hearing loss than those who don't.
T   F   15.37   People in the deaf community do not see hearing loss as a disability.
T   F   15.38   The age of onset of hearing loss is critical in determining the type and extent of interventions indicated.
T   F   15.39   The prevalence of hearing loss decreases as family income and education increase.
T   F   15.40   By 2006, virtually all new TV programming will be captioned.
T   F   15.41   Rubella during pregnancy has dramatically increased.
T   F   15.42   Facial expressions are considered part of sign language.
T   F   15.43   Cued speech is the same as sign language.
T   F   15.44   A rock concert registers at about 110 dB.
T   F   15.45   The range of human hearing is approximately 0 to 40 dB.
T   F   15.46   Most people with a hearing loss use sign language.

Chapter Review – Practice Test

In the following activity, select the most appropriate of the four answers provided for each item. Try to do this without looking at your text in order to get an idea of your comprehension level.

15.47 A hearing loss occurring before the age of two or the time of speech development is a
    A.   postlingual loss.
    B.   prelingual loss.
    C.   sensorineural loss.
    D.   conductive loss.

15.48 In American schools there are more than _____ special education students between the ages of 6 and 21 with hearing impairments.
    A.   71,000
    B.   61,000
    C.   21,000
    D.   11,000

15.49 Which of the following phrases is not accurate?
   A. People with a hearing loss are less satisfied with their life.
   B. People with a hearing loss are underemployed.
   C. People with a hearing loss are less ambitious.
   D. People with a hearing loss are less healthy.

15.50 The purpose of the eustachian tube is to
   A. equalize air pressure on the eardrum.
   B. transmit the vibrations from the external ear to the inner ear.
   C. protect the inner ear.
   D. trap foreign materials before they infect the middle ear.

15.51 Motion and gravity are detected through the
   A. cochlea.
   B. eustachian tube.
   C. spinal fluid.
   D. vestibular mechanism.

15.52 In the U.S. approximately how many are deaf?
   A. 11 million
   B. 8 million
   C. 3 million
   D. 1 million

15.53 Conversational speech registers at
   A. 10 to 30 dB.
   B. 40 to 60 dB.
   C. 70 to 100 dB.
   D. 100 to 120 dB.

15.54 When a person is hard-of-hearing, he/she
   A. can usually hear small children's voices.
   B. can hear the ring of a phone.
   C. can hear with the use of a hearing aid.
   D. can usually qualify for a cochlear implant.

15.55 When determining if a person is deaf or hard-of-hearing, _____ are measured.
   A. loudness, pitch, current age, and educational level
   B. loudness, pitch, age of onset, and anatomical site of the loss
   C. pitch, language disorder, intellectual level, and the age of onset
   D. medical condition, age of onset, and educational level

15.56 When a person can hear sound but manifests problems with auditory perception, comprehension of sounds, and language development, he/she may have a
   A. central auditory problem.
   B. sensorineural hearing problem.
   C. conductive hearing problem.
   D. middle ear problem.

15.57 When a person registers a hearing loss of 40-55 decibels, he/she has
   A. minimal difficulty with soft speech.
   B. frequent difficulty with normal speech.
   C. occasional difficulty with loud speech.
   D. frequent difficulty with loud speech.

15.58 All but which of the following can be said about otitis media?
   A. Otitis media is highly correlated with hearing loss.
   B. Otitis media is an inflammation of the membranes that cover the spinal cord.
   C. Otitis media ranks second to the common cold for preschoolers' health problems.
   D. Otitis media is the most common cause of conductive hearing loss in younger children.

15.59 According to your text, most children with a hearing loss
   A. have lower IQs than their peers who can hear.
   B. have higher IQs in lower grades than they do in higher grades.
   C. have IQs that are basically the same as their peers who can hear.
   D. have higher IQs than their peers who can hear.

15.60 Gallaudet Research indicates that by the time students who are deaf reach 13 years of age, their reading performance is about
   A. two years below that of their peers with normal hearing.
   B. a year above that of their peers with normal hearing.
   C. three to four years above that of their peers with normal hearing.
   D. three to four years below that of their peers with normal hearing.

15.61 American Sign Language (ASL) has the same grammatical structure as
   A. French Sign Language (FSL).
   B. spoken English.
   C. Spanish Sign Language (SSL).
   D. None of the above.

15.62 Which of the following statements is not true?
   A. Hearing individuals are usually not welcomed into the Deaf community.
   B. People who are deaf tend to be animated in their expressions of affections.
   C. Members of the deaf culture are known for their tact during discussions.
   D. The Deaf community expects its children to marry within the Deaf group.

Cryptogram

A	B	C	D	E	F	G	H	I	J	K	L	M	N	O	P	Q	R	S	T	U	V	W	X	Y	Z
			10	21				8			18									19					

D E _ _ _ E _ _ I _ _ _ _ _ E E _ _ _ _
10 21 4 20 22 21 11 11 8 11 22 17 24 11 21 21 22 4 11 4

D I _ _ _ I _ L _ I _ _ _ _ I _ _ I _ _ _ E D E _ _
10 8 11 4 5 8 18 8 24 13 6 8 24 23 8 22 24 23 21 10 21 4 20

_ U _ L _ _ U _ E .
12 19 18 24 19 26 21

Scramble

Unscramble the tiles to reveal a message.

A R I N	M O S T	G L O	P E E R	U A L S	G L O
H H E	T H O U	S S .	A V E	E I R	O T H
I V I D	T H E	V A L E	I Q S	S S H	W I T
I N D	E Q U I	S W I	N T T	A R I N	

Double Puzzle

Unscramble each of the clue words. Copy the letters in the numbered cells to other cells with the same number.

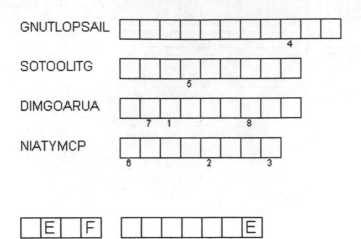

GNUTLOPSAIL

SOTOOLITG

DIMGOARUA

NIATYMCP

Crossword Puzzle

Across

3. Hearing loss greater than 90 dB or greater
4. _____ media is an inflammation of the middle ear
7. Hearing loss occurs after speech acquisition
9. Type of speech that combines hand signals with speechreading
10. Gender in which most hearing losses occur

Down

1. Absence of normal opening
2. Outer ear canal
5. Ringing in the ears
6. Group that is bonded together through traditions and common language
8. Third most commonly used language in the U.S.

Best Practices

Case Study

Joseph was born profoundly deaf. He was identified at 3 months of age, and has been receiving special services since. During his toddler years he received weekly speech-language services. As part of those special services, Joseph received language instruction in American Sign Language (ASL) and lip reading. Joseph's parents also learned ASL so that they could communicate with their son. The family raised Joseph in the same manner that they raised their other hearing children, expecting him to do chores, attend church with the family, and do his best in school.

Joseph is a 4th grader at the State School for the Deaf where he has attended since kindergarten. Joseph is one of the top students in his class, but when compared to hearing peers his achievement is not as good. His reading, writing, and math achievement ranges between the 40th and 50th percentile ranks.

The school uses a total communication approach. Teachers at the State School for the Deaf use visual images and signals to get Joseph and his classmates' attention. For example, when it is time to come in from recess the teacher waves a red flag around until all the children come to her and line up. The teachers make sure that they have students' attention and are facing the students when they give directions or deliver instruction.

1. What are some common learning issues for children like Joseph with severe hearing loss?

_____

_____

2. What instructional strategies are particularly effective when teaching children and youth with hearing loss? _____

_____

_____

3. What is total communication? _____
_____
_____

Community Activities

1. Arrange with local school to observe in a special education classroom that serves children with hearing loss or deafness. While observing the classroom and the interactions that occur, answer the following questions: What are some of the student's characteristics? How does the teacher address those differences? How successful is the child in this environment? _____
_____
_____
_____

2 Arrange with local school to observe in a general education classroom that has a child or children with hearing loss or deafness. While observing the classroom and the interactions that occur, answer the following questions. What are some of his/her learning, social, and behavioral characteristics? How does the general education teacher address those differences? How successful is the child in this environment?_____
_____
_____
_____

3. Observe the child with the hearing loss of deafness in settings other than the classroom, such as in the cafeteria or during art, physical education, and music. How does the child compare to his/her peers in terms of social interaction, class participation, and attention? _____
_____
_____
_____

Resources

Books
A Loss for Words: The Story of Deafness in a Family by Lou Ann Walker. Published by Perennial.
Deaf Like Me by Thomas S. Spradley and James P. Spradley. Published by Gallaudet University Press.

Videos
Children of a Lesser God. Produced by Paramount Studios.
Breaking the Silence: Cochlear Implants. Available from Films for the Humanities and Arts.

Websites
Deafness Research Foundation: www.drf.org
National Institute on Deafness and Other Communication Disorders: www.nidcd.nih.gov

Vision links an individual to the world, helping him or her to gain information beyond the range of other senses and to integrate information acquired through hearing, touch, smell, and taste. The way in which visual stimuli are perceived shapes a person's interaction with and reactions to the environment, and provides a foundation for developing a more complex learning structure.

This chapter defines vision loss from different perspectives. The medical and legal professions base their definitions on visual acuity and field of vision. The education profession focuses on a student's ability to use vision as an avenue for learning. In explaining the characteristics of people with vision loss, six areas are examined: intelligence, speech and language skills, academic achievement, social development, orientation and mobility, and perceptual-motor development.

Educators concern themselves with assessment, placement, mobility training, daily living skills, instructional content, and training in alternative communication media. Medical, social, and educational services are all involved in assessment and intervention strategies. The medical profession focuses on prevention and treatment of impairments; social services promote social adjustment and community participation.

Concept Reflection

A. What did I know about vision loss before reading this chapter?	B. How did reading the chapter enhance or change what I already knew? (Relate this to Column A.)	C. What new information did I learn? (This may or may not be associated with your responses in A or B.)
1.	1.	1.
2.	2.	2.
3.	3.	3.
4.	4.	4.

Keep the following questions in mind as you read this chapter.

16.1 Why is it important to understand the visual process, as well as to know the physical components of the eye?
A.
B.

16.2 Distinguish between the terms *blind* and *partially sighted*.
A.
B.
C.
D.

16.3 What are the distinctive features of refractive eye problems, muscle disorders of the eye, and receptive eye problems?
A.
B.
C.

16.4 What are the estimated prevalence and causes of vision loss?
A.
B.
C.
D.
E.
F.

16.5 Describe how a vision loss can affect intelligence, speech and language skills, educational achievement, social development, physical orientation and mobility, and perceptual motor development.

A.

B.

C.

D.

E.

F.

G.

H.

16.6 What is a functional approach to assessment for students with a vision loss?

A.

B.

16.7 Describe two content areas that should be included in educational programs for students with vision loss.

A.

B.

16.8 How can communication media facilitate learning for people with vision loss?

A.

B.

C.

16.9 What educational placements are available to students with vision loss?
A.
B.
C.

16.10 What steps can be taken to prevent and medically treat vision loss?
A.
B.
C.

16.11 Why is the availability of appropriate social services important for people with vision
A.

Guided Review

Read – Matching Vocabulary

Following are a number of the key terms and concepts used in this chapter. Try to complete this matching exercise before you read the chapter. Match each term with the phrase that you think most closely describes or defines it.

A. Web-Braille
B. Pupil
C. Tunnel
D. Trachoma

E. Cornea
F. Iris
G. Snellen
H. Verbalisms

16.12 _____ System that allows individuals who use Braille to read items posted on the Internet.

16.13 _____ External covering of the eye that refracts visual stimuli.

16.14 _____ The _____ dilates or constricts to control the light entering the eye.

16.15 _____ Membranous tissue and muscles that adjust the size of the pupil.

16.16 _____ Chart used to determine visual acuity.

16.17 _____ A person with a field of vision restricted to 20 degrees or less at its widest angle is said to have _____ vision.

16.18 _____ A slow-progressing infectious bacterial disease associated with inadequate hygiene.

16.19 _____ Excessive use of speech in which words may be used that have little meaning.

This exercise is intended to provide practice in recalling what you have just read. Try not to refer back to the chapter as you match the following items with their descriptions below. As you work through this exercise, consider how this new information relates to other knowledge, concepts, and/or principles you learned before taking this course.

A. Refractive
B. Cataracts
C. Retinopathy of prematurity
D. Mowat Sensor

E. Astigmatism
F. Genetic
G. Xeropthalmia
H. Retinitis pigmentosa

16.20 _____ The most common type of vision loss problems are _____.
16.21 _____ Light rays are prevented from converging at one point due to an uneven cornea.
16.22 _____ An individual's lens becomes opaque.
16.23 _____ The most common hereditary condition associated with the loss of vision.
16.24 _____ When too much oxygen is administered to premature infants and light rays are prevented from reaching the retina.
16.25 _____ Albinism and glaucoma are examples of _____ disorders.
16.26 _____ The leading cause of acquired blindness in children.
16.27 _____ An ultrasound aid that uses high-frequency sound to detect objects.

Supply a word/phrase in each sentence in order to make sense out of the statement of a concept, definition, or principle that is otherwise incomplete or lacks closure. Several answers, other than those listed in the key, may be acceptable for an item. Focus on whether or not your answer is equivalent to the answer supplied and be prepared to explain why you completed the statement(s) as you did.

16.28 Anatomical disorders of the eyes include impairment of the refractive structures of the eye, problems of the receptive structures of the eye, and _____ anomalies in the visual system.

16.29 Four types of refractive problems include (1) hyperopia, (2) myopia, (3) astigmatism, and (4)_____.

16.30 The condition in which the eyes are pulled toward the ears is known as external _____.

16.31 _____ _____ starts out as night blindness and degenerates to totoal blindness.

16.32 Retinopathy of prematurity is associated with speech, behavior, and _____ problems.

16.33 Diseases that can cause blindness in the fetus include (1) mumps, (2) syphilis, (3) rubella, (4) measles, and (5)_____.

16.34 Visual capacity includes the response of an individual to visual information, field of vision, and _____.

16.35 The American Foundation for the Blind _____ a continuum of placements.

Please indicate whether the statements are true (T) or false (F) by circling the corresponding letter. You should be able to briefly describe the rationale for your answer.

T	F	16.36	Braille readers can read their books on the Internet through Web-Braille.
T	F	16.37	Definitions of vision loss vary because they are based on their intended use.
T	F	16.38	Residual vision combined with visual stimulation training improves a person's ability to use sight as an avenue for learning.
T	F	16.39	Academic achievement of students with vision loss often resembles that of children with learning disabilities.
T	F	16.40	One of the common early skills developed by a young child who is blind is efficient use of a cane.
T	F	16.41	Excessive school absences due to medical needs is a possible explanation for delayed academic performance.
T	F	16.42	In the Language Experience Approach, it is recommended to read a story only once in order to increase a student's listening skills.
T	F	16.43	IDEA mandates that schools must make provision for instruction in Braille and the use of Braille for every student who has a vision loss.
T	F	16.44	No matter where a child who is blind attends class, a vision specialist must be available.
T	F	16.45	The only effective treatment for glaucoma is surgery.
T	F	16.46	Glare is not regarded as a hindrance for individuals with vision loss.
T	F	16.47	Speech and language skills may be delayed due to vision loss.

Chapter Review – Practice Test

In the following activity, select the most appropriate of the four answers provided for each item. Try to do this without looking at your text in order to get an idea of your comprehension level.

16.48 Vision loss encompasses people with a wide range of conditions such as
    A. those who have never experienced sight.
    B. those who have become partially or totally blind.
    C. those who have restricted vision.
    D. All of the above.

16.49 When vision cannot be corrected to better than 20/200 in the better eye, or when the visual field is 20 degrees or less, even with corrective lens, the condition is called
    A. blindness.
    B. tunnel vision.
    C. visual acuity deficit.
    D. legal blindness.

16.50 Students with vision loss may
    A. lag up to two years behind their sighted peers.
    B. excel in math at an early age.
    C. develop sophisticated social skills.
    D. be more affectionate toward their family members than their sighted peers.

16.51 Tunnel vision can severely limit a person's ability to
    A. play cards.
    B. participate in fine arts activities.
    C. drive a car.
    D. participate in athletics.

16.52 _____ as well as acquisition of daily living skills are unique needs of young students with vision loss.
    A. Telephone skills
    B. Mobility and orientation training
    C. Bathing and eating skills
    D. Language skills acquisition

16.53 The primary purpose of labeling a child as functionally blind is to ensure that he/she receives an instructional program that
    A. assists the student in utilizing other senses as a means of succeeding.
    B. meets the requirements of the federal regulations.
    C. places him in a classroom with other students who are also functionally blind.
    D. is built on social skills training.

16.54 People with partial sight have a visual acuity greater than
    A. 20/20 but not greater than 20/70 in their best eye after correction.
    B. 20/60 but not greater than 20/20 in their best eye after correction.
    C. 20/200 but not greater than 20/70 in their best eye after correction.
    D. 20/70 but not greater than 20/200 in their best eye after correction.

16.55 One of the reasons children with vision loss use Braille is that
    A. they need the use of tactile channels to learn best.
    B. it helps increase their IQ.
    C. it is a requirement of an IEP for a students with vision loss.
    D. it is how a vision therapist is justified for availability in their education.

16.56 When the eyes appear pulled inward, giving the appearance of being crossed, the condition is known as
    A. exotropia.
    B. nystagmus.
    C. esotropia.
    D. amblyopia.

16.57 Retinal detachment can occur as a result of
   A. glaucoma and extreme myopia.
   B. retinal degeneration.
   C. a strike to the face .
   D. All of the above.

16.58 Approximately _____ of American children have a serious eye disorder.
   A. 1%
   B. 2%
   C. 8%
   D. 20%

16.59 The most common cause of preventable blindness is
   A. xeropthalmia.
   B. retinoblastoma.
   C. trachoma.
   D. anophthalmia.

16.60 A symptom of macular degeneration is
   A. blurred central vision.
   B. increased myopia.
   C. light sensitivity.
   D. acute color awareness.

16.61 Useful visual imagery may disappear if sight is lost prior to age
   A. 3.
   B. 5.
   C. 7.
   D. It makes no difference.

16.62 Children who are blind have a restricted oral vocabulary in comparison to their sighted peers
   A. due to the lower level of intelligence that accompanies vision loss.
   B. because most teachers are ill-equipped to teach students with vision loss.
   C. due to the articulation disorders commonly present in students with vision loss.
   D. because they lack the visual input to piece together all information in an experience.

16.63 Conversion of printed matter into synthetic speech and/or Braille can by done with
   A. an Optacon Scanner.
   B. a PDA and CCTV.
   C. a Note teller.
   D. a Kurzweil Reading Machine.

A	B	C	D	E	F	G	H	I	J	K	L	M	N	O	P	Q	R	S	T	U	V	W	X	Y	Z
4				22				7										20		16					

```
    S     U     E        S     I           I  S  I              S  S
   20  8  16  11  22   1   8  20      21   7   8  14     15   7  20   7  10   1      23  10  20  20

      A        A     U                          E  A     S        E        I
   6   4  24     23   4  26     16  25     8  10   8  21  10     24  22   4   2  20     3  22  14   7   1  11

              E  I        S  I        E        E  E     S  .
            8  14  22   7   2     20   7  26  14   8  22  11     25  22  22   2  20
```

Unscramble the tiles to reveal a message.

C A U S	B L I E	E O F	L E A D	I A .	N C H
S S I	R O P T	T H E	S X E	I L D R	N D N E
I N G	H A L M	E N I			

Double Puzzle

Unscramble each of the clue words. Copy the letters in the numbered cells to other cells with the same number.

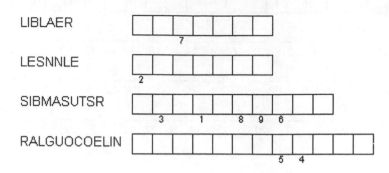

LIBLAER

LESNNLE

SIBMASUTSR

RALGUOCOELIN

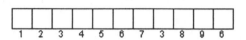

Crossword Puzzle

200

Across

4. Most common type of vision loss problem
6. Glaucoma and albinism are this type of disorder
8. Lens become opaque
9. Chart used to determine visual acuity
10. Type of sensor that uses high-frequency sound to detect objects

Down

1. Type of vision that has a visual field limit of 20 degrees or less
2. Most common cause of preventable blindness
3. Excessive use of words that may have little meaning
5. Type of vision used as a primary channel of learning
7. Tissue and muscles that adjust the size of the pupil

Best Practices

Case Study

As a result of being born 10 weeks premature, Janet is blind. Because her visual impairment was identified very early in her life, her parents were able to obtain early intervention services for her immediately. As a result of the ongoing services that Janet has received, at 16 years of age, she is very independent, active, and confident. Janet attends her local high school and is a straight-A student. She is a member of Pep Club, sings with the choir, and is in her 3rd year of German.

Janet is very mobile and uses a cane to assist with navigation around the school and classrooms. Classroom teachers meet with Janet at the beginning of each semester to identify environmental and instructional issues that they need to address so that the environment is safe and accessible to her. In class, Janet takes notes and completes all assignments using a Braille keyboard. The school purchased the software and hardware to allow Janet to print in Braille as well.

1. What are some common learning issues for individuals like Janet with visual impairments?

_____
_____
_____

2. What instructional strategies are particularly effective when teaching children and youth with visual impairments? _____

_____
_____

3. What environmental accommodations would be important for the classroom to be safe and accessible for Janet? _____

_____
_____
_____

1. Arrange with local school to observe in a special education classroom that serves children with visual impairments. While observing in the classroom think about the following questions: What are some of the student'learning characteristics? What are his/her mobility issues? How does the teacher address those differences? How successful is the child in this environment?

_____

_____

_____

2. Arrange with local school to observe in a general education classroom that has a child or children with visual impairments. While observing in the classroom think about the following questions: What are some of his/her learning characteristics? What are his/her mobility issues? How does the general education teacher address those differences?   How successful is the child in this environment? _____

_____

_____

3. Observe the child with the visual impairment in settings other than the classroom, such as in the cafeteria or during art, physical education, and music. How does the child compare to his/her peers in terms of social interaction, class participation, and attention? _____

_____

_____

_____

_____

Resources

Books
A Different Way of Seeing: Youth with Blindness and Vision Impairment by Patti Souder.
Published by Mason Crest Publishers.
Coping with Vision Loss: Maximizing What You Can See and Do by Bill G. Chapman.
Published by Hunter House.

Videos
If You Could See What I Hear. Available from www.rottentomatoes.com
At First Sight. Produced by MGM.

Websites
Foundation Fighting Blindness: www.blindness.org
National Federation of the Blind: www.nfb.org

Physical Disabilities and Health Disorders

Physical disabilities is a term generally used to refer to impairments that interfere with a person's mobility, coordination, communication, learning, or personal adjustment. This chapter discusses a representative sample of disabling physical conditions, including cerebral palsy, seizure disorders (epilepsy), spina bifida, spinal cord injuries, and muscular dystrophy.

Health disabilities are conditions resulting in "limited strength, vitality, or alertness," which are "due to chronic or acute health problems." The chapter discusses diabetes, cystic fibrosis, sickle cell anemia, human immunodeficiency virus (HIV) and acquired immune deficiency syndrome (AIDS). Other health-relevant conditions, including child abuse, adolescent pregnancy, suicide, and maternal drug and alcohol abuse, are described as well. Such health disabilities significantly alter not only the life of the person who develops one of them, but also the lives of that person's family and friends.

For each major condition the authors furnish details, definitions, and concepts. They explain causation, prevalence, and interventions. Current interventions or prevention strategies are explained. The authors emphasize that with appropriate and comprehensive treatment, people with physical and/or health disabilities can achieve personal independence and other goals necessary for a full and independent life.

Concept Reflection

A. What did I know about physical disabilities and health disorders before reading this chapter?	B. How did reading the chapter enhance or change what I already knew? (Relate this to Column A.)	C. What new information did I learn? (This may or may not be associated with your responses in A or B.)
1.	1.	1.
2.	2.	2.
3.	3.	3.
4.	4.	4.

Keep the following questions in mind as you read this chapter.

17.1 Identify the disabilities that may accompany cerebral palsy.
A.

17.2 What is spina bifida myelomeningocele?
A.
B.

17.3 Identify specific treatments for individuals with spinal cord injuries.
A.
B.
C.
D.
E.
F.
G.

17.4 Describe the physical limitations associated with muscular dystrophy.
A.

17.5 What steps should be taken to assist infants and children with AIDS?
A.
B.

17.6 **Describe the immediate treatment for a person who is experiencing a tonic/clonic seizure.**

A.

B.

C.

D.

E.

F.

G.

17.7 **Identify three problems that individuals with diabetes may eventually experience.**

A.

17.8 **Identify present and future interventions for the treatment of children and youth with cystic fibrosis.**

A.

B.

C.

D.

E.

F.

G.

17.9 **Describe the impact of the sickling of cells on body tissues.**

A.

17.10 Identify five factors that may contribute to child abuse and neglect.
A.
B.
C.
D.
E.
17.11 Identify factors that may contribute to the increased prevalence of adolescent pregnancy.
A.
B.
17.12 Identify the major causes of youth suicide.
A.
B.
C.
D.

Guided Review

Read – Matching Vocabulary

Following are a number of the key terms and concepts used in this chapter. Try to complete this matching exercise before you read the chapter. Match each term with the phrase that you think most closely describes or defines it.

A. Acquired immune deficiency
B. Fetal alcohol syndrome
C. Chest infections
D. Absence
E. Myelomeningocele
F. Diabetes

G. Fatty
H. Mortality
I. Sickle cell anemia
J. Muscular dystrophy
K. Electroencephalogram
L. Cystic fibrosis

17.13 _____ The most serious form of spina bifida, in which the sac contains nerve tissue.
17.14 _____ The presence of human immunodeficiency and recurrent bacterial infections.
17.15 _____ Test to detect abnormalities in the electrical activity of the brain.
17.16 _____ The leading known cause of mental retardation.
17.17 _____ Type of seizure that may appear to be daydreaming.
17.18 _____ The loss of ability in muscular dystrophy is due to muscle tissue that is gradually replaced by _____ tissue.
17.19 _____ Chronic disorder that is characterized by gradual wasting and weakening of the voluntary skeletal muscles.
17.20 _____ Hunger, thirst, and frequent urination are typical symptoms associated with _____.
17.21 _____ Genetically transmitted, systemic disease characterized by glue-like mucus in the lungs.
17.22 _____ The treatment goals of cystic fibrosis include early diagnosis, adequate nutrition, suitable education, and control of _____.
17.23 _____ Condition in which the red blood cells become distorted and cause obstructions in vessels, which can lead to stroke and organ damage.
17.24 _____ Children born to mothers who are 15 years of age or younger experience higher rates of _____.

Reflect – Matching Vocabulary

This exercise is intended to provide practice in recalling what you have just read. Try not to refer back to the chapter as you match the following items with their descriptions below. As you work through this exercise, consider how this new information relates to other knowledge, concepts, and/or principles you learned before taking this course.

A. Athetoid   E. Health disorders
B. Hemiplegia   F. Spinal cord injury
C. Paraplegia   G. Methylprednisolone
D. Opportunistic   H. Tonic

17.25 _____ Tuberculosis, leukemia, and sickle cell anemia are classified by IDEA as _____.
17.26 _____ Cerebral palsy characterized by involuntary and uncontrolled movements.
17.27 _____ Result of the spinal cord being severed or traumatized.
17.28 _____ Lower body and both legs paralyzed .
17.29 _____ Paralytic condition that affects one side of the body.
17.30 _____ Medication used to reduce the severity of a spinal cord injury.
17.31 _____ As the HIV turns into AIDS, children are attacked by life-threatening _____ infections.
17.32 _____ Stiffening of the body.

Supply a word/phrase in each sentence in order to make sense out of the statement of a concept, definition, or principle that is otherwise incomplete or lacks closure. Several answers, other than those listed in the key, may be acceptable for an item. Focus on whether or not your answer is equivalent to the answer supplied and be prepared to explain why you completed the statement(s) as you did.

17.33   The most frequently occurring permanently disabling birth defect is _____ _____.

17.34   Excess glucose, maternal hyperthermia, and radiation are examples of _____ that may induce malformation in the spine.

17.35   Signs of a shunt malfunctioning include a decline in school performance, reduced alertness, neck pain, vomiting, irritability, and _____.

17.36   The seriousness of the various dystrophies is influenced by the rate at which the condition progresses, physical location and nature of onset, age of onset, and _____.

17.37   By definition, a health disorder must be manifested as limiting strength, vitality, or alertness and adversely affecting the _____ performance of a student.

17.38   Symptoms of a damaged immune system include (1) weight loss, (2) night sweats, (3) skin rashes, and (4)_____.

17.39   HIV is passed from one person to another through sexual contact, blood exchange, breast milk, perinatal contact, and _____.

17.40   Many types of seizures can be controlled through stress management, rest, diet modifications, and _____.

17.41   _____ onset diabetes tends to be more severe and progresses more quickly than _____ onset diabetes.

17.42   The average lifespan for over 50% of the individuals with cystic fibrosis is beyond _____ years of age.

17.43   Substance abusers are _____ times more likely to commit suicide.

17.44   The three types of cerebral palsy include ataxic, spastic, and _____.

Please indicate whether the statements are true (T) or false (F) by circling the corresponding letter. You should be able to briefly describe the rationale for your answer.

T   F   17.45   Preventing unplanned pregnancies in HIV mothers is the best way to reduce the number of children who become infected with HIV.

T   F   17.46   The degree to which individuals with physical disabilities become integral participants in the communities is directly related to the timeliness of treatment received from professionals.

T   F   17.47   School-centered services by OTs and PTs for individuals with cerebral palsy always includes direct treatment in out-of-class settings.

T   F   17.48   The purpose of surgery for infants with spina bifida myelomeningocele is to prevent further damage to the spinal column.

T	F	17.49	When a spinal cord injury occurs in the neck, the paralysis is usually confined to the legs.
T	F	17.50	Education for individuals with spinal cord injury is similar to that for those without spinal cord injury.
T	F	17.51	The focus of treatment for individuals with muscular dystrophy is preserving ambulatory independence.
T	F	17.52	Spina bifida originates in the first days of pregnancy.
T	F	17.53	Suicide notes are not necessarily a sign of danger.
T	F	17.54	Spina bifida occulta has little impact on a developing infant.
T	F	17.55	The primary cause of spinal cord injury is sporting activities.
T	F	17.56	Over half of the children who test positive for HIV thrive.

Chapter Review – Practice Test

In the following activity, select the most appropriate of the four answers provided for each item. Try to do this without looking at your text in order to get an idea of your comprehension level.

17.57 Sudden, unexpected happiness may indicate a person is profoundly relieved and has made a decision to
   A. commit suicide.
   B. take drugs.
   C. become more balanced.
   D. All of the above.

17.58 For individuals 15–24 years old, suicide is the _____ leading cause of death.
   A. second
   B. third
   C. fourth
   D. fifth

17.59 IDEA describes individuals with physical disabilities as those with
   A. physical handicaps.
   B. health disorders.
   C. orthopedic impairments.
   D. crippled limbs.

17.60 The term used to describe the neurological disorder characterized by motor problems, general physical weakness, lack of coordination, and perceptual difficulties is
   A. other health impairment.
   B. cerebral palsy.
   C. physical disability.
   D. medically fragile.

17.61 Triplegia usually involves
    A. lower body.
    B. both halves of the body.
    C. lower body and both arms.
    D. both legs and one arm.

17.62 Spinal cord injuries are usually accompanied by
    A. head trauma and significant chest injuries.
    B. chest injuries and neck pain.
    C. fractures of some portion of the trunk and hydrocephalus.
    D. head trauma and paralysis of the left arm.

17.63 Which of the following statements about spinal cord injuries (SCI) is not true?
    A. Most individuals with SCI are men.
    B. SCI usually occur between the hours 8:00 p.m. and midnight.
    C. A majority of SCI are due to motor vehicle accidents.
    D. Alcohol is a contributing factor in approximately 25% of the SCI that occur.

17.64 The first phase of treatment for SCI includes
    A. identifying signs of depression and despondency.
    B. rehabilitation including activation of any residual muscle strength.
    C. transport to a medical facility specializing in SCI.
    D. management of shock and immobilization.

17.65 Life expectancy for individuals with Duchenne-type muscular dystrophy is around
    A. 45 to 60 years of age.
    B. 38 to 50 years of age.
    C. 20 to 35 years of age.
    D. 10 to 18 years of age.

17.66 Symptoms of Duchenne-type muscular dystrophy usually first appear
    A. during pregnancy.
    B. at birth.
    C. during preschool years.
    D. during late elementary years.

17.67 Compassionate Friends is a program for parents of children with muscular dystrophy and primarily addresses
    A. the child's perception of death.
    B. the causes of muscular dystrophy.
    C. the parent's medical background.
    D. financial needs of families.

17.68 During what stage of AIDS does a person first manifest symptoms?
   A. Second
   B. Third
   C. Fourth
   D. Fifth

17.69 The best cure for AIDS in children and youth is
   A. daily gammaglobulin injections.
   B. prevention.
   C. counseling.
   D. mega-doses of vitamin c.

17.70 Tonic/clonic seizures were formerly known as
   A. seizure disorders.
   B. petit mal seizures.
   C. grand mal seizures.
   D. involuntary contractions.

17.71 The explicit cause of most seizure disorders is
   A. drugs.
   B. alcohol.
   C. automobile accidents.
   D. unknown.

17.72 When an individual with sickle cell anemia is in crisis, the teacher should attempt to employ all but which of the following treatments?
   A. Ensuring good blood oxygenation
   B. Starting transfusions
   C. Keeping the individual warm
   D. Increasing liquid intake

17.73 Classic symptoms of Type I diabetes include
   A. weight loss, fatigue, and excessive urination.
   B. high blood sugar levels.
   C. blurred vision, excessive thirst and hunger.
   D. All of the above.

17.74 Use of an insulin infusion pump allows individuals to
   A. exercise vigorously without concern for their glucose level.
   B. eat as they please without concern for their glucose level.
   C. "control" diabetes when used in conjunction with diet and exercise control.
   D. eliminate concern for nerve damage and kidney disease.

17.75 State laws designate educators and other professionals who work with children as mandated reporters who must
A. report suspected abuse or neglect.
B. report and be prepared to provide proof of suspected abuse or neglect.
C. be willing to sign an affidavit attesting to their suspicion of abuse or neglect.
D. be willing to confront the parents about suspected abuse or neglect.

17.76 Teachers of students with cystic fibrosis must help students make up past due work, feel at home at school, and
A. develop friendships.
B. communicate with their parents.
C. learn appropriate learning strategies.
D. adjust to their medical needs.

Cryptogram

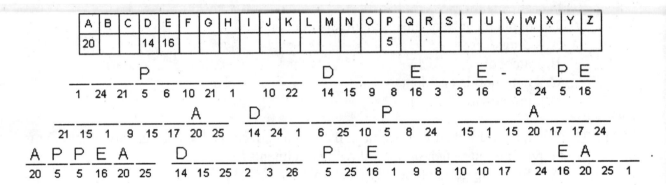

Unscramble the tiles to reveal a message.

BY	AL C	ALLY	OMPA	ARE	T IN
SPIN	ES .	RIES	INJU	AND	ACC
ORD	UMA	CHES	TRA	USU	HEAD
NIED	JURI				

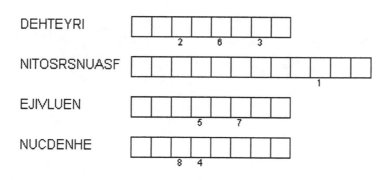

Double Puzzle

Unscramble each of the clue words. Copy the letters in the numbered cells to other cells with the same number.

DEHTEYRI   ☐☐☐☐☐☐☐☐
          2   6   3

NITOSRSNUASF   ☐☐☐☐☐☐☐☐☐☐☐☐
                1

EJIVLUEN   ☐☐☐☐☐☐☐☐
       5   7

NUCDENHE   ☐☐☐☐☐☐☐☐
     8 4

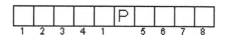

☐☐☐☐☐P☐☐☐☐
1 2 3 4 1 5 6 7 8

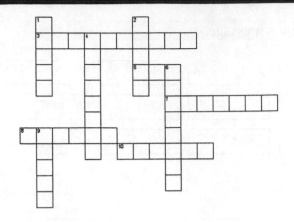

Across

3. Paralysis of lower body and both legs
5. Human immunodeficiency with recurrent bacterial infections
7. Type of seizure that gives the appearance of daydreaming
8. One of three types of cerebral palsy
10. _____ fibrosis is characterized by glue-like mucus in the lungs

Down

1. _____ bifida is the most frequently occurring permanently disabling birth defect
2. _____ alcohol syndrome is the leading known cause of mental retardation
4. Type of cerebral palsy characterized by involuntary movements
6. Symptoms associated with this include hunger, thirst, and frequent urination
9. Stiffening of the body

Dionna is a junior in high school who has been on the school's honor roll every semester and is completing a college preparatory curriculum. She is a popular student with her peers and her teachers and is a favorite math tutor among the underclass students. Dionna's academic skills are above many in her class, her ability to think abstractly is unmatched, and her motivation to learn is very high.

In classes, it is easy to find Dionna because she is usually sitting in the front of the classroom in her wheelchair. Dionna has cerebral palsy, which interferes with her mobility and communication. She uses a voice-controlled laptop computer to participate in instructional activities because her writing is slow, laborious, and illegible.

Dionna spends all of her school time in the general classroom with her same-age peers and participates fully in the curriculum and class instruction. However, many of her teachers and peers will tell you that when they first met Dionna they expected someone entirely different. Now, as Dionna is preparing for college the counselors are concerned about her success on a university campus and those unique issues that might be problematic for her.

1. What law would address Dionna's rights to a barrier-free educational environment? What kinds of barriers might Dionna face in a school setting? _____
_____
_____
_____
_____

2. How could the school address those barriers? _____
_____
_____
_____
_____

3. What kinds of problems might Dionna face in a university setting that other students without physical differences would not? _____
_____
_____
_____
_____

4. How could the university address those barriers? _____
_____
_____
_____
_____

1. Interview a school superintendent or principal who has been in education since before 1975. Ask them to describe what special education was like before PL 94-142 and what it is like today in terms of: integration with same-age peers, curriculum expectations, assessment, and parental expectations. What did you find out? _____

_____

_____

_____

2. Visit a local children's shelter and spend time reading to a small group of children. As you are reading and interacting with them, observe their social/emotional and communication skills. Then, repeat this experience with a similar group of children who come from homes with involved, active parents. Compare the developmental skills of these two groups of children. How were these children alike and different in terms of language skills, interpersonal competence, and peer relationships? How was your behavior/experience with the two groups?

_____

_____

_____

Resources

Books
Savage Inequalities: Children in America's Schools by Jonathan Kozol. Available through HarperCollins Publishers.
Helping the Child Who Doesn't Fit In by Stephen Nowicki and Marshall P. Duke. Available from Peachtree Publishers.

Videos
As I Am by James Brodie, www.fanlight.com
Kiss My Wheels by Thunder Road Productions, www.fanlight.com

Websites
Council for Exceptional Children: www.cec.sped.org
American Psychological Association: www.apa.org
Office of Special Education and Rehabilitation Services:
www.ed.gov/about/offices/list/osers/osep/index.html
Curry School of Education, University of Virginia: curry.edschool.virginia.edu
The Disability Rag: www.ragged-edge-mag.com
National Information Center for Children and Youth with Disabilities (NICHCY):
www.nichcy.org/

Gifted, creative and *talented* are terms associated with a group of people who have extraordinary abilities in one or more areas of performance. This chapter begins with a historical look at the study of giftedness and examines research efforts to explore intelligence.

Definitions of giftedness are important since the concept of giftedness that is being used has a profound impact on the kind of education provided to students with exceptional ability. For example, definitions influence the number of students selected for gifted programs, the types of instruments and selection procedures used, the scores one must obtain to qualify for specialized instruction, the types of different education provided, the amount of funding allotted for services, and the types of training required of those who teach gifted and talented programs. Definitions of giftedness are a function of our educational, societal, and political priorities at a given time.

This chapter covers the prevalence, characteristics, and origins of giftedness. Gifted people vary significantly in characteristics; they are not a homogeneous group. Techniques of assessment that are explored include teacher nomination, intelligence and achievement tests, and creativity tests.

Intervention strategies focus on helping gifted/talented children and youth to develop their abilities during early childhood, childhood, and adolescence. A number of service delivery systems, such as acceleration, enrichment, special programs and schools, career education, and mentoring, are used to provide differentiated education to gifted and talented students. Parents play a major role in advancing their children's development by providing varied opportunities suited to the child's strengths and interests.

Concept Reflection		
A. What did I know about individuals who are gifted, creative, and talented before reading this chapter?	B. How did reading the chapter enhance or change what I already knew? (Relate this to Column A.)	C. What new information did I learn? (This may or may not be associated with your responses in A or B.)
1.	1.	1.
2.	2.	2.
3.	3.	3.

Keep the following questions in mind as you read this chapter.

18.1 Briefly describe several historical developments directly related to the measurement of various types of giftedness.
A.
B.
C.
D.
E.
F.
G.
18.2 Identify six major components of definitions that have been developed to describe giftedness.
A.
B.
C.
D.
E.
F.
18.3 Identify four problems inherent in accurately describing the characteristics of individuals who are gifted.
A.
B.
C.
D.

18.4 **Identify three factors that appear to contribute significantly to the emergence of various forms of giftedness.**

A.

B.

C.

18.5 **Describe the range of assessment devices used to identify the various types of giftedness.**

A.

B.

C.

D.

E.

F.

G.

H.

18.6 **Identify eight strategies that are utilized to foster the development of children and adolescents who are gifted.**

A.

B.

C.

D.

E.

F.

G.

H.

18.7 What are some of the social-emotional needs of students who are gifted?

A.

B.

C.

D.

E.

F.

G.

18.8 Identify four challenges females face in dealing with their giftedness.

A.

B.

C.

D.

18.9 Identify eight important elements of programs for gifted children who come from diverse backgrounds and who may live in poverty.

A.

B.

C.

D.

E.

F.

G.

H.

Read – Matching Vocabulary

Following are a number of the key terms and concepts used in this chapter. Try to complete this matching exercise before you read the chapter. Match each term with the phrase that you think most closely describes or defines it.

A. Multiple intelligences
B. Renzulli
C. Differentiated
D. Talented

E. Transformation
F. Chance
G. Multidimensional
H. Underachievers

18.10 _____ The capacity to change an idea into something new.
18.11 _____ Individuals who demonstrate remarkable skills in the visual or performing arts or excel in other areas of performance.
18.12 _____ Intelligence manifested in linguistics, logical-mathematical, spatial, musical, bodily-kinesthetic, interpersonal, and intrapersonal behaviors.
18.13 _____ One of the five elements identified by Tannenbaum as contributing to gifted behavior.
18.14 _____ Identification of individuals who are gifted has become a _____ approach.
18.15 _____ Model that focuses on continuous identification of students who are gifted.
18.16 _____ One of the advantages of intelligence testing is identification of students who are _____.
18.17 _____ Type of education uniquely suited to the natural abilities and interests of students who are gifted.

Reflect – Matching Vocabulary

This exercise is intended to provide practice in recalling what you have just read. Try not to refer back to the chapter as you match the following items with their descriptions below. As you work through this exercise, consider how this new information relates to other knowledge, concepts, and/or principles you learned before taking this course.

A. Spatial
B. Advantaged
C. Low

D. Disadvantaged
E. Creative
F. Perfectionism

18.18 _____ Architects demonstrate _____ intelligence
18.19 _____ Early research reflected characteristics of gifted individuals from _____ environments.
18.20 _____ _____ individuals are known to be risk-takers.
18.21 _____ Intelligence tests with _____ ceilings do not allow the child to demonstrate his/her full potential.
18.22 _____ Syndrome in which students feel compelled to contribute with excellence.
18.23 _____ Students who are come from _____ backgrounds are underrepresented in gifted programs.

Supply a word/phrase in each sentence in order to make sense out of the statement of a concept, definition, or principle that is otherwise incomplete or lacks closure. Several answers, other than those listed in the key, may be acceptable for an item. Focus on whether or not your answer is equivalent to the answer supplied and be prepared to explain why you completed the statement(s) as you did.

18.24   Capacities associated with creativity include elaboration, transformation, and _____.

18.25   Students identified as gifted may be compared with others of their own age, experience, or _____.

18.26   Definitions of giftedness are often a function of educational, societal, and _____ priorities at a particular time.

18.27   The controversy regarding the respective contributions of heredity and environment to intelligence is known as _____ versus _____.

18.28   The five elements of the "Star Model" that explain the causes and antecedents of giftedness include superior general intellect, distinctive special aptitudes, nonintellective factors, chance, and _____ _____.

18.29   Factors that appear to contribute significantly to the emergence of various forms of intelligence include interaction of innate abilities with environmental influences, environmental stimulation, and _____ endowment.

18.30   The keys to effective enrichment programs are high student interest, excellent teaching, and superb _____.

18.31   In elementary school, most gifted students have mastered _____% to _____% of the curriculum to be offered before they begin the school year.

Please indicate whether the statements are true (T) or false (F) by circling the corresponding letter. You should be able to briefly describe the rationale for your answer.

T   F   18.32   Educators are correct in their assumption that gifted individuals will reach their potential without specialized programs or assistance.

T   F   18.33   No Child Left Behind legislation mandates that each state provide educational services for students who are gifted and talented, just as services are provided for students with special needs.

T   F   18.34   Critics report that many local definitions are elitist in nature

T   F   18.35   Most intelligence tests have been revised to fairly assess students who are substantially different from the core culture for whom the tests were designed.

T   F   18.36   Developmental checklists need to be included in assessments for giftedness.

T   F   18.37   Programs for gifted students must focus on their strengths as well as their deficits in order to be effective.

T   F   18.38   Gifted students must be able to differentiate between excellence and perfection.

T	F	18.39	Individuals with cerebral palsy can be gifted.
T	F	18.40	True giftedness may appear in different forms in different cultures.
T	F	18.41	Terman found that people who are gifted are well adjusted adults.
T	F	18.42	Gagne recommends acknowledgment of talents like farming.
T	F	18.43	Creative individuals like to work in pairs.

Chapter Review – Practice Test

In the following activity, select the most appropriate of the four answers provided for each item. Try to do this without looking at your text in order to get an idea of your comprehension level.

18.44 Intelligence quotient is obtained by dividing a child's mental age by
 A. his chronological age.
 B. his chronological age and multiplying that figure by 50.
 C. his chronological age and multiplying that figure by 100.
 D. 100 then multiplying that figure by the child's chronological age.

18.45 It is anticipated that the term *talent development* will be interpreted to reflect
 A. individuals who are gifted and have high IQs.
 B. programming directed at all students.
 C. educational opportunities that stress the arts for identified individuals.
 D. teachers who have been specifically trained to teach visual and performing arts.

18.46 Definitions of giftedness have an influence on all but which of the following?
 A. Number of teachers needed to provide services
 B. Types of instruments and selection procedures
 C. Funding required to provide services
 D. Number and kinds of students ultimately selected in a school system

18.47 Sternberg's triarchic theory of human intelligence claims that an individual with the ability to be an unconventional thinker who is creative, intuitive, and insightful has
 A. analytic intelligence.
 B. synthetic intelligence.
 C. practical intelligence.
 D. conceptual intelligence.

18.48 The theory of multiple intelligences was developed by
 A. Piirto.
 B. Ramos-Ford and Gardner.
 C. Gagne.
 D. Sternberg.

18.49 A superb storyteller is said to have what type of intelligence?
 A. Musical
 B. Interpersonal
 C. Intrapersonal
 D. Linguistic

18.50 In defining giftedness, researchers, professionals, and policy makers have
   A. come to an agreed-upon definition of giftedness.
   B. determined that 2% of the general population can be regarded as gifted.
   C. agreed that IQ should be the definitive condition for identifying giftedness.
   D. fluctuated over the years and continue to do so.

18.51 Gifted students are developmentally advanced in their
   A. math ability.
   B. language and thought.
   C. reading and writing.
   D. physical accomplishments.

18.52 Positive characteristics identified by Rimm and Davis as being associated with students who are gifted include all but
   A. perfectionism.
   B. overexcitability.
   C. excellent sense of humor.
   D. expanded awareness.

18.53 As gifted children age and move to adulthood, they
   A. actively select and create environments that are conducive to the development of genetic proclivities.
   B. increase their intelligence quotient by challenging themselves to pursue new information.
   C. tend to gravitate toward careers in mathematics and sciences.
   D. seek to identify other individuals who are gifted in the same areas of interest.

18.54 One of the problems with teachers' nomination of gifted students is that they
   A. identify more students from lower socioeconomic backgrounds.
   B. notice more students whose parents demonstrate a vested interest.
   C. overlook bright underachievers.
   D. tend to nominate more males than females.

18.55 Social, cognitive, and linguistic skills can be enhanced through interactions such as
   A. feeding, bathing, changing, and dressing a baby.
   B. encouraging children to make up stories.
   C. engaging in discussions that address analysis, synthesis, and evaluation.
   D. All of the above.

18.56 Successful programs for gifted students include all but teachers who
   A. have been identified as gifted themselves.
   B. enjoy the excitement of change.
   C. practice collaboration with other professionals.
   D. have a disposition for some autonomy in teaching.

18.57 Research suggests that gifted students
- A. are best served when they delay college entrance until their same-age peers.
- B. tend to become socially maladjusted and withdrawn as they grow older.
- C. come from encouraging homes.
- D. experience trouble with law enforcement at a young age.

18.58 The enrichment approach is the most
- A. effective of all approaches.
- B. abused system.
- C. well-planned of all approaches utilized.
- D. directly correlated with grade skipping.

18.59 One of the reasons cited for the disappearance of giftedness in girls is
- A. the lack of a differentiated curriculum.
- B. realization of their innate need to nurture and cooperate.
- C. the increased identification of giftedness in boys.
- D. gender-role socialization.

Cryptogram

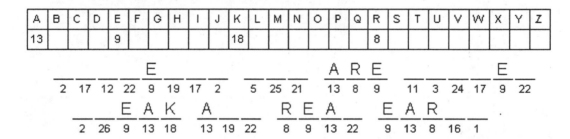

A	B	C	D	E	F	G	H	I	J	K	L	M	N	O	P	Q	R	S	T	U	V	W	X	Y	Z
13			9							18							8								

```
_  _  _  _  E  _  _  _      _  _  _      A  R  E      _  _  _  _  E  _
2 17 12 22  9 19 17  2      5 25 21     13  8  9     11  3 24 17  9 22

_  E  A  K  _      A  _  _      R  E  A  _      E  A  R  _  _  .
2 26  9 13 18     13 19 22      8  9 13 22      9 13  8 16  1
```

Scramble

Unscramble the tiles to reveal a message.

```
| G I F T | S S   C | N Y   F | N T   I | . |         | R E S E |
| E D N E | A N   P | N   M A | O R M S |
```


Unscramble each of the clue words. Copy the letters in the numbered cells to other cells with the same number.

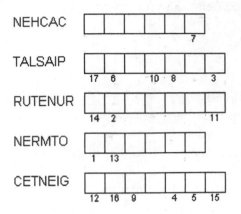

NEHCAC

TALSAIP

RUTENUR

NERMTO

CETNEIG

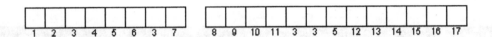

Across

    2. Type of intelligence demonstrated by architects

    6. Individuals known to be risk-takers

    7. First step in identifying gifted individuals

    8. Model that focuses on continuous identification of gifted students

Down

    1. Type of education uniquely suited to natural abilities and interests

    3. Approach used to identify individuals who are gifted

    4. Remarkable skills demonstrated in visual and/or performing arts

    5. Compulsion to accept only excellence

Case Study

Kasia is in the 1st grade. She is a very sweet child, but she is presenting a significant challenge to the teacher. On the first day of school the teacher told the class that they would be learning to read this year. Kasia already knows how to read; she taught herself to read when she was 4 and is now reading on the 3rd grade level. The teacher gave the class a math worksheet to complete that required the students to count items and write the number on the line. Not only can Kasia count, she can multiply and divide. Some of Kasia's classmates do not know how to write their name; Kasia can write complete sentences and loves to write and illustrate her own books. Kasia likes school, but spends much of her day reading independently at her desk because she completes the assigned work so quickly. When Kasia is asked about school she complains that she already knows all the things they are doing in first grade.

On the last day of the first week of school, students brought items to share during Show and Tell. Many of the 1st graders brought their favorite toys. Kasia brought a book about Egyptian Mummies and talked about how to make a mummy at home, a project that she and her mother did in the summer. The first grade teacher decides to schedule a meeting with Kasia's parents to talk about how to meet her needs.

1. What are common characteristics of gifted children like Kasia? _____
_____
_____
_____

2. What challenges will the teacher face in meeting Kasia's needs in her classroom? _____
_____
_____
_____

3. What can the school do to accommodate Kasia? _____
_____
_____
_____

Community Activities

1. Arrange with local school to observe in a gifted classroom or an activity (e.g., academic competitions like Quiz Bowl) that includes children with high ability or unusual talents. While observing the classroom or events, think about the following questions: What are some of the student's characteristics? How does the teacher address those differences? How successful is the child in this environment? _____
_____
_____
_____

2. Arrange with local school to observe in a general education classroom that has a child or children with giftedness. While observing the classroom and the interactions that occur, answer the following questions: What are some of his/her learning, social, and behavioral characteristics? How does the general education teacher address those differences? How successful is the child in this environment?_____

_____

_____

_____

_____

3. Observe the child with giftedness in settings other than the classroom, such as in the cafeteria or during art, physical education, and music. How does the child compare to his/her peers in terms of social interaction, class participation, and attention? _____

_____

_____

_____

_____

Resources

Books
The Drama of the Gifted Child: The Search for the True Self by Alice Miller. Available from Basic Books.
Helping Gifted Children Soar: A Practical Guide for Parents and Teachers by Carol Ann Strip & Gretchen Hirsch. Available from Great Potential Publishers.
Teaching Young Gifted Children in the Regular Classroom by Joan Franklin Smutny, Sally Yahnke Walker (Contributor), Elizabeth A. Meckstroth. Available from Free Spirit Publishers.

Videos
Amazing Grace and Chuck. HBO.
Little Man Tate. MGM/UA

Websites
National Association for Gifted Children: www.nagc.org.
The Gifted Child Society: www.gifted.org
Prufrock Press, Inc.: www.prucfrock.com

1
Understanding Exceptionality

1.1 Why do we label people?
- A. Labels are an attempt to describe, identify, and distinguish one person from another.
- B. Many medical, psychological, social, and educational services require that an individual be labeled in order to determine who is eligible to receive special services.
- C. Labels help professionals communicate more effectively with one another and provide a common ground for evaluating research findings.
- D. Labels enable professionals to differentiate more clearly the needs of one group of people from those of another.

1.2 Identify three approaches to describe human differences.
- A. The developmental approach is based on differences in the course of human development from what is considered normal physical, social, and intellectual growth. Human differences are the results of interaction between biological and environmental factors. Observing large numbers of individuals and looking for characteristics that occur most frequently at any given age can explain normal growth.
- B. The cultural approach defines *normal* according to established cultural standards. Human differences can be explained by examining the values of any given society. What is considered normal will change over time and from culture to culture.
- C. Self-labeling reflects how we perceive ourselves, although those perceptions may not be consistent with how others see us.

1.3 Describe the services for people with disabilities through most of the 20th century.
- A. People with disabilities were viewed as being deviant or defective and were considered social problems.
- B. State laws were passed that prevented people with disabilities from marrying, mandated sterilization, and eventually segregated them into large institutions.
- C. Many families who had a child with a disability were unable to get help for basic needs, such as medical and dental care, social services, or education.
- D. In the 1960s, parent and professional organizations were established to fight for rights of people with disabilities to be included in the community.
- E. Through the advocacy of parent and professional organizations, the civil rights of people with disabilities were finally recognized with the passage of the Americans with Disabilities Act (ADA) in 1990.

1.4 What is the purpose of the Americans with Disabilities Act?
- A. To provide a national mandate to end discrimination against individuals with disabilities in private-sector employment, all public services, and public accommodations, transportation, and telecommunications.

1.5 What services and supports must be available to ensure that an individual with a disability is able to live and learn successfully in a community setting?
- A. Comprehensive community services must be available, including access to housing, employment, public transportation, recreation, and religious activities.
- B. The individual should be able to purchase services such as medical and dental care as well as adequate life insurance.

1.6 How did the work of the 19th century physicians and philosophers contribute to our understanding of people with disabilities?
- A. Early nineteenth-century physicians emphasized that people with disabilities should be treated humanely.
- B. Jean-Marc Itard demonstrated that an individual with a severe disability could learn new skills through physiological stimulation.

1.7 Distinguish between abnormal behavior and social deviance.
- A. Human behavior is the focus of psychology. When the behavior of an individual does not meet the criteria of normal, it is labeled abnormal.
- B. Sociology is concerned with modern culture, group behaviors, societal institutions, and inter-group relationships. When people are unable to adapt to social roles or establish interpersonal relationships, their behaviors are labeled deviant.

Guided Review

Read – Matching Vocabulary

1.8 H	1.10 G	1.12 E	1.14 F
1.9 D	1.11 C	1.13 A	1.15 B

Reflect – Matching Vocabulary

1.16 G	1.18 E	1.20 B	1.22 C
1.17 A	1.19 F	1.21 H	1.23 D

Recite – Fill in the Blank

1.24 Narrow, negative	1.28 Cultural
1.25 Exceptional	1.29 Disabilities
1.26 Discrimination	1.30 Pathology
1.27 Ourselves	1.31 Psychology

Review – True/False

1.32 T	1.36 T	1.40 T	1.44 T
1.33 F	1.37 F	1.41 T	1.45 F
1.34 T	1.38 F	1.42 F	1.46 F
1.35 T	1.39 T	1.43 T	1.47 T

Chapter Review – Practice Test

1.48 D (6)	1.52 A (11)	1.56 A (16)	1.60 D (20)
1.49 C (5)	1.53 D (13)	1.57 C (16)	1.61 A (22)
1.50 A (6)	1.54 B (16)	1.58 D (18)	1.62 C (5)
1.51 C (10)	1.55 A (16)	1.59 B (20)	1.63 B (22)

Cryptogram

Labels attempt to identify one from another.

Double Puzzle

pathology, deviant, developmental, differences, discrimination

Scramble

ADA recognized the civil rights of people with disabilities.

Crossword Puzzle

Across
1. Deviance
5. Psychology
6. ADA
7. Disability
8. Geneticist

Down
2. Neurotic
3. Exceptional
4. Itard

2
Education for All

Focus Questions

2.1 What educational services were available to students with disabilities during most of the 20th century?

A. Educational programs at the beginning of the 20th century were provided primarily in separate, special schools.
B. For the first 75 years of the 20th century, the availability of educational programs for students with disabilities was sporadic and selective. Special education was allowed in many states but required in only a few.
C. Research on the efficacy of special classes for students with mild disabilities suggested that there was little or no benefit in removing students from general education classrooms.

2.2 Identify the principal issues in the right-to-education cases that led to eventual passage of the national mandate to educate students with disabilities.
A. The U.S. Supreme Court reaffirmed education as a right and not a privilege.
B. In Pennsylvania, the court ordered the schools to provide a free public education to all children with mental retardation of ages 6 to 21.
C. The *Mills* case extended the right to a free public education to all school-age children with disabilities.

2.3 Identify five major provisions of the Individuals with Disabilities Education Act.
A. The labeling and placement of students with disabilities in educational programs required the use of nondiscriminatory and multidisciplinary assessment.
B. Parental safeguards and involvement in the educational process included consent for testing and placement and participation as a team member in the development of an IEP.
C. Procedural safeguards (e.g., due process) were included to protect the child and family from decisions that could adversely affect their lives.
D. Every student with a disability is entitled to a free and appropriate public education.
E. The delivery of an appropriate education occurs through an individualized education program (IEP).
F. All children have the right to learn in an environment consistent with their academic, social, and physical needs. The law mandated that children with disabilities receive their education with peers without disabilities to the maximum extent appropriate.

2.4 Identify the four phases of the special education referral, planning, and placement process.
A. Initiating the referral.
B. Assessing student eligibility and educational need.
C. Developing the individualized education program (IEP).
D. Determining the least restrictive environment (LRE).

2.5 Identify three characteristics of effective special education that enhance learning opportunities for students with disabilities.
A. Individualization: A student-centered approach to instructional decision-making.
B. Intensive instruction: Frequent instructional experiences of significant duration.
C. The explicit teaching of academic, adaptive, and/or functional life skills.

2.6 Identify four principles for school accountability as required in *No child Left Behind*. Under IDEA, what must a student's IEP include relative to accessing the general curriculum?
A. The four principles include:
   1. A focus on student achievement as the primary measure of school success.
   2. An emphasis on challenging academic standards that specify the knowledge and skills students should acquire and the levels at which they should demonstrate mastery of that knowledge.
   3. A desire to extend the standards to all students, including those for whom expectations have been traditionally low.
   4. Heavy reliance on achievement testing to spur the reforms and to monitor their impact.
B. IDEA requires that a student's IEP must describe how the disability affects the child's involvement and progress in the general curriculum. IEP goals must enable the child to access the general curriculum when appropriate.

2.7 Distinguish between students with disabilities eligible for services under Section 504/ADA and those eligible under IDEA
A. Students eligible under ADA are entitled to accommodations and/or modifications to their educational program that will ensure that they receive an appropriate education comparable to that of their peers without disabilities.
B. Students eligible under IDEA are entitled to special education and related services to ensure they receive a free and appropriate education.

2.8 Distinguish between the principles of zero tolerance and zero exclusion in America's schools.
A. The principle of zero tolerance states that the consequences for a student's misbehavior are predetermined (e.g., a one-year expulsion) and any individual reasons or circumstances are not considered.

B.   The principle of zero exclusion states that no students with a disability can be denied a free and appropriate public education regardless of the nature, type, or extent of his or her disabling condition. As such, a student with a disability cannot be expelled from school for misbehavior.

Guided Review

Read – Matching Vocabulary

2.9 D	2.11 E	2.13 B	2.15 C
2.10 A	2.12 G	2.14 H	2.16 F

Reflect – Matching Vocabulary

2.17 H	2.19 B	2.21 F	2.23 D
2.18 E	2.20 A	2.22 G	2.24 C

Recite – Fill in the Blank

2.25 Full participation	2.31 Learn
2.26 Segregated	2.32 Disability
2.27 Right, privilege	2.33 Primary
2.28 People first, disabilities	2.34 Individualization.
2.29 autism	2.35 Functional
2.30 5	2.36 Excluded

Review – True/False

2.37 T	2.40 F	2.43 F	2.46 F
2.38 T	2.41 T	2.44 F	2.47 T
2.39 T	2.42 F	2.45 T	2.48 T

Chapter Review – Practice Test

2.49 A (25)	2.54 A (32)	2.59 B (33,34)	2.64 D (32)
2.50 A (48)	2.55 D (30)	2.60 D (34)	2.65 B (34)
2.51 A (27)	2.56 A (33)	2.61 C (31)	2.66 A (30)
2.52 B (28)	2.57 D (44)	2.62 B (47)	2.67 C (34)
2.53 D (26)	2.58 C (33)	2.63 D (32)	2.68 A (44)

Cryptogram

ADA, IEP, LRE, IDEA, IFSP,FAPE

Double Puzzle

prereferral, adaptive, functional, self-determination, people first language

Scramble

The goal of education is full participation for everyone.

Crossword

Across	Down
3. Individualization	1. Functional
4. IFSP	2. IEP
7. Right	5. FAPE
8. Learn	6. Primary
10. Disabilities	7. Related
12. Disability	9. LRE
13. IDEA	11. Adaptive

3
Inclusion and Collaboration in the Early Childhood and Elementary School Years

3.1 Define inclusive education
   A. Inclusive education may be defined as placing students with disabilities in a general education setting within their home or neighborhood school while making available both formal and natural supports to ensure an appropriate educational experience.
   B. Full inclusion is where the student with a disability receives all instruction and support within the general education classroom. Partial inclusion is where the student with a disability receives most instruction within the general education classroom but is pulled out for specialized services part of the school day.

3.2 Describe the characteristics of effective inclusive schools.
   A. Promote the values of diversity, acceptance, and belonging.
   B. Ensure the availability of formal and natural supports within the general education setting.
   C. Provide services and supports in age-appropriate classrooms in neighborhood schools.
   D. Ensure access to the general curriculum while meeting the individualized needs of each student.
   E. Provide a schoolwide support system to meet the needs of all students.

3.3 Define collaboration and identify its key characteristics.
   A. Collaboration is defined as professionals, parents, and students working together to achieve the mutual goal of delivering an effective educational program designed to meet individual needs. Collaboration is not what those involved do, it is how they do it.
   B. In an inclusive school, effective collaboration has several key characteristics:
      1. parents are viewed as active partners in the education of their children
      2. team members share responsibility; individual roles are clearly understood and valued
      3. team members promote peer support and cooperative learning

3.4 Why is it so important to provide early intervention services as soon as possible to young children at risk?
   A. The first years of life are critical to the overall development of all children – normal, at-risk, and disabled.
   B. Early stimulation is crucial to the later development of language, intelligence, personality, and self-worth.
   C. Early intervention may prevent and lessen the overall impact of disabilities as well as counteract the negative effects of delayed intervention.
   D. Early intervention may in the long run be less costly and more effective than providing services later in the individual's life.

3.5 Identify the components of the Individualized Family Service Plan (IFSP).
   A. The infant's or toddler's present levels of physical development, cognitive development, communication development, social or emotional development, and adaptive development.
   B. The family's resources, priorities, and concerns relating to enhancing the development of the young child with a disability.
   C. The major outcomes to be achieved for the infant or toddler and the family, and the criteria, procedures, and timelines used to determine progress toward achieving the outcomes.
   D. Specific early intervention services necessary to meet the unique needs of the infant or toddler and the family.
   E. The natural environments in which early intervention services are to be provided, including a justification of the extent, if any, to which the services will not be provided in a natural environment.
   F. The projected dates for initiation of services and the anticipated duration of the services.
   G. The identification of the service coordinator.
   H. The steps to be taken to support the transition of the toddler with a disability to preschool or other appropriate services

3.6 Identify effective instructional approaches for preschool-age children with disabilities.
   A. A child-find system in each state to locate young children at risk and make referrals to appropriate agencies for preschool services.
   B. An individualized education program plan that involves specialists across several disciplines.
   C. Instruction that reflects developmentally appropriate practice, age appropriate practice, and the teaching of functional skills.
   D. Inclusive preschool classrooms where young children with disabilities are educated side-by-side with peers without disabilities.

3.7 Describe the roles of special education and general education teachers in an inclusive classroom setting

    A. Special education teachers have multiple roles that may be referred to as the "three Cs": collaborator, consultant, and coordinator.

    B. In the role of *collaborator,* special educators work with school to assess students' needs, develop the IEP, determine appropriate accommodations and instructional adaptations, and deliver intensive instruction in academic, behavioral, and/or adaptive functional areas. Special education teachers use effective problem-solving strategies to facilitate students learning, co-teach with general educators, and apply effective accountability measures to evaluate individual student progress and long-term results.

    C. In the role of *consultant*, the special education teacher serves as a resource to general educators and parents on effective instructional practices for students with disabilities.

    D. In the role of *coordinator,* the special education takes the lead responsibility for organizing the activities of the school team in developing, implementing, and evaluating student IEPs. They may also be responsible for organizing school resources; professional development activities; supervision of paraprofessionals, peer support, and volunteers; and facilitation of positive communication with parents.

    E. General educators must be able to identify and refer students who may be in need of additional support; understand each student's individual strengths and limitations, and the affects on learning; implement an appropriate individualized instructional program that is focused on supporting student success in the general education curriculum and initiate and maintain ongoing communication with parents.

3.8 Why are multilevel instruction, universal design for learning, direct instruction, assistive technology, and curriculum-based assessment considered effective practice in an inclusive classroom?

    A. Students of the same level are clearly not alike in how they learn or their rate of learning. As such, teachers must use multilevel instruction (also referred to as *differentiated instruction*) in which multiple teaching approaches within the same curriculum are *adapted* to individual need and functioning level.

    B. Universal design goes one step beyond multilevel instruction, creating instructional programs and environments that work for all students, to the greatest extent possible, without the need for adaptation or specialized design.

    C. A primary characteristic of special education is the *explicit teaching* of academic, adaptive, and functional skills. Research suggests that students with disabilities learn more efficiently in a structured, teacher-directed approach, often referred to as *direct instruction.*

    D. Assistive technology can take many forms and be helpful to students with disabilities in several different ways (e.g., high-tech digital textbook, low-tech language board, a joystick to guide a power wheelchair.)

    E. While traditional assessments may be useful in determining a student's eligibility for special education, many educators question their use in planning for instruction and measuring day-to-day students learning. An alternative approach to traditional tests is the use of curriculum-based assessments (CBAs). CBAs provide direct and frequent measurement of observable student behaviors toward progress within the curriculum.

Guided Review

Read – Matching Vocabulary

3.9 F	3.11 A	3.13 E	3.15 B
3.10 C	3.12 H	3.14 D	3.16 G

Reflect – Matching Vocabulary

3.17 B	3.19 E	3.21 D	3.23 H
3.18 G	3.20 A	3.22 F	3.24 C

Recite – Fill in the Blank

3.25 Participation	3.30 Critical
3.26 Adults	3.31 Interruptions
3.27 Respected	3.32 Family
3.28 Professional collaboration	3.33 Individual need
3.29 Transdisciplinary	3.34 Family needs, strengths
	3.35 Functional assessments

Review – True/False

3.36 F	3.38 F	3.40 F	3.42 T
3.37 T	3.39 T	3.41 T	3.43 F

Chapter Review – Practice Test

3.44 D (77)	3.50 B (64)	3.56 A (63)	3.62 C (73)
3.45 D (77,78)	3.51 D (59)	3.57 B (68)	3.63 B (73)
3.46 D (63,64)	3.52 D (60)	3.58 D (68)	3.64 D (73)
3.47 A (57)	3.53 C (62)	3.59 C (71)	3.65 A (73)
3.48 B (59)	3.54 A (67)	3.60 A (72)	3.66 C (76)
3.49 D (69)	3.55 C (62)	3.61 A,B,C,D (72)	3.67 A (75)

Cryptogram

The first years of life are critical to the overall development of all children.

Double Puzzle

functional, families, participation, individual, transdisciplinary

Scramble

Effective schools promote the values of diversity, acceptance, and belonging.

Crossword

Across
3. IFSP
5. Individualized

Down
1. Transcisciplinary
2. Partial
4. Early
6. Inclusion
7. Intensity

4
Transition and Adult Life

Focus Questions

4.1 What do we know about access to community living and employment for people with disabilities after they leave school?
  A. Special education graduates are often unable to participate fully in community activities and are socially isolated in comparison to people without disabilities.
  B. Many current graduates are not adequately prepared for employment and are unable to get help to enroll in higher education. The majority of adults with disabilities are unemployed.
  C. Adult service systems do not have the resources to meet the needs of students with disabilities following the school years.
  D. The capabilities of adults with disabilities are often underestimated

4.2 What are the requirements for transition planning in IDEA?
  A. IDEA requires that every student with a disability receive transition services.
  B. Transition services must be designed within an outcome-oriented process, which promotes movement from school to post-school activities.
  C. Transition services must be based upon the individual student's needs, taking into account the student's preferences and interests.

4.3 Identify the purpose of an ITP and the basic steps in its formulation.
  A. An ITP is developed to ensure each student's access to the general education curriculum and/or a focus on the adaptive and functional skills that will facilitate life in the community following school. The ITP identifies the type and range of needed transitional services, and establishes timelines and personnel responsible.
  B. The basic steps in the formulation of the ITP include:
    1. convening the IEP Team, individualized around the wants and needs of each transition-age student.
    2. reviewing assessment data and conducting additional assessment activities.

3. developing and implementing the ITP.
4. updating the ITP annually during IEP meetings and implementing follow-up procedures.
5. holding an exit meeting.

4.4 Why it is important for students with disabilities to receive instruction in self-determination, academics, adaptive and functional life skills, and employment preparation during the secondary school years?

A. Self-determination skills help students to solve problems, consider options, and make appropriate choices as they make the transition into adult life.

B. Academic skills are essential in meeting high school graduation requirements and preparing students with disabilities for college. A functional academic program helps students learn applied skills in daily living, leisure activities, and employment preparation.

C. Adaptive and functional life skills help students learn how to socialize with others, maintain personal appearance, and make choices about how to spend free time.

D. Employment preparation during high school increases the probability of success on the job during the adult years and places the person with a disability in the role of a contributor to society.

4.5 Describe government-funded and natural supports for people with disabilities.

A. Income support programs are direct cash payments to people with disabilities, providing basic economic assistance.

B. Medicaid and Medicare are government supported health care programs. The Medicaid program can pay for inpatient and outpatient hospital services, laboratory services, and early screening, diagnosis, treatment, and immunization for children. Medicare is a national insurance program with two parts: hospital insurance and supplementary medial insurance.

C. Residential services indicate a trend toward smaller, community-based residences located within local neighborhoods and communities. These residences may include group homes, semi-independent homes and apartments, or foster family care. The purpose of residential services is to provide persons with disabilities a variety of options for living in the community.

D. There are essentially three approaches to competitive employment with time-limited support services, and employment with ongoing support services. The purpose of all three approaches is to assist people with disabilities obtain a job and maintain it over time.

E. Natural supports include family, friends, neighbors, and coworkers.

Guided Review

Read – Matching Vocabulary

4.6 B	4.8 A	4.10 C
4.7 E	4.9 G	4.11 F

Reflect – Matching Vocabulary

4.12 A	4.14 D	4.16 B
4.13 F	4.15 E	4.17 C

Recite – Fill in the Blank

4.18 Accommodations	4.24 Self-determination
4.19 Formal, natural supports	4.25 High, low
4.20 14	4.26 Occupational
4.21 Needs and preferences	4.27 Support
4.22 Timelines, personnel	4.28 Group
4.23 Adult service agencies	

Review – True/False

4.29 T	4.31 T	4.33 T	4.35 T
4.30 T	4.32 F	4.34 F	4.36 F

Crossword

Across
3. Group
5. High
6. Medicare
7. Self-determination
8. Transition
9. Accommodations

Down
1. Government
2. Fourteen
4. Occupational

5
Multicultural and Diversity Issues

Focus Questions

5.1 Identify three ways in which the purposes of and approaches to general education I the United States sometimes difer from those of special and multicultural education..
  A. A major purpose of general education is to provide education for everyone and to bring all students to a similar level of performance.
  B. Special education focuses on individual differences and often evaluates performance on an individually set or prescribed performance level.
  C. Multicultural education promotes cultural pluralism and, therefore, promotes differences.

5.2 Describe the population and trends among culturally diverse groups in the United States. How do they have an impact on the educational system?
  A. Ethnically and culturally diverse groups, such as Latinos, African Americans, and others, represent substantial portions of the U.S. population.
  B. Population growth in ethnically and culturally diverse groups is increasing at a phenomenal rate, in some cases, at twice that of Caucasians. Both immigration and birthrates contribute to this growth.
  C. Increased demands for services will be placed on the educational system as culturally diverse populations gradually acquire appropriate services and as significant growth rates continue.

5.3 Identify two ways in which assessment may contribute to the overrepresentation of culturally diverse students in special education programs.
  A. Using assessment instruments that are designed and constructed with specific language and content favoring the cultural majority.
  B. Using assessment procedures (and perhaps due to personnel) that are negatively biased, either implicitly or explicitly, toward people from culturally different backgrounds.

5.4 Identify three ways in which language diversity may contribute to assessment difficulties with students who are from a variety of cultures.
  A. Students with limited or no English proficiency may be thought to have speech or language disorders and be referred and tested for special education placement.
  B. A child's native language may appear to be English because of conversational fluency at school, but he or she may not be proficient enough to engage in academic work or assessment in English.
  C. A child's academic or psychological assessment may inaccurately portray ability because of his or her language differences.

5.5 Identify three ways in which differing sociocultural customs may affect the manner in which parents become involved in the educational process
  A. Parents from some cultural backgrounds may have a different view of special assistance than educational institutions do.
  B. Parents from certain cultural backgrounds may be reluctant to take an active role in interacting with the educational system.

C. Certain behaviors that ma suggest a disabling condition needing special education assistance are viewed as normal in some cultures and parents may not see them as problematic.

5.6 Identify two areas that require particular attention when developing an individualized education plan (IEP) for a student from a culturally diverse background.
    A. Coordination of different services and professional personnel becomes crucial.
    B. Cultural stereotypes should not be perpetuated by assumptions that are inappropriate for an IEP or otherwise improper for education.

5.7 Identify two considerations that represent difficulties in serving children from culturally diverse backgrounds in the least restrictive environment (LRE).
    A. Cultural or language instruction may be needed in addition to other teaching that focuses on remediation of a learning problem, making integration into the educational mainstream more difficult.
    B. Training limitations of school staff, rather than the child's needs, may influence placement decisions.

5.8 Identify two ways in which poverty may contribute to the academic difficulties of children from culturally diverse backgrounds, often resulting in their referral to special education.
    A. Circumstances resulting in disadvantages prenatal development and birth complications occur much more frequently among those of low socioeconomic status and nonmainstream populations.
    B. Environmental circumstances, such as malnutrition and the presence of toxic agents, that place children at risk are found most frequently in impoverished households, and poverty is most frequently evident among ethnic minority populations.

5.9 Identify two ways in which migrancy among culturally diverse populations may contribute to academic difficulties.
    A. In many cases, migrant families are characterized by economic disadvantages and language differences.
    B. Children in migrant households may move and change educational placements several times a year, contributing to limited continuity and inconsistent educational programming.

5.10 Identify three conceptual factors that have contributed to heightened attention and concern regarding the placement of children from ethnic and cultural groups in special education.
    A. A stigma is attached to special education.
    B. Special education placement for children from culturally and ethnically diverse groups may not be educationally effective in meeting their academic needs.
    C. A self-fulfilling prophecy may occur, results in youngsters' becoming what they are labeled.

Guided Review

Read – Matching Vocabulary

5.11 E	5.13 A	5.15 B	5.17 D
5.12 F	5.14 C	5.16 G	5.18 H

Reflect – Matching Vocabulary

5.19 H	5.21 B	5.23 C	5.25 D
5.20 G	5.22 E	5.24 A	5.26 F

Recite – Fill in the Blank

5.27 literate	5.31 health
5.28 roles	5.32 nondiscriminatory
5.29 diversity	5.33 explicit/focused
5.30 parental involvement	5.34 religious

Review – True/False

5.35 T	5.37 T	5.39 T	5.41 F
5.36 F	5.38 T	5.40 F	5.42 T

Chapter Review – Practice Test

5.43	C (131)	5.48	B (116)	5.53	D (122)	5.58	B (125)
5.44	B (113)	5.49	A (117)	5.54	A, C (122)	5.59	A (126)
5.45	A (113)	5.50	C (118)	5.55	B (122)	5.60	C (126)
5.46	D (114)	5.51	B (121-122)	5.56	D (122)	5.61	D (129)
5.47	D (115)	5.52	C (122)	5.57	A (124)	5.62	B (131)

Cryptogram

Multicultural education promotes learning about multiple cultures and values.

Double Puzzle

prevalence, acculturation, overrepresentation, assessment, self-fulfilling, nondiscriminatory

Scramble

Minorities are overrepresented in special education.

Crossword Puzzle

Across
2. Integrated
5. Special
6. Assess
7. Normbased
8. Bias

Down
1. Prevalence
2. Impoverished
3. Acculturation
4. General

6
Exceptionality and the Family

Focus Questions

6.1 Identify five factors that influence the ways in which families respond to infants with birth defects or disabilities.
    A.   The emotional stability of each family member.
    B.   Religious values and beliefs.
    C.   Socioeconomic status.
    D.   The severity of the disability.
    E.   The type of disability.

6.2 What three statements can be made about the stages parents may experience in responding to infants or young children with disabilities?
    A.   The stage approach needs further refinement and validation before it can be used accurately to understand, predict, or help parents deal with young infants and children with disabilities.
    B.   Parental responses are highly variable.
    C.   The adjustment process, for most parents, is continuous and distinctively individual.

6.3 Identify three ways in which a newborn child with disabilities influences the family social/ecological system.
    A.   The communication patterns within the family may change.
    B.   The power structure within the family may be altered.
    C.   The roles and responsibilities assumed by various family members may be modified.

6.4 Identify three factors in raising a child with a disability that contribute to spousal stress.
    A.   A decrease in the amount of time available for the couple's activities.
    B.   Heavy financial burdens.
    C.   Fatigue.

6.5 Identify four general phases that parents may experience in rearing a child with a disability.
    A. The diagnostic period: Does the child truly have a disability?
    B. The school period (elementary and secondary, with their inherent challenges: dealing with teasing and other peer-related behaviors, as well as learning academic, social, and vocational skills). Included in this period are the challenges of adolescence.
    C. The post school period: The child makes the transition from school to other educational or vocational activities.
    D. The period when the parents are no longer able to provide direct care and guidance for their son or daughter.

6.6 Identify four factors that influence the relationship that develops between infants with disabilities and their mothers.
    A. The mother may be unable to engage in typical feeding and caregiving activities because of the intensive medical care being provided.
    B. Some mothers may have difficulty bonding to children with whom they have little physical and social interaction.
    C. Some mothers are given little direction as to how they might become involved with their children. Without minimal involvement, some mothers become estranged from their children and find it difficult to begin the caring and bonding process.
    D. The expectations that others have about their children and their functions in nurturing them play a significant role in the relationship that develops.

6.7 Identify three ways in which fathers may respond to their children with disabilities.
    A. Fathers are more likely in internalize their feelings than are mothers.
    B. Fathers often respond to sons with disabilities differently from how they respond to daughters.
    C. Fathers may resent the time their wives spend in caring for their children with disabilities.

6.8 Identify four ways in which siblings respond to a brother or sister with a disability.
    A. Siblings tend to mirror the attitudes and behaviors of their parents toward a child with disabilities.
    B. Siblings may play a crucial role in fostering the intellectual, social, and affective development of the child with a disability.
    C. Some siblings respond by eventually becoming members of helping professions that serve populations with disabilities.
    D. Some siblings respond with feelings of resentment or deprivation.

6.9 Identify three types of support grandparents and other extended family members may render to families with children with disabilities.
    A. They may provide their own children with weekend reprieves from the pressures of the home environment.
    B. They may assist occasionally with baby-sitting or transportation.
    C. They may help their children in times of crisis by listening and helping them deal with seemingly unresolvable problems and by providing short-term and long-term financial assistance.

6.10 Describe five behaviors skilled collaborators exhibit when interacting and relating to families with children with disabilities.
    A. They establish rapport.
    B. They create supportive environments.
    C. They demonstrate sensitivity to the needs of families and seek to understand the culture and ecology of each family.
    D. They share valuable information.
    E. They listen well.

6.11 What are the five goals of family support systems?
    A. Enhancing the caregiving capacity of the family.
    B. Giving parents and other family members respite from the demands of caring for a child with a disability.
    C. Assisting the family with persistent financial demands related to the child's disability.
    D. Providing valuable training to families, extended family members, concerned neighbors, and caring friends.
    E. Improving the quality of life for all family members.

6.12 What are five potential thrusts of parent training?
    A. To help them with specific needs such as feeding their children; teaching them language skills; helping them become toilet trained; accessing adult services; finding appropriate housing; and locating appropriate postsecondary vocational training.
    B. To help them understand their legal rights.
    C. To contribute to their understanding of the nature of the disability or disabilities.

D. To make them aware of services in the community.
E. To alert them to financial assistance that is available.

Guided Review

Read – Matching Vocabulary

6.13 A	6.15 F	6.17 E	6.19 D
6.14 C	6.16 B	6.18 G	6.20 H

Reflect – Matching Vocabulary

6.21 G	6.23 C	6.25 B	6.27 H
6.22 A	6.24 F	6.26 D	6.28 E

Recite – Fill in the Blank

6.29 Confusion	6.33 Marital
6.30 Intermittently	6.34 Acknowledgment state
6.31 Die	6.35 Power structure
6.32 Defensive retreat	6.36 Satisfaction or contentment

Review – True/False

6.37 T	6.39 F	6.41 T	6.43 T
6.38 T	6.40 T	6.42 T	6.44 F

Chapter Review – Practice Test

6.45 C (161)	6.49 D (140)	6.53 C (161)	6.57 D (152)
6.46 A (148)	6.50 C (141)	6.54 B (159)	6.58 C (149)
6.47 A (139)	6.51 B (142)	6.55 A,B,C (147)	6.59 B (152)
6.48 B (139)	6.52 B (143)	6.56 C (149)	6.60 A (156)

Cryptogram

Fathers react differently than mothers to a child born with a disability.

Double Puzzle

Dyadic, respite, stages, support, "Relationships are important."

Scramble

Most individuals with hearing loss have IQs equivalent to their peers without hearing

Crossword Puzzle

Across	Down
3. Dyadic	1. Family
5. Acknowledgment	2. Realization
6. Shock	4. Defensive
7. Emotional	

7
Learning Disabilities

Focus Questions

7.1 Identify four reasons why definitions of learning disabilities have varied.

A. *Learning disabilities* is a broad, generic term that encompasses many different specific problems.
B. The study of leaning disabilities has been undertaken by a variety of different disciplines.
C. The field of learning disabilities per se has existed for a relatively short period of time and are therefore relative immature with respect to conceptual development and terminology.
D. The field of learning disabilities has grown at a very rapid pace.

7.2 Identify three ways in which classification has been used with people having learning disabilities and state how research evidence supports them.
A. Discrepancy approaches to classification are based on notions that there is an identifiable IQ-achievement gap in particular areas such as reading, math, language, and other areas. Though the evidence is not strong, some of the literature supports this approach.
B. Exclusion basically contends that the learning disabilities cannot be due to selected other conditions. There is a contention that the approach to defining learning disabilities should be inclusive where the focus is on identifying special attributes that need attention.
C. Heterogeneity classification addresses the differing array of academic domains where these children often demonstrate performance problems   Research most strongly supports the parameters of this approach to classification.

7.3 Identify two current estimated ranges for the prevalence of learning disabilities.
A. Prevalence estimates range from 2.7% to 30% of the school-age population.
B. The most reasonable estimates for school-age children range from 5% to 10%. The prevalence variation is partially due to the changing definition statements as well as pressing needs to provide service to a large number of students.

7.4 Identify eight characteristics attributed to those with learning disabilities and explain why it is difficult to characterize this group.
A. Typically, average or near-average intelligence.
B. Uneven skill levels in various areas.
C. Hyperactivity.
D. Perceptual problems.
E. Visual and auditory discrimination problems.
F. Cognition deficits, such as memory.
G. Attention problems.
H. The group of individuals included under the umbrella term *learning disabilities* is so varied that it defies simple characterization denoted by a single concept or term.

7.5 Identify four causes thought to be involved in learning disabilities.
A. Neurological damage or malfunction.
B. Maturational delay of the neurological system.
C. Genetic abnormality.
D. Environmental factors .

7.6 Identify four questions that are addressed by screening assessment in learning disabilities.
A. Is there a reason to investigate the abilities of the child fully?
B. Is there a reason to suspect that the child in any way has disabilities?
C. If the child appears to have disabilities, what are the characteristics and what sort of intervention is appropriate?
D. How should we plan for the future of the individual?

7.7 Identify three types of intervention or treatment employed with people diagnosed as having learning disabilities.
A. Medical treatment, in some circumstances involving medication to control hyperactivity.
B. Academic instruction and support in a wide variety of areas that are specifically aimed at building particular skill areas.
C. Behavioral interventions aimed at improving social skills or remediating problems in this area (behavioral procedures may also be a part of academic instruction).

7.8 How are the services and supports for adolescents and adults with learning disabilities different from those used with children?
A. Services and supports for children focus primarily on building the most basic skills.
B. Instruction during adolescence may include skill building but also may involved assistance in compensatory skills to circumvent deficit areas.
C. Services during adolescence should include instruction and assistance in transition skills that will prepare students for adulthood, employment, and further education, based on their own goals.

Guided Review

Read – Matching Vocabulary

7.9 E	7.11 B	7.13 C	7.15 H
7.10 A	7.12 G	7.14 F	7.16 D

Reflect – Matching Vocabulary

7.17 B	7.19 A	7.21 F	7.23 G
7.18 D	7.20 E	7.22 C	7.24 H

Recite – Fill in the Blank

7.25	Direct instruction	
7.26	Deficits	
7.27	Legal	
7.28	Fundamental	
7.29	Memory	
7.30	Visual	
7.31	Auditory	
7.32	51%	

Review – True/False

7.33 T	7.35 T	7.37 T	7.39 F
7.34 F	7.36 T	7.38 F	7.40 F

Chapter Review – Practice Test

7.41 C (166)	7.45 B (170)	7.49 A (176)	7.53 D (178)
7.42 D (166)	7.46 C (175)	7.50 B (176)	7.54 A (180)
7.43 A (168)	7.47 A (189)	7.51 C (176)	7.55 B (195)
7.44 B (189)	7.48 D (175)	7.52 D (189)	7.56 C (165)

Cryptogram

People with learning disabilities usually achieve at low levels in reading.

Double Puzzle

deficit, memory, auditory, direct instruction

Scramble

The field of learning disabilities reflects a strong interdisciplinary nature.

Crossword Puzzle

Across	Down
2. Kirk	1. Brief
5. Lifelong	3. Hyperactivity
6. Achievement	4. Cognition
7. Retarded	5. Learning
8. Overused	

8
Attention-Deficit/Hyperactivity Disorder (ADHD)

Focus Questions

8.1 Identify three behavioral symptoms commonly associated with ADHD.

    A.   Impulsive behavior.

    B.   Fidgeting or hyperactivity.

    C.   Inability to focus attention.

8.2 Identify two ways the behavior of children with ADHD detrimentally affects instructional settings.

    A.   Children with ADHD challenge teachers' skills in classroom management as they are in and out of their seats, pestering their classmates, and perhaps exhibiting aggressive behavior toward other students.

    B.   Children with ADHD challenge teachers' skills in instruction in that they may be unable to focus on instructions, they may impulsively start an assignment before directions are complete, and they may submit incomplete assignments because they did not listen to all the instructions.

8.3 Identify four other areas of disability that are often found to be comorbid with ADHD.

    A.   Learning disabilities.

    B.   Tourette's syndrome.

    C.   Conduct disorders.

    D.   Emotional disorders.

8.4 Identify the three major types of ADHD according to the *DSM-IV*.

    A.   Attention-deficit/hyperactivity disorder, combined type.

    B.   Attention-deficit/hyperactivity disorder, predominantly inattentive type.

    C.   Attention-deficit/hyperactivity disorder, predominantly hyperactive-impulsive type.

8.5 Identify two prevalence estimates for ADHD that characterize the difference in occurrence by gender.

    A.   Some estimates of gender differences range from 2:1 to 10:1 with males outnumbering females.

    B.   On the average, the male/female ratio appears to be about 3.5:1.

8.6 Identify the two broad categories of assessment information useful in diagnosing ADHD.

    A.   Information about medical terms.

    B.   Information about educational, behavioral, and contextual circumstances.

8.7 Identify three areas of characteristics that present challenges for individuals with ADHD.

    A.   Difficulties in self-regulation, impulsivity, and hyperactivity.

    B.   Difficulties in social relationships.

    C.   Significant challenges in academic performance.

8.8 Identify three possible causes of ADHD.

    A.   Neurological dysfunction that is trauma-based.

    B.   Neurological dysfunction due to brain structure differences.

    C.   Hereditary transmission.

8.9 Identify two approaches to intervention that appear to show positive results with individuals having ADHD.

    A.   Medication

    B.   Behavior modification

Guided Review

Read – Matching Vocabulary

8.10 A	8.12 B	8.14 D	8.16 H
8.11 G	8.13 F	8.15 C	8.17 E

Reflect – Matching Vocabulary

8.18 E	8.20 G	8.22 H	8.24 B
8.19 F	8.21 C	8.23 A	8.25 D

Recite – Fill in the Blank

8.26 Learning disabilities	8.28 Identical, fraternal
8.27 Parents/caregivers, teachers	8.29 Medical

Review – True/False

8.30 F	8.32 T	8.34 T	8.36 F
8.31 T	8.33 F	8.35 F	8.37 F

Chapter Review – Practice Test

8.38 A (209)	8.43 B (215)	8.48 A (219)	8.53 D (223)
8.39 D (211)	8.44 A (217)	8.49 D (220)	8.54 C (223)
8.40 D (212)	8.45 C (219)	8.50 A (220)	8.55 A (224)
8.41 A (213)	8.46 B (219)	8.51 C (221)	8.56 B (225)
8.42 C (214)	8.47 C (219)	8.52 D (222)	8.57 B (207)

Cryptogram

Behavior modification is an effective approach with students with ADHD.

Double Puzzle

structure, impulsivity, hyperactivity, comorbid, "ADHD is a lifelong disability."

Scramble

Impulsivity, fidgeting, and inability to focus are common characteristics of ADHD.

Crossword Puzzle

Across
3. Structure
4. Impulsivity
5. Referral
6. Identical
7. Comorbid
8. Executive

Down
1. Hyperactivity
2. Substance
6. Inclusion

9

Emotional/Behavioral Disorders

Focus Questions

9.1 Identify six essential parts of the definitions describing emotional/behavioral disorders.
- A. The behaviors in question must be exhibited to a marked extent.
- B. Learning problems that are not attributable to intellectual, sensory, or health deficits are common.
- C. Satisfactory relationships with parents, teachers, siblings, and others are few.
- D. Behaviors occur in many settings and under normal circumstances are considered inappropriate.
- E. A pervasive mood of unhappiness or depression is frequently displayed by children with E/BD.
- F. Physical symptoms or fears associated with the demands of school are common in some children.

9.2 Identify five factors that influence the ways in which others' behaviors are perceived.
- A. Our personal beliefs, standards, and values.
- B. Our tolerance for certain behaviors and our emotional fitness at the time the behaviors are exhibited.
- C. Our perceptions of normalcy, which are often based on personal perspective rather than on an objective standard of normalcy as established by consensus or research.
- D. The context in which a behavior takes place.
- E. The frequency with which the behavior occurs or its intensity.

9.3 Identify three reasons why classification systems are important to professionals who identify, treat, and educate individuals with E/BD.
- A. They provide a means of describing and identifying various E/BD.
- B. They provide a common language for communicating about various types and subtypes of E/BD.
- C. They sometimes provide a basis for treating a disorder and making predictions about treatment outcomes.

9.4   What differentiates externalizing disorders from internalizing disorders?
    A.   Externalizing disorders involve behaviors that are directed at others (e.g., fighting, assaulting, stealing, vandalizing).
    B.   Internalizing disorders involve behaviors that are directed inwardly or at oneself more that at others (e.g., fears, phobias, depression).

9.5   Identify five general characteristics (intellectual, adaptive, social, and achievement) of children and youth in E/BD.
    A.   Children and youth with E/BD tend to have average to below-average IQs compared to their normal peers.
    B.   Children and youth with E/BD have difficulties in relating socially and responsibly to persons such as peers, parents, teachers, and other authority figures.
    C.   Three out of four children with E/BD show clinically significant language deficits.
    D.   More than 40% of the youth with disabilities in correctional facilities are youngsters with identified E/BD.
    E.   In contrast with other students with disabilities, students with E/BD are absent more often, fail more classes, are retained more frequently, and are less successful in passing minimum competency examinations.

9.6   What can be accurately said about the causes of E/BD?
    A.   E/BD are caused by sets of continuously interacting biological, genetic, cognitive, social, emotional, and cultural variables.

9.7   What four important outcomes are achieved through a functional behavioral assessment?
    A.   A complete description of all of the problem behaviors, including their intensity, their length, their frequency, and their impact.
    B.   A description of the events that seem to set off the problem behaviors.
    C.   One or more predictions regarding when and under what conditions the problem behaviors occur.
    D.   Identification of the functions or consequences that are achieved by the problem behaviors.

9.8   What five guiding principles are associated with systems of care?
    A.   Children with emotional disturbances have access to services that address physical, emotional, social, and educational needs.
    B.   Children receive individualized services based on unique needs and potentials and guided by an individualized service plan.
    C.   Children receive services within the least restrictive environment that is appropriate.
    D.   Families are full participants in all aspects of the planning and delivery of services.
    E.   Children receive integrated services with connections between child-serving agencies and programs and mechanisms from planning, developing, and coordinating services.

9.9   What five factors should be considered in placing a child or youth with E/BD in general education settings and related classes?
    A.   Will the child or youth be able to achieve his or her IEP goals and objectives in the general education environment?
    B.   Will the child or youth pose significant management problems for teachers and others in the general education setting?
    C.   Will the behavior(s) of the child or youth pose significant safety problems for other students?
    D.   Will the behavior(s) of the child or youth interfere significantly with the learning of other classmates?
    E.   Will the child or youth benefit from the curriculum delivered in the general education setting?

9.10   What are several promising practices for dealing with challenging behavior in children and youth?
    A.   Behavioral assessment must be linked with interventions that follow the student through all placements.
    B.   Multiple interventions are necessary for most students. Any positive effect of a single strategy is likely to be temporary.
    C.   Interventions must address not only the behavior that led to disciplinary action but a constellation of related behaviors and contributing factors.
    D.   Interventions must promote maintenance over time and generalization across settings.
    E.   Combined proactive, corrective, and instructive classroom management strategies must target specific prosocial and antisocial behaviors and the "thinking skills" that mediate such behaviors.
    F.   Interventions must be developmentally appropriate and address strengths and weaknesses of the individual student and his or her environment.
    G.   Parent education and family therapy are critical components of effective programs for antisocial children and youth.
    H.   Interventions are most effective when provided early in life.

I. Interventions should be guided by schoolwide and districtwide policies that emphasize positive interventions over punitive ones.
J. Interventions should be fair, consistent, culturally and racially nondiscriminatory, and sensitive to cultural diversity.
K. Interventions should be evaluated as to their short-term and long-term effectiveness.
L. Teachers and support staff need to be well trained with respect to assessment and intervention.
M. The school, home, and community agencies must collaborate to help children and youth.

Guided Review

Read – Matching Vocabulary

9.11 F	9.13 H	9.15 E	9.17 B
9.12 D	9.14 A	9.16 G	9.18 C

Reflect – Matching Vocabulary

9.19 A	9.21 D	9.23 G	9.25 B
9.20 F	9.22 H	9.24 E	9.26 C

Recite – Fill in the Blank

9.27 Incompleteness	9.31 Rumination
9.28 Multiple, emotional	9.32 75%
9.29 School	9.33 Self-esteem
9.30 Common	9.34 Performance

Review – True/False

9.35 F	9.37 T	9.39 T	9.41 T
9.36 F	9.38 T	9.40 F	9.42 T

Chapter Review – Practice Test

9.43 B (259)	9.48 A (236)	9.53 B (242)	9.58 B (246-247)
9.44 C (262)	9.49 D (264)	9.54 A (242)	9.59 A (248)
9.45 A (253)	9.50 D (236)	9.55 D (243)	9.60 D (250-251)
9.46 A (234)	9.51 B (238)	9.56 C (243)	9.61 B (252)
9.47 C (235)	9.52 C (239)	9.57 C (245)	9.62 C (252)

Cryptogram

Three out of four children with E/BD show clinically significant language deficits.

Double Puzzle

wraparound, pica, functional, behavioral, "Behavioral assessments must be linked with treatment."

Scramble

Students with E/BD are retained more frequently than their nondisabled peers.

Crossword Puzzle

Across
2. Four
7. Socialized
9. Involuntary
10. Emotional

Down
1. Autism
3. Family
4. Reactive
5. Pica
6. Wraparound
8. Early

10
Mental Retardation (Intellectual Disabilities)

10.1 Identify the major components of the AAMR definition of mental retardation.
- A. Significant limitations in intellectual abilities.
- B. Significant limitations in adaptive behavior as expressed in conceptual, social, and practical adaptive skills.
- C. Disability originates before the age of 18.
- D. The severity of the condition is tempered by each individual's participation, interactions, and social roles within the community; their overall physical and mental health; and the environmental context.

10.2 Identify four approaches to classifying people with mental retardation.
- A. Severity of the condition may be described in terms of mild, moderate, severe, and profound mental retardation.
- B. Educability expectations are designated for groups of children who are educable, trainable, and custodial.
- C. Medical descriptors classify mental retardation on the basis of the origin of the condition (e.g., infection, intoxication, trauma, chromosomal abnormality).
- D. Classification based on the type and extent of support needed categorizes people with mental retardation according to intermittent, limited, extensive, or pervasive needs for support in order to function in natural settings.

10.3 What is the prevalence of mental retardation?
- A. Over 600,000 students between the ages of 6 and 21 are labeled as having mental retardation and are receiving service under IDEA. Approximately 11% of all students with disabilities between the ages of 6 and 21 have mental retardation.
- B. The National Health Survey-Disability Supplement found that people with mental retardation constitute 0.83% of the total populations, or 2 million people.
- C. The President's Committee on Mental Retardation (2000) estimated that between 6.2 and 7.5 million Americans of all ages, or 3% of the general population, experience mental retardation. These figures are considerably higher that the 2 million people reported in the National Health Survey.

10.4 Identify intellectual, self-regulation, and adaptive skills characteristics of individuals with mental retardation.
- A. Intellectual characteristics may include learning and memory deficiencies, difficulties in establishing learning sets, and inefficient rehearsal strategies.
- B. Self-regulation characteristics include difficulty in mediating or regulation behavior.
- C. Adaptive skills characteristics may include difficulties in coping with the demands of environment, developing interpersonal relationships, developing language skills, and taking care of personal needs.

10.5 Identify the academic, motivational, speech and language, and physical demands of environment, developing interpersonal relationships, developing language skills, and taking care of personal needs.
- A. Students with mental retardation exhibit significant deficits in the areas of reading and mathematics.
- B. Students with mild mental retardation have poor reading mechanics and comprehension, compared to their same-age peers.
- C. Students with mental retardation may be able to learn basic computations but be unable to apply concepts appropriately in a problem-solving situation.
- D. Motivational difficulties may reflect learned helplessness – "No matter what I do or how hard I try, I will not succeed."
- E. The most common speech difficulties involve articulation problems, voice problems, and stuttering.
- F. Language differences are generally associated with delays in language development rather than the bizarre use of language.
- G. Physical differences generally are not evident for individuals with mild mental retardation because the retardation is usually not associated with genetic factors.
- H. The more severe the mental retardation, the greater the probability of genetic causation and compounding physiological problems.

10.6 Identify the causes of mental retardation.
- A. Mental retardation is the result of multiple causes, some known, many unknown. The cause of mental retardation is generally not known for the individual with mild retardation.
- B. Causes associated with moderate to profound mental retardation include sociocultural influences, biomedical factors, behavioral factors, and unknown prenatal influences.

10.7 Why are early intervention services for children with mental retardation so important?
    A.   Early intervention services are needed to provide a stimulating environment for the child to enhance growth and development.
    B.   Early intervention programs focus on the development of communication skills, social interaction, and readiness for formal instruction.

10.8 Identify five skills areas that should be addressed in programs for elementary-age children with mental retardation.
    A.   Motor development skills
    B.   Self-help skills
    C.   Social skills
    D.   Communication skills
    E.   Academic skills

10.9 Identify four educational goals for adolescents with mental retardation.
    A.   To increase the individual's personal independence.
    B.   To enhance opportunities for participation in the local community.
    C.   To prepare for employment.
    D.   To facilitate a successful transition to the adult years.

10.10 Why is the inclusion of students with mental retardation in general education settings important to an appropriate educational experience?
    A.   Regardless of the severity of their condition, students with mental retardation benefit from placement in general education environments where opportunities for inclusion with nondisabled peers are systematically planned and implemented.

Guided Review

Read – Matching Vocabulary

10.11 C	10.13 G	10.15 D	10.17 H
10.12 E	10.14 F	10.16 A	10.18 B

Reflect – Matching Vocabulary

10.19 E	10.21 C	10.23 B	10.25 G
10.20 H	10.22 A	10.24 F	10.26 D

Recite – Fill in the Blank

10.27 Profound	10.31 Prenatal
10.28 Adaptive	10.32 Cultural-familial
10.29 Intermittent	10.33 Chromosomal
10.30 6.6	10.34 Stuttering

Review – True/False

10.35 T	10.37 T	10.39 T	10.41 F
10.36 T	10.38 T	10.40 F	10.42 F

Chapter Review – Practice Test

10.43 A (273)	10.48 C (278)	10.53 C (284)	10.58 C (290)
10.44 B (274)	10.49 B (281)	10.54 A (285)	10.59 C (294)
10.45 A (274)	10.50 D (282)	10.55 B (287)	10.60 D (296)
10.46 C (277)	10.51 B (282)	10.56 D (287)	10.61 A (282)
10.47 D (278)	10.52 A (284)	10.57 B (275)	10.62 C (289)

Cryptogram

The cause of mild retardation is generally unknown.

biomedical, metabolic, metacognitive, intellectual, neurofibromatosis

Scramble

Students with mental retardation benefit from inclusion when it is systematically planned and implemented.

Crossword Puzzle

Across
1. Birth
4. Norm
6. Greater
9. Medical
10. Memory

Down
2. Reading
3. Most
5. Mental
7. Rubella
8. Two

11
Communication Disorders

Focus Questions

11.1 Identify four ways in which speech, language, and communication are interrelated.
   A.   Both speech and language from part, but not all, of communication.
   B.   Some components of communication involved language but not speech.
   C.   Some speech does not involve language.
   D.   The development of communication, language, and speech overlap to some degree.

11.2 Identify two ways in which language delay and language disorder are different.
   A.   In language delay, the sequence of development is intact, but the rate is interrupted.
   B.   In language disorder, the sequence of development is interrupted.

11.3 Identify three factors thought to cause language disorders.
   A.   Defective or deficient sensory systems.
   B.   Neurological damage occurring through physical trauma or accident.
   C.   Deficient or disrupted learning opportunities during language development.

11.4 Describe two ways in which treatment approaches for language disorders generally differ for children and for adults.
   A.   Treatment for children generally addresses initial acquisition or learning of language.
   B.   Treatment for adults involves relearning or reacquiring language function.

11.5 Identify three factors thought to cause stuttering.
   A.   Learned behavior, emotional problems, and neurological problems can contribute to stuttering.
   B.   Some research has suggested that people who stutter have a brain organization differing from those who do not.
   C.   People who stutter may learn their speech patterns as an outgrowth of the normal nonfluency evident when speech development first occurs.

11.6 Identify two ways in which learning theory and home environments relate to delayed speech.
   A.   The home environment may provide little opportunity to learn speech.
   B.   The home environment may interfere with speech development when speaking is punished.

11.7 Identify two reasons why some professionals are reluctant to treat functional articulation disorders in young school children.
   A.   Many articulation problems evident in young children are developmental in nature, so speech may improve with age.
   B.   Articulation problems are quite frequent among young children and treatment resources are limited.

Guided Review

Read – Matching Vocabulary

11.8 D	11.10 E	11.12 G	11.14 H
11.9 F	11.11 B	11.13 C	11.15 A

Reflect – Matching Vocabulary

11.16 C	11.18 G	11.20 E	11.22 D
11.17 A	11.19 F	11.21 H	11.23 B

Recite – Fill in the Blank

11.24 Developmental, acquired
11.25 Morphology
11.26 Speech, language
11.27 R, s, th
11.28 Age, development
11.29 Speech

Review – True/False

11.30 T	11.32 F	11.34 T	11.36 F
11.31 T	11.33 F	11.35 T	11.37 T

Chapter Review – Practice Test

11.38 B (303)	11.43 C (309)	11.48 B (318)	11.53 A (321)
11.39 C (312)	11.44 B (313)	11.49 A (319)	11.54 C (326)
11.40 D (305)	11.45 C (315)	11.50 C (310)	11.55 C (328)
11.41 B (307)	11.46 B (314)	11.51 D (320)	11.56 D (330)
11.42 D (308)	11.47 C (317)	11.52 B (321)	11.57 A (318)

Cryptogram

Disrupted learning opportunities can cause problems with language.

Double Puzzle

emphysema, augmentative, cleft, functional, neurological

Scramble

Speech often improves with age.

Crossword Puzzle

Across
1. Syntax
5. Neurological
7. Acquired
8. Delayed
9. Th

Down
1. Semantics
2. Stutter
3. Pragmatics
4. Hoarse
6. Cleft

12
Severe and Multiple Disabilities

Focus Questions

12.1 What are the three components of the TASH definition of severe disabilities?
    A. The relationship of the individual with the environment (adaptive fit).
    B. The inclusion of people of all ages.

C. The necessity of extensive ongoing support in life activities.

12.2 Define the terms *multiple disabilities* and *deaf-blindness* as described in IDEA.
  A. *Multiple disabilities* refers to concomitant impairments (such as mental retardation-orthopedic impairments, etc.). The combination causes educational problems so severe that they cannot be accommodated in special education programs solely for one impairment. One such combination is "dual diagnosis," a condition characterized by serious emotional disturbance (challenging behaviors) in conjunction with severe mental retardation.
  B. *Deaf-blindness* involves concomitant hearing and visual impairments. The combination causes communication and other developmental and educational problems so severe that they cannot be accommodated in special education programs solely for children who are dear or blind.

12.3 Identify the estimated prevalence and causes of severe and multiple disabilities.
  A. Prevalence estimates generally range from 0.1% to 1% of the general population.
  B. Students with multiple disabilities accounted for about 2% of the 5.5 million students with disabilities served in the public schools. Approximately 0.0002% of students with disabilities were labeled *deaf-blind.*
  C. Many possible causes of severe and multiple disabilities exist. Most severe and multiple disabilities are evident at birth. Birth defects may be the result of genetic or metabolic problems. Most identifiable causes of severe mental retardation and related developmental disabilities are genetic in origin. Factors associated with poisoning, accidents, malnutrition, physical and emotional neglect, and disease are also known causes.

12.4 What are the characteristics of persons with severe and multiple disabilities?
  A. Mental retardation is often a primary condition.
  B. Most children will not benefit from basic academics instruction in literacy and mathematics. Instruction in functional academics is the most effective approach to learning academic skills.
  C. People with severe and multiple disabilities often do not have age-appropriate adaptive skills and need ongoing services and supports to facilitate learning in this area.
   Significant speech and language deficits and delays are a primary characteristic.
   Physical and health needs are common, involving conditions such as congenital heart disease, epilepsy, respiratory problems, spasticity, athetoses, and hypotonia. Vision and hearing loss are also common.

12.5 Identify three types of educational assessments for students with severe and multiple disabilities.
  A. Traditionally, there has been a heavy reliance on standardized measurements, particularly the IQ test, in identifying people with severe and multiple disabilities.
  B. Assessments that focus on valued skills to promote independence and quality of life in natural settings are referred to as *functional, ecological,* or *authentic assessment.*
  C. Students with disabilities must participate in statewide or district-wide assessments of achievement or provide a statement of why that assessment is not appropriate for the child. For many students with severe disabilities, these assessments are inappropriate and they are excluded from taking them. Alternate assessments are conducted instead.

12.6 Identify the features of effective services and supports for children with severe and multiple disabilities during the early childhood years.
  A. Services and supports must begin at birth.
  B. Programs for infants and toddlers are both child- and family-centered.
  C. The goals for preschool programs are to maximize development across several developmental areas, to develop social interaction and classroom participation skills, to increase community participation through support to family and caregivers, and to prepare the child for inclusive school placement.
  D. Effective and inclusive preschool programs have a holistic view of the child, see the classroom as a community of learners, base the program on a collaborative ethic, use authentic assessment, create a heterogeneous environment, make available a range of individualized supports and services, engage educators in reflective teaching, and emphasize multiple ways of teaching and learning.

12.7 Identify the features of effective services and supports for children with severe and multiple disabilities during the elementary school years.
  A. Self-determination – students' preferences and needs are taken into account in developing educational objectives.
  B. The school values and supports parental involvement.
  C. Instruction focuses on frequently-used functional skills related to everyday life activities.
   Assistive technology and augmentative communication are available to maintain or increase the functional capabilities of the students with severe and multiple disabilities.

12.8 Describe four outcomes that are important in planning for the transition from school to adult life for adolescents with severe and multiple disabilities.

    A.   Establishing a network of friends and acquaintances.
    B.   Developing the ability to use community resources on a regular basis.
    C.   Securing a paid job that supports the use of community resources and interaction with peers.
    D.   Establishing independence and autonomy in making lifestyle choices.

12.9 Describe four features that characterize successful inclusive education for students with severe and multiple disabilities.
    A.   Physical placement of students with severe and multiple disabilities in the general education schools and classes they would attend if they didn't have disabilities.
    B.   Systematic organization of opportunities for interaction between students with severe and multiple disabilities and students without disabilities.
    C.   Specific instruction to increase the competence of students with severe and multiple disabilities in interacting with students without disabilities.
    D.   Highly trained teachers competent in the necessary instructional and assistive technology to facilitate social interaction between students with and without disabilities.

12.10 Describe four bioethical dilemmas that can affect people with severe disabilities and their families.
    A.   Genetic engineering may be used to conquer disease or as a means to enhance or perfect human beings.
    B.   Genetic screening may be effective in preventing disease but can also be used by insurance companies, employers, courts, schools, adoption agencies, law enforcement, and the military to discriminate against people with severe disabilities.
    C.   Genetic counselors can provide important information to families but may also lose neutrality and give their own personal beliefs about that the family should do.
    D.   Selective abortion and options for the withholding of medical treatment may allow parents to make the very personal decision about whether the quality of life for their unborn child may be so diminished that life world not be worth living. However, it can also be argued that no one has the right to decide for someone else whether a life is worth living.

Guided Review

Read – Matching Vocabulary

12.11 A	12.13 C	12.15 G	12.17 B
12.12 E	12.14 F	12.16 H	12.18 D

Reflect – Matching Vocabulary

12.19 C	12.21 G	12.23 B	12.25 F
12.20 H	12.22 E	12.24 A	12.26 D

Recite – Fill in the Blank

12.27 Respiratory ventilation	12.30 Adaptability
12.28 Dual sensory	12.31 Peers
12.29 Inclusion	Neutrality

Review – True/False

12.33 T	12.35 F	12.37 T	12.39 T
12.34 T	12.36 F	12.38 F	12.40 F

Chapter Review – Practice Test

12.41 B (340)	12.46 D (342)	12.51 A (344)	12.56 B (350)
12.42 C (340)	12.47 A (358)	12.52 A, B, D (346)	12.57 A (351)
12.43 D (341)	12.48 C (342)	12.53 C (347)	12.58 B (357)
12.44 A (341)	12.49 B (342)	12.54 A (347)	12.59 A (348)
12.45 B (341)	12.50 C (341)	12.55 D (357)	12.60 C (344)

Cryptogram

The greater the retardation, the greater the speech and language needs.

epilepsy, adaptive, functional, gastronomy, respite care

Early intervention is of key importance for individuals with severe disabilities.

Across
  5. Retardation
  8. Hypotonia
  9. Respite
  10. Adaptive

Down
  1. Gastronomy
  2. Natural
  3. Epilepsy
  4. Genetic
  6. Athetosis
  7. Bioethics

13
Autism

13.1 Identify four areas of functional challenge often found in children with autism.
  A.   Language
  B.   Interpersonal skills
  C.   Emotional or affective behaviors
  D.   Intellectual functioning

13.2 What is the general prevalence estimated for autism?
  A.   Approximately 5 cases per 10,000

13.3 Identify six characteristics of children with autism.
  A.   As infants, they are often unresponsive to physical contact or affection from their parents and later have extreme difficulty relating to other people.
  B.   Most have impaired or delayed language skills, with about half not developing speech at all.
  C.   Those who have speech often engage in echolalia and other inappropriate behavior.
  D.   They frequently engage in self-stimulatory behavior.
  E.   Changes in their routine are met with intense resistance.
  F.   Most have a reduced level of intellectual functioning.

13.4 Identify the two broad theoretical views regarding the causes of autism.
  A.   The psychoanalytic view places a great deal of emphasis on the interaction between the family and the child.
  B.   The biological view has included neurological damage and genetics.

13.5 Identify four major approaches to the treatment of autism.
  A.   Psychoanalytic-based therapy focuses on repairing the emotional damage presumed to have resulted from faulty family relationships.
  B.   Medically based treatment often involves the use of medication.
  C.   Behavioral interventions focus on enhancing specific appropriate behaviors or on reducing inappropriate behaviors.
  D.   Educational interventions employ the full range of educational placements.

13.6 G	13.8 D	13.10 E	13.12 C
13.7 B	13.9 A	13.11 F	13.13 H

Reflect – Matching Vocabulary

13.14 C	13.16 A	13.18 G	13.20 D
13.15 E	13.17 B	13.19 H	13.21 F

Recite – Fill in the Blank

13.22 5	13.26 Behavioral
13.23 High	13.27 Facilitated communication
13.24 Low	13.28 Disability
13.25 Delivery	13.29 Savant-like

Review – True/False

13.30 F	13.32 F	13.34 T	13.36 F
13.31 T	13.33 F	13.35 T	13.37 F

Chapter Review – Practice Test

13.38 D (363)	13.43 A (366)	13.48 C (370)	13.53 A (379)
13.39 D (362)	13.44 D (367)	13.49 D (373)	13.54 B (379)
13.40 C (364)	13.45 A (367)	13.50 D (367)	13.55 C (381)
13.41 B (366)	13.46 B (366)	13.51 B (373)	13.56 D (363)
13.42 A (367)	13.47 A (370)	13.52 C (375)	13.57 A (364)

Cryptogram

Two broad theoretical views regarding the causes of autism include psychoanalytical and biological

Double Puzzle

medical, educational, psychoanalytical, medical, four major approaches to treatment

Scramble

Behavioral treatment can be used effectively for teaching language development and social skills

Crossword Puzzle

Across	Down
4. Generalization	1. Transition
6. Flat	2. IDEA
8. Prevalence	3. Social
9. Asperger	5. Ultimate
	7. Eye

14
Traumatic Brain Injury

Focus Questions

14.1 Identify three key elements of traumatic brain injury.
- A. The brain is damaged by external forces that cause tearing, bruising, or swelling.
- B. The injuries, open and/or closed head, dramatically influence the individual's functioning in several areas, including psychosocial behavior, speech and language, cognitive performance, vision and hearing, and motor abilities.
- C. The brain injury often results in permanent disabilities.

14.2 Identify four general characteristics of individuals with traumatic or acquired brain injuries.
- A. Individuals with traumatic or acquired brain injuries often exhibit cognitive deficits, including problems with memory, concentration, attention, and problem solving.
- B. Speech and language problems are frequently evident, including word retrieval problems, slurred or unintelligible speech, and aphasia.

    C.   These individuals may also present social and behavioral problems, including increased irritability, inability to suppress or manage socially inappropriate behaviors, low thresholds for frustration, and insensitivity to others.

    D.   Neuromotor and physical problems may also be present, including eye-hand coordination impairments, vision and hearing deficits, and paralysis.

14.3   Identify the most common causes of brain injury in children, youth, and adults.
    A.   The most common causes of brain injury in young children are falls, neglect, and physical abuse.
    B.   For children in the elementary grades, the most common causes are falls, pedestrian or bicycle accidents involving a motor vehicle, and sports.
    C.   For high school students and adults, the most common causes are motor vehicle accidents and sports-related injuries.

14.4   Describe the focus of educational interventions for individuals with traumatic or acquired brain injuries.
    A.   Educational interventions are directed at improving the general behaviors of the individual, including problems solving, planning and developing insight; building appropriate social behaviors such as working with others, suppressing inappropriate behaviors, and using appropriate etiquette; developing expressive and receptive language skills, including word retrieval, event description, and understanding instructions; and writing skills.
    B.   Other academic skills are also taught that are relevant to the students' needs and developmental level of functioning.
    C.   Transition planning for postsecondary education and training is also essential to the well-being of the individual with traumatic or acquired brain injury.

14.5   Identify four common types of head injuries.
    A.   Common head injuries include concussion, contusions, skull fractures, and epidural and subdural hemorrhages.

14.6   Describe five important elements of medical treatment for individuals with traumatic or acquired brain injuries.
    A.   The first stage of treatment is directed at preserving the individual's life, addressing swelling and bleeding, and minimizing complications.
    B.   Once the individual regains consciousness or can benefit from more active therapies, the learning and relearning of pre-injury skills begin.
    C.   The last stage focuses on preparing the individual to return to home, school, or work settings; and readying the individual to work with other health care and training providers.
    D.   The last stage is also characterized by the provision of psychological services directed at helping individuals and their families cope with the injuries and their effects.
    E.   Throughout all the stages of treatment, interdisciplinary collaboration and cooperation are essential to the individual's success.

Guided Review

Read – Matching Vocabulary

14.7 F	14.9 E	14.11 C
14.8 A	14.10 B	14.12 D

Reflect – Matching Vocabulary

14.13 A	14.15 F	14.17 H	14.19 G
14.14 E	14.16 C	14.18 D	14.20 B

Recite – Fill in the Blank

14.21 Traumatic Brain Injury	14.23 Seizures
14.22 Blood	14.24 Cognition

Review – True/False

14.25 T	14.27 T	14.29 T	14.31 F
14.26 T	14.28 F	14.30 T	14.32 F

Chapter Review – Practice Test

14.33 D (400)	14.38 C (387)	14.43 A (388)	14.48 C (397)
14.34 C (387)	14.39 B (387)	14.44 C (390)	14.49 C (397)
14.35 A (385)	14.40 C (388)	14.45 A (390)	14.50 A (403)
14.36 D (386)	14.41 B (388)	14.46 B (391)	14.51 D (397)
14.37 C (387)	14.42 A (388)	14.47 D (397)	14.52 D (392)

Cryptogram

Following a TBI, it may be difficult to retrieve new information.

Double Puzzle

concussion, contusion, aphasia, fracture, magnetic resonance imaging

Scramble

Social behaviors are frequently impacted by traumatic brain injury.

Crossword Puzzle

Across
2. Aphasia
7. Neuromotor
8. Coma
9. Expressive
10. Blood

Down
1. Fracture
3. Helmets
4. Contusion
5. Judgment
6. Concussiion

15
Hearing Loss

Focus Questions

15.1 Describe how sound is transmitted through the human ear.
- A. A vibrator – such as a string, reed, or column or air – causes displacement of air particles.
- B. Vibrations are carried by air, metal, water, or other substances.
- C. Sound waves are displaced air particles that produce a pattern of auricular waves that move away from the sources to a receiver.
- D. The human ear collects, processes, and transmits sounds to the brain, where they are decoded into meaningful language.

15.2 Distinguish between the terms *deaf* and *hard-of-hearing*.
- A. A person who is deaf typically has profound or total loss of auditory sensitivity and very little, if any, auditory perception.
- B. For the person who is deaf, the primary means of information input is through vision; speech received through the ears is not understood.
- C. A person who is hard-of-hearing (partially hearing) generally has residual hearing through the use of a hearing aid, which is sufficient to process language through

15.3 Why is it important to consider age of onset and anatomical site when defining a hearing loss?
- A. Age of onset is critical in determining the type and extent of intervention necessary to minimize the effect of the hearing loss.
- B. Three types of peripheral hearing loss are associated with anatomical site: conductive, sensorineural, and mixed.
- C. Central auditory hearing loss occurs when there is a dysfunction in the cerebral cortex (outer layer of gray matter in the brain).

15.4   What are the estimated prevalence and causes of hearing loss?

A. It has been extremely difficult to determine the prevalence of hearing loss. Estimates of hearing loss in the United States go as high as 28 million people; approximately 11 million people have significant irreversible hearing loss, and 1 million are deaf.

B. Nearly 71,000 students between the ages of 6 and 21 have a hearing impairment and are receiving special education services in U.S. schools. These students account for approximately 1.5% of school-age students identified as having a disability.

C. Although more than 200 types of deafness have been related to hereditary factors, the cause of 50% of all hearing loss remains unknown.

D. A common hereditary disorder is otosclerosis (bone destruction in the middle ear).

E. Nonhereditary hearing problems evident at birth may be associated with maternal health problems: infections (e.g., rubella), anemia, jaundice, central nervous system disorders, the use of drugs, sexually transmitted disease, chicken pox, anoxia, and birth trauma.

F. Acquired hearing losses are associated with postnatal infections, such as measles, mumps, influenza, typhoid fever, and scarlet fever.

G. Environmental factors associated with hearing loss include extreme changes in air pressure caused by explosions, head trauma, foreign objects in the ear, and loud noise. Loud noise is rapidly becoming one of the major causes of hearing problems.

15.5 Describe the basic intelligence, speech and language skills, educational achievement, and social development associated with people who are deaf or hard-of-hearing.

A. Intellectual development for people with hearing loss is more a function of language development than cognitive ability. Any difficulties in performance appear to be closely associated with speaking, reading, and writing the English language, but are not related to level of intelligence.

B. Speech and English language skills are the areas of development most severely affected for those with a hearing loss. The effects of a hearing loss on English language development vary considerably.

C. Most people with a hearing loss are able to use speech as the primary mode for language acquisition. People who are congenitally deaf are unable to receive information through the speech process unless they have learned to speechread.

D. Reading is the academic area most negatively affected for students with a hearing loss.

E. The social and psychological development in children with a hearing loss if different in comparison to children who can hear. Different or delayed language acquisition may lead to more limited opportunities for social interaction. Children who are deaf may have more adjustment challenges when attempting to communicate with children who can hear, but appear to be more secure when conversing with children who are also deaf. For some people who are deaf, social isolation from the hearing world is not considered an adjustment problem. It is a natural state of being where people are bonded together by a common language, customs, and heritage.

15.6 Identify four approaches to teaching communication skills to persons with a hearing loss.

A. The auditory approach to communication emphasizes the use of amplified sound and residual hearing to develop oral communication skills.

B. The oral approach to communication emphasizes use of amplified sound and residual hearing but may also employ speechreading, reading and writing, and motokinesthetic speech training.

C. The manual approach stresses the use of signs in teaching children who are deaf to communicate.

D. Total communication employs the use of residual hearing, amplification, speechreading, speech training, reading, and writing in combination with manual systems to teach communication skills to children with a hearing loss.

15.7 Describe the uses of closed-caption television, computers, and the Internet for people with a hearing loss.

A. Closed-caption television translates dialogue from a television program into captions (subtitles) that are broadcast on the television screen. Closed-caption television provides the person with a hearing loss greater access to information and entertainment.

B. Computers place people with a hearing loss in interactive settings with access to vast amounts of information. Computer programs are now available for instructional support in a variety of academic subject areas, from reading and writing to leaning basic sign language. Certain software can display a person's speech in visual form on the screen to assist in the development of articulation skills.

C. E-mail, interactive chatrooms, and the infinite number of web sites provide people with a hearing loss access to many kinds of visual information.

D. TT systems provide efficient ways for people who are deaf to communicate over long distances. TTY devices allow people who are deaf to use a personal computer or typewriter, modem, and printer to communicate over the phone.

15.8 Why is the early detection of a hearing loss so important?

259

    A.   Early detection of hearing loss can prevent or minimize the impact of the disability on the overall development of an individual.

15.9 Distinguish between an otologist and an audiologist.
    A.   An otologist is a medical specialist who is concerned with the hearing organ and its diseases.
    B.   An audiologist is concerned with the measurement of hearing loss and its sociological and educational impact on an individual.
    C.   Both the audiologist and otologist assist in the process of selected and using a hearing aid.

15.10 Identify factors that may affect the social inclusion of people who are deaf into the hearing world.
    A.   The inability to hear and understand speech has isolated some people who are deaf from those without hearing loss.
    B.   Societal views of deafness may reinforce isolation.

Guided Review

Read – Matching Vocabulary

15.11 A	15.13 G	15.15 B	15.17 D
15.12 E	15.14 H	15.16 C	15.18 F

Reflect – Matching Vocabulary

15.19 A	15.21 F	15.23 C	15.25 G
15.20 B	15.22 D	15.24 E	15.26 H

Recite – Fill in the Blank

15.27 Postlingual	15.31 Mixed
15.28 English, Spanish	15.32 Increases, men
15.29 Cochlea	15.33 Oral
15.30 Deaf	15.34 Signed English

Review – True/False

15.35 F	15.38 T	15.41 F	15.44 T
15.36 T	15.39 T	15.42 T	15.45 F
15.37 T	15.40 T	15.43 F	15.46 F

Chapter Review – Practice Test

15.47 B (411)	15.51 D (410)	15.55 B (411)	15.59 C (416)
15.48 A (407)	15.52 D (407)	15.56 A (412)	15.60 D (416)
15.49 C (408)	15.53 B (411)	15.57 B (413)	15.61 D (418)
15.50 A (410)	15.54 C (411)	15.58 B (415)	15.62 C (418)

Cryptogram

Deafness is not seen as a disability within the Deaf culture.

Double Puzzle

postlingual, otologist, audiogram, tympanic, deaf culture

Scramble

Most individuals with hearing loss have IQs equivalent to their peers without hearing loss.

Across
3. Deaf
4. Otitis
7. Postlingual
9. Cued
10. Men

Down
1. Atresia
2. Meatus
5. Tinnitus
6. Culture
8. Sign

16
Vision Loss

Focus Questions

16.1 Why is it important to understand the visual process as well as know the physical components of the eye?
    A.   The visual process is an important link to the physical world, helping people to gain information beyond that provided by the other senses and also helping to integrate the information acquired primarily through sound, touch, smell, and taste.
    B.   Our interactions with the environment are shaped by the way we perceive visual stimuli.

16.2 Distinguish between the terms *blind* and *partially sighted.*
    A.   Legal blindness is visual acuity of 20/200 or worse in the best eye with best correction, or a field of vision of 20% or less.
    B.   Educational definitions of blindness focus primarily on the student's inability to functionally use vision as an avenue for learning.
    C.   A person who is partially sighted has a visual acuity greater than 20/200 but not greater than 20/70 in the best eye after correction.
    D.   A person who is partially sighted can still use vision as a primary means of learning.

16.3 What are the distinctive features of refractive eye problems, muscle disorders of the eye, and receptive eye problems?
    A.   Refractive eye problems occur when the refractive structures of the eye (cornea or lens) fail to focus light rays properly on the retina. Refractive problems include hyperopia (farsightedness), myopia (nearsightedness), astigmatis (blurred vision), and cataracts.
    B.   Muscle disorders occur when the major muscles within the eye are inadequately developed or atrophic, resulting in a loss of control and an inability to maintain tension. Muscle disorders include nystagmus (uncontrolled rapid eye movement), strabismus (crossed eyes), and amblyopia (loss of vision due to muscle imbalance).
    C.   Receptive eye problems occur when the receptive structures of the eye (retina and optic nerve) degenerate or become damaged. Receptive eye problems include optic atrophy, retinitis pigmentosa, retinal detachment, retrolental fibroplasia, and glaucoma.

16.4 What are the estimated prevalence and causes of vision loss?
    A.   Approximately 20% of all children and adults have some vision loss; 3% (9 million people) have a significant vision loss that will requires some type of specialized services and supports.
    B.   Fifty percent of people over the age of 65 experience a significant loss of vision (includes cataracts).
    C.   Over 26,000 students have visual impairments and received specialized services in the U.S. public schools.
    D.   A number of genetic conditions can result in vision loss, including albinism, retinitis pigmentosa, retinoblastoma, optic atrophy, cataracts, severe myopia associated with retinal detachment, lesions of the cornea, abnormalities of the iris, microphthalmia, hydrocephalus, anophthalmia, and glaucoma.
    E.   Acquired disorders that can lead to vision loss prior to birth include radiation, the introduction of drugs into the fetal system, and infections, inflammations, and tumors.
    F.   The leading cause of acquired blindness in children worldwide is vitamin A deficiency (xerophthalmia). Cortical visual impairment (CVI) is also a leadng cause of acquired blindness.

16.5 Describe how a vision loss can affect intelligence, speech and language skills, educational achievement, social development, physical orientation and mobility, and perceptual-motor development.
    A.   Performance on tests of intelligence may be negatively affected in areas ranging from spatial concepts to general knowledge of the world.
    B.   Children with vision loss are at a distinct disadvantage in developing speech and language skills because they are unable to visually associate words with objects. They cannot learn speech by visual imitation but must

rely on hearing or touch for input. Preschool-age and school-age children with vision loss may develop a phenomenon known as verbalisms, or the excessive use of speech (wordiness), in which individuals may use words that have little meaning to them.

C.   In the area of written language, students with vision loss have more difficulty organizing thoughts to write a composition. Decoding for reading may be delayed because such students often use Braille or large-print books as the media to decode. Decoding is a much slower process when using these two media. Reading comprehension is also affected because it depends so much on the experiences of the reader.

D.   Other factors that may influence the academic achievement include (1) late entry to school; (2) failure in inappropriate school programs; (3) loss of time in school due to illness, treatment, or surgery; (4) lack of opportunity; and (5) slow rate of acquiring information.

E.   People with vision loss are unable to imitate the physical mannerisms of sighted peers and thus do not develop body language, an important from of social communication. A person with sight may misinterpret what is said by a person with a vision loss because his or her visual cues may not be consistent with the spoken word.

F.   People with vision loss are often excluded from understanding his or her own relative position in space. A vision loss may affect fine motor coordination and interfere with a person's ability to manipulate objects.

G.   The perceptual discrimination abilities of people with vision loss in the areas of texture, weight, and sound are comparable to those of sighted peers.

H.   People who are blind do not perform as well as people with sight on complex tasks of perception, including form identification, spatial relations, and perceptual-motor integration.

16.6   What is a functional approach to assessment for students with a vision loss?
A.   Assessment focuses specifically on how the student utilized any remaining vision (visual efficiency) in conjunction with other senses to acquire information.
B.   A functional approach to assessment goes beyond determining visual acuity and focuses on capacity, attention, and processing.

16.7   Describe two content areas that should be included in educational programs for students with vision loss.
A.   Mobility and orientation training: The ability to move safely, efficiently, and independently through the environment enhances the individual's opportunities to learn more about the world and thus be less dependent on others for survival. Lack of mobility restricts individuals with vision loss in nearly every aspect of educational life.
B.   The acquisition of daily living skills: For children with a vision loss, routine daily living skills are not easily learned through everyday experiences. These children must be encouraged and supported as they develop life skills and not overprotected from everyday challenges and risks by family and friends.

16.8   How can communication media facilitate learning for people with vision loss?
A.   Through communication media, such as optical aids in conjunction with auditory and tactile stimuli, individuals with vision loss can better develop an understanding of themselves and the world around them.
B.   Tactile media, including the raised-dot Braille system and the Optacon Scanner, can greatly enhance the individual's access to information.
C.   Specialized media – including personal readers, microcomputers with voice output, closed-circuit TV systems, personal digital assistants, talking calculators, talking-book machines, CD players, and audiotape recorders – provide opportunities for people with vision loss that were not thought possible even a few years ago.

16.9   What educational placements are available to students with vision loss?
A.   Residential facilities provide children who are blind with opportunities for the same kinds of experiences that would be available if they were growing up in their own communities.
B.   The vast majority of people with vision loss live at home, attend public schools, and interact within their own communities.
C.   Services available within the public schools range from general education class placement, with little or no assistance, to special day schools.

16.10   What steps can be taken to prevent and medically treat vision loss?
A.   Vision loss can be prevented through genetic screening and counseling, appropriate prenatal care, and early developmental assessment.
B.   The development of optical aids, including corrective glasses and contact lenses, has greatly improved access to the sighted world for people with vision loss.
C.   Medical treatment may range from complex laser surgical procedures and corneal transplants to drug therapy (e.g., atropinization).

16.11 Why is the availability of appropriate social services important for people with vision loss?
    A.   Social services address issues of self-esteem and feelings of inferiority that may stem from having a vision loss.

Guided Review

Read – Matching Vocabulary

16.12 A	16.14 B	16.16 G	16.18 D
16.13 E	16.15 F	16.17 C	16.19 H

Reflect – Matching Vocabulary

16.20 A	16.22 B	16.24 C	16.26 G
16.21 E	16.23 H	16.25 F	16.27 D

Recite – Fill in the Blank

16.28 Muscle	16.32 Neurological
16.29 Cataracts	16.33 Influenze
16.30 Strabismus/Exotropia	16.34 Acuity
16.31 Retinitis pigmentosa	16.35 Supports

Review – True/False

16.36 T	16.39 T	16.42 F	16.45 F
16.37 T	16.40 F	16.43 F	16.46 F
16.38 T	16.41 T	16.44 T	16.47 T

Chapter Review – Practice Test

16.48 D (444)	16.52 B (452)	16.56 C (446)	16.60 A (448)
16.49 D (444)	16.53 A (444)	16.57 D (447)	16.61 B (448)
16.50 A (449)	16.54 C (444)	16.58 B (447)	16.62 D (449)
16.51 B (444)	16.55 A (445)	16.59 C (448)	16.63 D (457)

Cryptogram

Students with vision loss may lag up to two years behind their sighted peers.

Double Puzzle

Braille, Snellen, strabismus, neurological, astigmatism

Scramble

The leading cause of blindness in children is xeropthalmia.

Crossword Puzzle

Across
4. Refractive
6. Genetic
8. Cataracts
9. Snellen
10. Mowat

Down
1. Tunnel
2. Trachoma
3. Verbalisms
5. Functional
7. Iris

17
Physical Disabilities and Health Disorders

16.10 What steps can be taken to prevent and medically treat vision loss?
    A.   Vision loss can be prevented through genetic screening and counseling, appropriate prenatal care, and early developmental assessment.

17.1 Identify the disabilities that may accompany cerebral palsy.
    A.   Often, individuals with cerebral palsy have several disabilities, including hearing impairments, speech and language disorders, intellectual deficits, visual impairments, and general perceptual problems.

17.2 What is spina bifida myelomeningocele?
    A.   Spina bifida myelomeningocele is a defect in the spinal column. The meningocele type presents itself in the form of a tumor-like sac on the back of the infant, which contains spinal fluid and nerve tissue.
    B.   Myelomeningocele is also the most serious variety of spina bifida in that it generally includes paralysis or partial paralysis of certain body areas, causing lack of bowel and bladder control.

17.3 Identify specific treatments for individuals with spinal cord injuries.
    A.   Immediate pharmacological interventions with high and frequent doses of methylprednisolone. These doses reduce the severity of the injury and improve the functional outcome over time.
    B.   Stabilization of the spine is critical to the overall outcome of the injury.
    C.   Once the spine has been stabilized, the rehabilitation process begins. Physical therapy helps the affected individual make full use of any and all residual muscle strength.
    D.   The individual is also taught to use orthopedic devices, such as handsplints, braces, reachers, headsticks, and other augmentative devices.
    E.   Psychological adjustment is aided by psychiatric an psychological personnel.
    F.   Rehabilitation specialists aid the individual in becoming retrained or reeducated; they may also help in securing employment.
    G.   Some individuals will need part-time or full-time attendant care for assistance with daily activities (e.g., bathing, dressing, and shopping).

17.4 Describe the physical limitations associated with muscular dystrophy.
    A.   Individuals with muscular dystrophy progressively lose their ability to walk and use their arms and hands effectively because fatty tissue begins to replace muscle tissue.

17.5 What steps should be taken to assist infants and children with AIDS?
    A.   Infants and children should be provided with the most effective medical care available, particularly care addressed as controlling opportunistic infections with appropriate medications.
    B.   Children with AIDS should attend school unless they exhibit behaviors that are dangerous to others or are at risk for developing infectious diseases that would exacerbate their condition.

17.6 Describe the immediate treatment for a person who is experiencing a tonic/clonic seizure.
    A.   Cushion the head
    B.   Loosen tight neck tie or collar
    C.   Turn on side
    D.   Put nothing in the mouth of the individual
    E.   Look for identification
    F.   Don't hold down
    G.   As seizure ends, offer help

17.7 Identify three problems that individuals with diabetes may eventually experience.
    A.   Structural abnormalities that occur over time may result in blindness, cardiovascular disease, and kidney disease.

17.8 Identify present and future interventions for the treatment of children and youth with cystic fibrosis.
    A.   Drug therapy for prevention and treatment of chest infections.
    B.   Diet management, use of replacement enzymes for food absorption, and vitamin intake.
    C.   Family education regarding the condition.
    D.   Chest physiotherapy and postural drainage.
    E.   Inhalation therapy.
    F.   Psychological and psychiatric counseling.
    G.   Use of mucus-thinning drugs, gene therapy, and lung or lung/heart transplant.

17.9 Describe the impact of the sickling of cells on body tissues.

A. Sickled cells are more rigid than normal cells; as such, they frequently block microvascular channels. The blockage of channels reduces or terminates circulation in these areas, and tissues in need of blood nutrients and oxygen die.

17.10 Identify five factors that may contribute to child abuse and neglect.
A. Unemployment, poverty, and substance abuse.
B. Isolation from natural and community support networks.
C. Marital/relationship problems.
D. Having a particularly challenging, needy, or demanding infant.
E. Poor impulse control.

17.11 Identify factors that may contribute to the increase prevalence of adolescent pregnancy.
A. General factors include a lack of knowledge about conception and sexuality, a desire to escape family control, an attempt to be more adult, a desire to have some to love, a means of gaining attention and love, and an inability to make sound decisions.
B. Societal factors include greater sexual permissiveness and freedom, social pressure from peers, and continual exposure to sexuality through the media.

17.12 Identify the major causes of youth suicide.
A. The causes of suicide are multidimensional. These causes involve biological, personal, family, peer, and community factors.
B. Alterations in brain chemistry put some individuals at risk for suicide.
C. Often, clinical depression or other psychiatric conditions precede suicide.
D. Other causative factors include extreme peer rejections, problems with sexual identity, and substance-abuse.

Guided Review

Read – Matching Vocabulary

17.13 E	17.16 B	17.19 J	17.22 C
17.14 A	17.17 D	17.20 F	17.23 I
17.15 K	17.18 G	17.21 L	17.24 H

Reflect – Matching Vocabulary

17.25 E	17.27 F	17.29 B	17.31 D
17.26 A	17.28 C	17.30 G	17.32 H

Recite – Fill in the Blank

17.33 Spina bifida	17.39 Transfusions
17.34 Teratogens	17.40 Drugs
17.35 Headache	17.41 Juvenile, adult
17.36 Heredity	17.42 31
17.37 Educational	17.43 6
17.38 Fatigue	17.44 Athetoid

Review – True/False

17.45 T	17.48 F	17.51 T	17.54 T
17.46 T	17.49 F	17.52 T	17.55 F
17.47 F	17.50 T	17.53 F	17.56 T

Chapter Review – Practice Test

17.57 A (504)	17.62 A (480)	17.67 A (484)	17.72 B (498)
17.58 B (471)	17.63 B (480)	17.68 C (488)	17.73 D (494)
17.59 C (472)	17.64 D (481)	17.69 B (489)	17.74 C (495)
17.60 B (473)	17.65 C (484)	17.70 C (491)	17.75 A (501)
17.61 D (480)	17.66 C (484)	17.71 D (492)	17.76 A (497)

Cryptogram

Symptoms of Duchenne-type muscular dystrophy usually appear during preschool years.

Double Puzzle

heredity, transfusions, juvenile, Duchenne, orthopedic

Scramble

Spinal cord injuries are usually accompanied by head trauma and chest injuries.

Crossword Puzzle

Across	Down
3. Paraplegia	1. Spina
5. AID	2. Fetal
7. Absence	4. Athetoid
8. Ataxic	6. Diabetes
10. Cystic	9. Tonic

18
Gifted, Creative, and Talented

Focus Questions

18.1 Briefly describe several historical developments directly related to the measurement of various types of giftedness.
- A. Alfred Binet developed the first developmental scale for children during the early 1900s. Gradually, the notion of mental age emerged, that is, a representation of what the child was capable of doing compared with age-specific developmental tasks.
- B. Lewis M. Terman translated the Binet scale and made modifications suitable for children in the United States.
- C. Gradually, the intelligence quotient, or IQ became the gauge for determining giftedness.
- D. Intelligence was long viewed as a unitary structure underlying ability. But this view gradually changed and researchers began to believe that intelligence was represented in a variety of distinct capacities and abilities.
- E. J.P. Guilford and other social scientists began to develop a multidimensional theory of intelligence, which prompted researchers to develop models and assessment devices for examining creativity.
- F. Programs were gradually developed to foster and develop creativity in young people.
- G. More recently V. Ramos-Ford and H. Gardner have developed the multiple intelligences perspective that includes linguistic, logical-mathematical, spatial, musical, bodily-kinesthetic, interpersonal, and intrapersonal behaviors.

18.2 Identify six major components of definitions that have been developed to describe giftedness.
- A. Children and adolescents who are gifted perform or show potential for performing at remarkably high levels when compared with others of their age, experience, or environment.
- B. Children who are gifted exhibit high performance capability in intellectual, creative, and/or artistic areas.
- C. Such children may possess unusual leadership capacity or excel in specific academic fields.
- D. Gifted children become extraordinarily proficient performers or creative producers, excelling in a wide range of potential activities from cooking to musical improvisation.
- E. Gifted children have the capacity over time to solve challenging problems and to crate products valued and needed by a culture.
- F. Such children and adolescents need well-designed environments and opportunities to realize their full intellectual and creative potential.

18.3 Identify four problems inherent in accurately describing the characteristics of individuals who are gifted.
- A. Individuals who are gifted vary significantly on a variety of characteristics; they are not a homogeneous group.
- B. Because research regarding the characteristics of people who are gifted has been conducted with different population groups, the characteristics that have surfaced represent the population studied rather than the gifted population as a whole.
- C. Many early studies of individuals who are gifted led to a stereotypical view of giftedness.

D. Historically, studies regarding the characteristics of individuals who are gifted have not included adequate samples of females, minority or ethnic groups, or socioeconomic groups.

18.4 Identify three factors that appear to contribute significantly to the emergence of various forms of giftedness.
A. Genetic endowment certainly contributes to manifestations of giftedness in all of its varieties.
B. Environmental stimulation provided by parents, teachers, coaches, tutors, and others contributes significantly to the emergence of giftedness.
C. The interactions of innate abilities with environmental influences and encouragement fosters the development and expression of giftedness.

18.5 Describe the range of assessment devices used to identify the various types of giftedness.
A. Developmental checklists and scales
B. Parents and teacher inventories
C. Intelligence and achievement tests
D. Creativity tests
E. Other diverse observational information provided by parents, grandparents, and other knowledgeable informants.

18.6 Identify eight strategies that are utilized to foster the development of children and adolescents who are gifted.
A. Environmental stimulation provided by parents from infancy through adolescence.
B. Differentiated education and specialized serviced delivery systems that provide enrichment activities and/or possibilities for accelerations: early entrance to kindergarten or school; grade skipping; early admission to college; honors programs at the high school and college levels; specialized schools in the performing and visual arts, math, and science; mentor programs with university professors and other talented individuals; and specialized counseling facilities.

18.7 What are some of the social-emotional needs of students who are gifted?
A. Understanding, appreciated and valuing their own uniqueness as well as that of others.
B. Understanding the importance and the development of relationship skills.
C. Expanding and valuing their high-level sensitivity.
D. Gaining a realistic understanding of their own abilities and talents.
E. Identifying ways of nurturing and developing their own abilities and talents.
F. Adequately distinguishing between pursuits of excellence and pursuits of perfection.
G. Developing the behaviors associated with negotiation and compromise.

18.8 Identify four challenges females face in dealing with their giftedness.
A. Fear of appearing "unfeminine" or unattractive when competing with males.
B. Competition between marital and career aspirations
C. Stress induced by traditional cultural and societal expectations
D. Self-imposed and/or culturally imposed restrictions related to educational and occupational choice.

18.9 Identify eight important elements of programs for gifted children who come from diverse backgrounds and who may live in poverty.
A. The programs are staffed with skilled and competent teachers and other support personnel.
B. The staff members work as teams.
C. Teachers and others responsible for developing the learning experience understand learning styles, students' interests, and how to build students' affective, cognitive, and ethical capacities.
D. The programs maintain and encourage ethnic diversity, provide extracurricular cultural enrichment, provide counseling, foster parent support groups, and provide children and youth access to significant models.
E. The programs focus on students' strengths, not their deficits.
F. The programs help parents understand their key role in developing talents and giftedness.
G. The programs provide many opportunities or hands-on learning; activities that foster self-expression, and generous use of mentors and role models from the child's cultural and ethnic group.
H. The programs are characterized by a team approach, involving parents, teachers, mentors, and other family members.

Guided Review

Read – Matching Vocabulary

18.10 E	18.12 A	18.14 G	18.16 H
18.11 D	18.13 F	18.15 B	18.17 C

Reflect – Matching Vocabulary

18.18 A	18.20 E	18.22 F
18.19 B	18.21 C	18.23 D

Recite – Fill in the Blank

18.24 Visualization	18.28 Environmental supports
18.25 Environment	18.29 Genetic
18.26 Political	18.30 Mentoring
18.27 Nature, nurture	18.31 35%, 50%

Review – True/False

18.32 F	18.35 F	18.38 T	18.41 T
18.33 F	18.36 T	18.39 T	18.42 T
18.34 T	18.37 F	18.40 T	18.43 F

Chapter Review – Practice Test

18.44 C (515)	18.48 B (519)	18.52 A (524)	18.56 A (535)
18.45 B (518)	18.49 D (520)	18.53 A (525)	18.57 C (537)
18.46 A (518)	18.50 D (521)	18.54 C (528)	18.58 B (539)
18.47 B (518)	18.51 B (522)	18.55 D (529)	18.59 D (541)

Cryptogram

Students who are gifted speak and read early.

Double Puzzle

chance, spatial, nurture, mentor, genetic, multiple intelligences

Scramble

Giftedness can present in many forms.

Crossword Puzzle

Across	Down
2. Spatial	1. Differentiated
6. Creative	3. Multidimensional
7. Screen	4. Talented
8. Renzuli	5. Perfection

NOTES

NOTES

NOTES

NOTES

NOTES

NOTES

NOTES

NOTES

NOTES

NOTES

NOTES

NOTES

NOTES